THE CASE FOR CHRIST

DEVOTIONS

FOR KIDS

ALSO BY LEE STROBEL

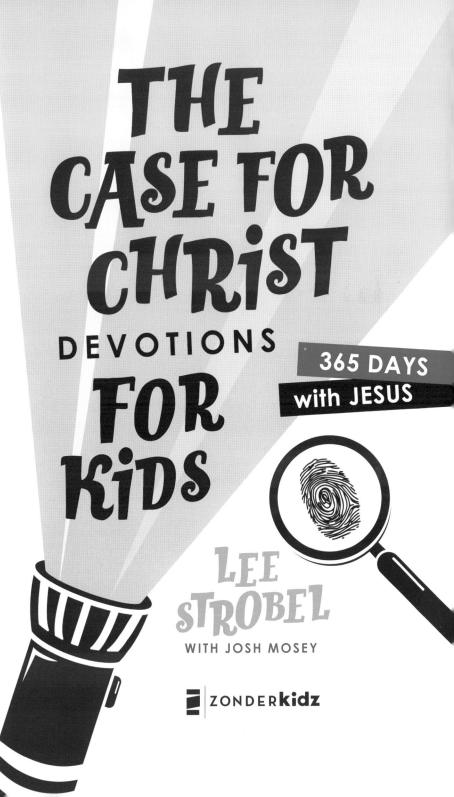

THE CASE FOR CHRIST

DEVOTIONS

FOR KIDS

365 DAYS
with JESUS

LEE STROBEL

WITH JOSH MOSEY

ZONDER**kidz**

ZONDERKIDZ

The Case for Christ Devotions for Kids
Copyright © 2021 by Lee Strobel

Published in Grand Rapids, Michigan, by Zonderkidz. Zonderkidz is a registered trademark of The Zondervan Corporation, L.L.C., a wholly owned subsidiary of HarperCollins Christian Publishing, Inc.

Requests for information should be addressed to customercare@harpercollins.com.

ISBN 978-0-310-77013-8 (hardcover)
ISBN 978-0-310-77014-5 (ebook)

Library of Congress Cataloging-in-Publication Data

Names: Strobel, Lee, 1952- author. | Mosey, Josh, author. | Strobel, Lee, 1952- Case for Christ for kids.
Title: The case for Christ devotions for kids: 365 days with Jesus / Lee Strobel, with Josh Mosey.
Description: Grand Rapids: Zonderkidz, 2021. | Series: The case for . . .series for kids | Audience: Ages 8–12 | Audience: Grades 4–6 | Summary: "The tough questions kids 8–12 ask about faith, Jesus, and Christianity are investigated and answered in this 365-day devotional that uses the historical facts and theological truths found in The Case for Christ to help young readers develop their faith and understand what it means to be a Christian. Each day's reading also includes reflection questions, helping kids think through what their faith personally means to them. Become an expert witness for Jesus! For kids who want to learn more about Christianity or simply have questions about the Bible, this devotional helps young readers understand why Jesus's ministry and miracles are true and why we can confidently believe in Jesus today. Includes 365 days of devotions for kids that use kid-friendly language, engaging illustrations, and clear examples to help kids understand faith and the proven truths that support Christianity, and mixes inspirational prose with facts, research, and true stories, all based around material from the New York Times bestselling The Case for Christ by Lee Strobel"—Provided by publisher.
Identifiers: LCCN 2021008832 (print) | LCCN 2021008833 (ebook) | ISBN 9780310770138 (hardcover) | ISBN 9780310770145 (ebook)
Subjects: LCSH: Jesus Christ—Person and offices—Prayers and devotions—Juvenile literature. | Bible—Evidences, authority, etc.—Juvenile literature. | Christian children—Religious life—Juvenile literature.
Classification: LCC BT203 .S759 2021 (print) | LCC BT203 (ebook) | DDC 242/.62—dc23
LC record available at https://lccn.loc.gov/2021008832
LC ebook record available at https://lccn.loc.gov/2021008833

Portions of this book contain quotes from:

The Case for Christ by Lee Strobel, ISBN: 9780310226468, 1998; *The Case for Christ for Kids 90-Day Devotional* by Lee Strobel, ISBN: 978-0310733928, 2013; *The Case for Christ Young Reader's Edition* by Lee Strobel, ISBN: 978-0310770046, 2020.

Cover Design: Michelle Lenger
Interior Design: Denise Froehlich
Content Contributor: Josh Mosey

Printed in India

---

24 25 26 27 28   REP   10 9 8 7 6 5 4 3

INTRODUCTION

Having questions about faith is something that happens to many people. They can have lots of serious concerns and questions about it all. Questions such as: "Does God really exist," "Was Jesus really the Son of God," and "Is the Bible all true." Some people are young when they start to wonder and want to dig deeper about things and some are older.

Here are some things to remember:

- You are not alone on your journey to answer questions you might have about God and Jesus and Christianity.

- There are many places you can go to look for evidence that will help you find the answers you need.

This year-long devotional is for anyone looking for encouragement and inspiration for the journey. God's own words from Scripture will assure you and in many devotions, clear evidence is presented to you, that will strengthen your faith and give you hope and peace as you explore that faith in Jesus.

So read the Scripture, reflect on the message, really think about the questions each day, and then pray with all your heart. This is going to be a great 365-day journey!

On Being Skeptical

But test them all; hold on to what is good.

1 THESSALONIANS 5:21

Truth is important. Journalists make their living by seeking the truth and presenting the facts accurately. Detectives look for clues in a crime scene to discover the truth of what happened. Kids need the truth too! But how do we know what's true and what isn't?

If someone said they got free pizza by saying the word "Flusterbuns" when calling in their order, would it be believable? We'd probably check the restaurant's website or ask some friends about it, but we wouldn't know until we called for pizza, said "Flusterbuns," and saw what happened.

To know something for sure, it has to be tested! A person who tests something before they believe it is called a skeptic. Some people think to be a Christian, we have to believe something without testing it. That's called blind faith. Having faith in God is important, but it doesn't need to be blind. He gives us lots of reasons to see He is real.

Proverbs 8:17 says, "I love those who love me, and those who seek me find me." God isn't worried about our questions or doubts. He knows when we seek the truth, we'll always come back to him. And finding God is much better than getting free pizza!

What's something you heard but didn't believe until you tested it?

What's something about God that seems too good to be true?

Lord, help me seek you. Make me skeptical of the things that aren't true.

7

Why Some People Doubt

Be merciful to those who doubt.

JUDE 1:22

According to *National Geographic Kids*, white-faced capuchin monkeys don't say hello by shaking hands or waving, but by sticking their fingers in each other's noses. Gross, right?

Some things are unbelievable because they are so different from our experience. People who don't believe in Jesus may think Christians are as weird as white-faced capuchin monkeys. We gather to sing and hear someone give a speech about the same book every week. Who else does that?

Other things are unbelievable because they sound too good to be true. Is it likely that the God who made the universe cares about every individual? Or that he became a human to take our punishment by dying a horrible death? Or that he rose again from the grave? Or that he loves us and wants to give us eternal life? It sounds like wishful thinking, but it isn't!

When people have a hard time believing, God tells us to be patient. Christians who look down on unbelievers make it harder for them to believe. When Christians treat others with love, it makes it easier to see Christ living in us. Our message will be backed up by our lives, making the truth a lot more believable.

What about Christianity makes it hard to believe?

How can you show by your actions, that Christianity is real?

So, let's greet each other with kindness all the time (but not like white-faced capuchin monkeys).

God, help my life make belief in you easier for the people around me.

So Many Religions

> *This is what the LORD says—Israel's King and*
> *Redeemer, the LORD Almighty: I am the first and*
> *I am the last; apart from me there is no God.*

ISAIAH 44:6

Think for a minute about all the different religions in the world. Along with Christianity, there's Judaism, Islam, Buddhism, and Hinduism, just to name a few. One of the fastest growing beliefs in the world is atheism, the denial that *any* religion is true. With so many different systems of belief, what makes Christianity right?

When God set aside the nation of Israel, he knew people would be tempted to mix their worship for him with the religions of countries around them. Throughout the Old Testament, God's chosen people fell into that temptation, only to be conquered by another nation before turning their worship back to the one true God.

God knew chasing after other gods would only hurt his people. It wasn't like he was scared of competition. God wanted to spare his people the consequences required to turn them back to himself.

Today, the God of Israel is still around. Even better, he's opened his arms and welcomed the whole world, not just Israel, to become his chosen people.

What makes Christianity right? Our God is alive and ready to show himself to those who are willing to look.

What sets Christianity apart from other world religions?

What do you think it means that God is the first and the last?

> *Lord, help me see that you are*
> *the one and only God.*

9

Good for Burritos, Bad for Beliefs

> *"Salvation is found in no one else, for there is no other name under heaven given to mankind by which we must be saved."*
>
> **ACTS 4:12**

We live in a mix-and-match world. For example, people may like the Jesus who hugged children and walked on water. But the Jesus who said to have faith and follow him makes them uncomfortable.

The blending of different religions is called *syncretism*. And it's a bad idea.

Being able to customize your beliefs, like ordering a meal with only the toppings you want, sounds enticing, but it will leave a bad taste in your mouth. The Bible teaches there is only one way—God's way.

After Jesus was crucified and rose from the dead, his disciples traveled around telling people the good news. In Acts 4, Peter and John appear before the religious leaders who ask, "By what name did you do this?"

Peter answers plainly. He explains that Jesus is the cornerstone of true faith and declares, "Salvation is found in no one else, for there is no other name under heaven given to mankind by which we must be saved" (Acts 4:12).

Picking and choosing is good for burritos, but when it comes to your beliefs, only one choice is right: Jesus Christ.

What are your favorite parts of Christianity?

Why shouldn't you cut out the bits that aren't your favorites?

> *Lord Jesus, you are more than the guy who walked on water. Help me know and love every part of you.*

10

Attractive Fruit

> *But the fruit of the Spirit is love, joy, peace, forbearance, kindness, goodness, faithfulness, gentleness and self-control. Against such things there is no law.*
>
> **GALATIANS 5:22–23**

Most people probably couldn't tell the difference between a pear tree sapling and an apple tree sapling. It isn't until saplings grow up a bit and start bearing fruit that telling them apart gets easier.

When someone enters into a relationship with Jesus, the Holy Spirit comes in and makes them a new creation. It's like God transforms them from one kind of fruit tree into another. By allowing the Spirit to work in and through them, that person grows up a bit and starts bearing Christian fruit.

Christians who grow the fruit of the Spirit start to look more like Jesus. They show more love, joy, peace, forbearance (a fancy word for patience), kindness, goodness, faithfulness, gentleness, and self-control. Who wouldn't want to be around someone like that?

When the Holy Spirit grows fruit in a believer's life, others may wonder what inspired the change. People don't change easily, after all. Fortunately, believers don't change themselves. It is God who does the transformation. It is God who grows the fruit in us. And it is God who opens the eyes of others to see the difference He makes in our lives.

Which fruit of the Spirit do you want God to grow in you?

Would it be obvious what kind of tree you are by the fruit you bear?

> *Creator God, I am a new creation because of you. Help me bear fruit to make it obvious what kind of tree I am.*

11

Copycat Faith?

This is how God showed his love among us: He sent his one and only Son into the world that we might live through him.

1 JOHN 4:9

Ten cats were in a boat. One jumped out. How many were left?

None. They were copycats.

That's an old joke. The problem of being a copycat is nothing new. Some people claim Christianity is a copycat religion; they say its beliefs and holidays are made up of earlier myths and other religions. But what does the evidence say?

Author and historian Michael Licona has studied the evidence. He speaks around the world and debates people who try to knock holes in Christianity. But solid scholarship conclusively shows that parallels between Christianity and other religions aren't accurate.

Then there's the biggest difference between Christianity and other religions: Jesus Christ. First John 4:9 tells us, "This is how God showed his love among us: He sent his one and only Son into the world that we might live through him."

"The consensus among modern scholars—*nearly universal*—is that there were no dying and rising gods that preceded Christianity," Licona says. Don't be confused. Christianity isn't copied. Its core beliefs are original, unique, and true.

How does it feel to be called a copycat?

What are some ways God shows his love to us?

Lord, thank you for being unique and for loving me.

Who is Jesus, Anyway?

> *Jesus and his disciples went on to the villages around Caesarea Philippi. On the way he asked them, "Who do people say I am?"*
>
> **MARK 8:27**

When Jesus asked his disciples who the people said he was, Jesus wasn't having an identity crisis. He knew who he was then and he still knows today. But as we develop the case for Christ, it would be helpful to understand what Christians believe about Jesus, so we can see if the beliefs line up with the available evidence.

Most people know Jesus as the baby born in Bethlehem whose birthday is celebrated at Christmas. Christians believe Jesus was born to the virgin Mary and fathered by God Himself. We also believe Jesus never sinned (did wrong or acted selfishly), that he was a teacher—or rabbi—who performed miracles, cast out demons, and fought with the established spiritual leaders of Israel in his day. Jesus's followers, or disciples, believed his arrival on earth was the answer to ancient prophecies about God coming in person to reign on his rightful throne.

Finally, Christians believe Jesus was crucified on a cross, buried in a tomb, and brought back to life to be seen by his followers.

And while our research will show us more of who Jesus was and who he claimed to be, in the end, we will face another question: If everything we find out about Jesus is true, what do we do about it?

> Who do you say Jesus is?
>
> How do you think developing the case for Christ will change your beliefs?

> *Lord, even though I think I know who you are, help me understand and believe in you on a whole new level.*

13

What is the Bible, Anyway?

All Scripture is God-breathed and is useful for teaching, rebuking, correcting and training in righteousness.

2 TIMOTHY 3:16

As we look at the question of who Jesus is, we won't get very far without understanding what the Bible is.

In addition to it being the bestselling book of all time, the Bible is the Word of God. It is made up of sixty-six individual books, written over the course of thousands of years by many different people, all of whom were inspired by the Holy Spirit.

The Bible is divided into two main parts: the Old and New Testaments. The Old Testament records the beginning of creation, the emergence of Israel as God's chosen people, the laws handed down from God, the establishment of kings, and stories of exile, prophets, and the hope of deliverance. The New Testament records stories about Jesus, the establishment of the church, letters to different churches and pastors, and a revelation of the end of the world.

Second Timothy 3:16 says "All Scripture is God-breathed and is useful for teaching, rebuking, correcting, and training in righteousness." By learning from the Bible, we get to know its author better. In the process, we grow to look more like Him.

As we get into the Word of God, the Word of God gets into us!

How do you feel about the Bible?

Do you believe it to be the Word of God? Why or why not?

Holy Author of the Bible, help me learn to be more like you.

14

God Rules

Obey the LORD's commands and rules. I'm giving them to you today for your own good.

DEUTERONOMY 10:13 (NIRV)

The Bible contains some seemingly strange laws as well. Leviticus 19:19 tells us, "Do not wear clothing woven of two kinds of material." Why is the Bible so concerned with fashion?

Some experts believe clothing woven from linen and wool would trap the desert heat and cause the wearer to get blisters. Others say God encouraged his people to wear "pure" fabrics as a reminder to keep themselves pure. In either case, God had a reason.

When Jesus came to earth, he proclaimed the rule of God. Not only does the heavenly Father rule over everything, but he also makes all the rules. God didn't give us his commandments to boss us around and ruin our fun.

In Deuteronomy 10:13 Moses says, "Obey the LORD's commands and rules. I'm giving them to you today *for your own good*" (NIrV, emphasis added). God's commands make us free to experience his love, free from the harm of making foolish choices, and free from the consequences of sin. We should think about that fact the next time we're bummed out about something we can't do. God made the rules for our own good.

What are some rules you think are silly?

Do you think those rules are made to protect you?

Lord, help me obey your rules. I know they're for my good.

15

Sweet Treat

How sweet are your words to my taste,
sweeter than honey to my mouth!

PSALM 119:103

For thousands of years, people have known about the health benefits of honey. Research shows honey has antibacterial and antifungal properties, reduces the risk of some cancers, helps with coughs, aids in healing wounds, and gives us better skin.

Numerous times in the Bible, God's Word is compared to honey. And the sweetness of God's Word always comes out on top. We normally relate sweet things with dessert or a reward. And that's exactly how we should view God's Word. Proverbs 24:14 reminds us, "Wisdom is like honey for you: If you find it, there is a future hope for you." And the best place to find wisdom is in the Bible.

If we're honest, we may have to admit we don't look at reading the Bible in the same way as eating a biscuit slathered with honey. But we should. Not only does spending time in God's Word give us greater benefits than antifungal properties and better skin, it helps us become more like the author of all creation.

What are some ways we can sweeten our experience with God's Word?

Keeping a journal, drawing pictures of Bible stories, even making up a song or poem based on a verse are great ways! Plus, when we apply what we learn in new ways, we remember what we learn even better.

> **Do you enjoy reading the Bible?**
>
> **Which method will you use to sweeten your experience with God's Word today?**

Lord, help me taste the sweetness of your wisdom.

Looking at the Evidence

> *We demolish arguments and every pretension that sets itself up against the knowledge of God, and we take captive every thought to make it obedient to Christ.*
>
> **2 CORINTHIANS 10:5**

For more than forty years, spies have used cameras that look like coat buttons to snap pictures. They've hidden transmitters in the heels of shoes. Complicated codes have been used to create, send, and translate information.

Spies do it. Detectives do it. People seeking the truth do it. What is it? It's following the facts.

Sometimes in criminal cases all the facts look stacked a certain way. But upon closer investigation, the evidence actually points to the exact opposite conclusion. The case many people make against the Bible is that way. Those who want to argue against God and his Word will put together evidence which appears convincing at first. But when we dig deeper, the Bible stands strong.

In 2 Corinthians 10:5, Paul tells us to "demolish arguments and every pretension that sets itself up against the knowledge of God, and we take captive every thought to make it obedient to Christ." We're bound to encounter ideas that oppose our belief in God. When that happens, we simply follow the facts and we'll find God's persuasive evidence demolishes all other arguments.

What kind of spy equipment do you wish you had?

How would you answer someone who disagrees with you about your beliefs?

> *Father God, help me follow the evidence where it leads.*

19

Beyond a Reasonable Doubt

*Trust in the LORD with all your heart and
lean not on your own understanding.*

PROVERBS 3:5

In a courtroom trial, before jurors can find someone guilty of a crime, they have to be convinced "beyond a reasonable doubt" the person accused actually did it. That phrase "beyond a reasonable doubt" can be kind of confusing, but it basically means we have to be as sure as humanly possible about something before we act on it.

People who don't think the Bible is true or that Jesus really did what the Bible says have lots of doubts about Christianity. Even Christians struggle with doubts sometimes. That's why Proverbs 3:5 tells us, "Trust in the LORD with all your heart and lean not on your own understanding."

Trusting in our own understanding when it comes to the incomprehensible God who created everything, has lived eternally, and is above all things is like an earthworm trying to figure out a human. Our understanding as Christians trusts that God is the ultimate truth.

When we struggle with belief in God, God doesn't struggle to believe in us. Besides, we aren't on the jury of our future. We are the ones on trial! Thank Jesus he's already taken our punishment and declared us not guilty of our sins. That's a kind of love worth trusting!

What are some things you don't understand about God?

How can you trust God, even when you don't understand him?

Lord, you are more awesome than I can understand. Thank you for believing in me when I struggle to believe in you.

18

Believing What is True

Guide me in your truth and teach me, for you are God my Savior, and my hope is in you all day long.

PSALM 25:5

Belief in something isn't what makes it true. Someone could believe refrigeration isn't needed for dairy products, but when their milk pours out in gloppy clumps and their cheese turns green with mold, they would find their belief to be wrong.

Paul Copan has studied the claims of Christ for years and written or edited over a dozen books, including *True for You But Not for Me.* "I can't stress this enough," Copan said. "What we believe about Jesus doesn't affect who he is. Whether we choose to believe it or not, Jesus is the unique Son of God.... So we have a choice: we can live in a fantasyland of our own making by believing whatever we want about him; or we can seek to discover who he really is."

By basing our beliefs on biblical truths, we can get to know the real Jesus. If we base our beliefs on our assumptions, we'll end up as sick spiritually as someone who drank curdled milk. And while we don't need more than the Bible to know what's true, God has left evidence throughout creation, history, and written accounts to help us know his word can be trusted.

How do you decide what to believe?

Have you ever believed something, then found out you were wrong?

For any who doubt, God is ready and willing to prove himself. After all, he is the truth! All we need to do is seek him.

Lord, may I not base my belief in you on assumptions, but on the truth in your Word.

Fingerprint Evidence

> *The LORD your God will raise up for you a prophet like me from among you, from your fellow Israelites. You must listen to him.*
>
> **DEUTERONOMY 18:15**

When fingerprint evidence was first introduced in a murder case against Thomas Jennings in 1910, the defense attorneys were skeptical. The science behind fingerprint evidence had only been introduced a few years earlier and had never been used to convict someone of murder. But when the trial was done, Jennings was found guilty and fingerprint evidence has been helping police put criminals in prison ever since.

The science is simple: Each person has unique ridges on his or her fingers. When a print is found on an object matching the pattern of ridges on a specific person's finger, investigators conclude with scientific certainty that this individual has touched the object.

What has this got to do with Jesus Christ?

Similar to fingerprints, investigators can look at the predictions of the Old Testament and see if they match Jesus's life. A coming Messiah, sent by God to redeem his people, would have his fingerprints all over the Old Testament. God did this on purpose so the Israelites could rule out any impostors and validate the identity of the true Messiah.

In the coming days, we'll look at different "ridges" in the Old Testament to see if God really did leave his fingerprints behind.

What thing in your house has more of your fingerprints on it than anything else?

Have you ever made a prediction that came true?

Creative God, you gave everyone unique fingerprints, but you love us all the same. How awesome you are!

20

What is a Messiah?

The woman said, "I know that Messiah"
(called Christ) "is coming. When he comes,
he will explain everything to us." Then Jesus
declared, "I, the one speaking to you—I am he."

JOHN 4:25–26

"Messiah" comes from the Hebrew verb *mashakh*, which means "to anoint." When translated from Hebrew to Greek, the work becomes *christos*, which in English is "Christ." But what was the Messiah expected to do?

In the days when King David reigned over Israel, God promised to raise up one of David's descendants to reign forever on his throne. After David's death, the nation of Israel was conquered and taken captive by the Babylonian empire. Still, the Jewish people remembered God's promised Messiah and prayed he would come in power to vanquish their enemies and set up a never-ending kingdom on Earth.

By the time Jesus showed up, Israel had gone from Babylonian to Roman control and the people were eager for the "anointed one" to claim his throne. As Jesus traveled through Israel casting out demons, healing the sick, and teaching with authority, people wondered if he was the Messiah they were promised.

And if he was, why didn't he go straight to Rome and set things straight? As the whole world would find out, Jesus *was* the Messiah, but he was unlike anything the people were expecting.

If you were expecting someone to take control of the world, what do you think they'd be like?

Why did the Jews think Jesus might be the Messiah?

Lord, thank you for rescuing us in
the way we least expected.

Waiting is Hard

I wait for the LORD, my whole being waits,
and in his word I put my hope.

PSALM 130:5

Researchers at the University of Rochester (N.Y.) tested a group of kids ages three to five to see how long they could wait to eat a marshmallow. They were promised another marshmallow if they could wait to eat the first one. Then the researcher left the room for fifteen minutes. Some kids licked the marshmallow. Others tried looking away. A few just popped the whole thing in their mouth without waiting.

Before the marshmallows though, the children were divided into two groups. Both groups started doing a craft project with poor art supplies. The researchers promised they'd return with better supplies. For one group, they came back with brand-new crayons and stickers. Researchers returned to the other group empty-handed. The kids who received the better art supplies waited around twelve minutes before eating the marshmallow. The disappointed group only waited an average of three minutes.

The nation of Israel had been waiting for a Messiah since King David left the throne. They dealt with many disappointments as they were conquered and exiled, but still they held out hope. When Jesus came performing miracles, some people claimed he was the Messiah, but many worried he'd be just another disappointment.

Which group in the experiment are you more like?

What is something you are waiting for?

As Christians, we know Jesus was the one we were waiting for, and he's so much better than a second marshmallow!

God, help me trust in your timing for my needs.

22

Abram's Promise

"I will bless those who bless you, and whoever curses you I will curse; and all peoples on earth will be blessed through you."

GENESIS 12:3

God had been planning his rescue plan for the world before Israel ever became a nation.

In Old Testament days when Abraham was still called Abram, God called Abram and his wife out of their home country to go on an adventure with him. Abram was seventy-five years old. But God gave Abram a promise which made everything he did during his seventy-five years worth leaving behind.

In Genesis 12:2–3, God told Abram, "I will make you into a great nation, and I will bless you; I will make your name great, and you will be a blessing. I will bless those who bless you, and whoever curses you I will curse; and all peoples on earth will be blessed through you."

God did make him into a great nation, changing his name from Abram, which means "exalted father," to Abraham, which means "father of many," in the process. But the promise God made was for more than just Abram or Abraham. It was for the whole world.

When Jesus was born on earth, he came from Abraham's family. That's the first ridge in the fingerprint God left pointing to Jesus being the Messiah.

If God asked you to leave your home and follow him, would you go?

What would you tell Abram about Jesus if you could?

Lord, your promises may take time, but they are worth waiting for.

23

David's Promise

> *When your days are over and you rest with your ancestors, I will raise up your offspring to succeed you, your own flesh and blood, and I will establish his kingdom.*
>
> **2 SAMUEL 7:12**

When sin entered the world, God set his rescue plan into motion. God's plan involved King David of Bethlehem.

David, the youngest of Jesse's children, was initially overlooked when the prophet came to anoint him as the future king. He wasn't the oldest or strongest. Jesse didn't even send for him until the prophet passed over his other kids. David was busy watching his father's sheep.

As an adult, David served God faithfully and God gave him victory in battle. Once peace was established, God gave David a promise.

Second Samuel says, "When your days are over and you rest with your ancestors, I will raise up your offspring to succeed you, your own flesh and blood, and I will establish his kingdom. He is the one who will build a house for my Name, and I will establish the throne of his kingdom forever."

God promised Abraham the Messiah would come from his family, and God promised David one of his descendants would set up a kingdom which will last forever. Matthew 1:1 introduces Jesus Christ as "the son of David, the son of Abraham." That's the second ridge of the fingerprint pointing to Jesus being the Messiah.

How do you think a king is supposed to look?

Why would a shepherd make a good king?

> *God, make me faithful and victorious like David was.*

Ahaz's Sign

Therefore the LORD himself will give you a sign: The virgin will conceive and give birth to a son, and will call him Immanuel.

ISAIAH 7:14

Ahaz was the king of Judah. He was a descendant of David after the nation of Israel split in two. Surrounded by enemies, Ahaz made a deal with the leader of Assyria to protect him. When the prophet Isaiah offered to show Ahaz a sign that God would protect Judah instead, Ahaz refused.

Ahaz could have asked for any sign, however impossible. Despite his refusal, Isaiah gave him a sign anyway. A girl who couldn't possibly be pregnant would give birth to a son. The child's name would be Immanuel, or "God with us." The message for Ahaz was this: Stop trusting in human abilities because God himself is with you.

But the sign wasn't just for Ahaz. Many years later, a girl named Mary who was a descendant of King David would become impossibly pregnant. The child would be named Jesus and he would be God in human form, literally "God with us."

When we are tempted to rely on our human strength instead of God's power, we need to remember Ahaz's sign. The impossible is possible for God. Mary's impossible pregnancy is the third ridge of the fingerprint pointing to Jesus being the Messiah.

When a situation seems impossible, do you ask God for help or rely on your own strength?

What are some ways God is with us?

Lord God, thank you for always being with us. Help me trust you more than human powers.

Oh, Little Town of Bethlehem

> *"But you, Bethlehem Ephrathah, though you are small among the clans of Judah, out of you will come for me one who will be ruler over Israel, whose origins are from of old, from ancient times."*
>
> **MICAH 5:2**

It would be easy to think Bethlehem was an important town in the Old Testament. The Book of Ruth is set there. Israel's most famous king, David, is from there. But aside from those things, it was just known as a small shepherding town.

When Micah announced Bethlehem was to be the birthplace of the Messiah, it was probably a bit of a shock. Little Bethlehem? Sure, it was where David was born, but it was so small and insignificant!

It's possible God chose Bethlehem *because* it was small and insignificant. After all, when the prophet Samuel anointed David to be king, David was considered too small and insignificant for the job. But God loves to defy expectations.

Why? Because by using the weak and small, he can show just how big and powerful he is! When we feel too weak for a job, it would be good to remember this: God loves to use people just like us to prove his power. Today, we know even though Jesus grew up in Nazareth, he was born in Bethlehem, just like his ancestor David, which is the fourth ridge of the fingerprint pointing toward him being the Messiah.

What is one way God has shown his strength in your weakness?

Why do you think God likes defying expectations?

> *Lord, when I'm feeling small and insignificant, remind me that you chose both David and Bethlehem to do big things for you.*

26

The King on a Donkey's Colt

Rejoice greatly, Daughter Zion! Shout, Daughter Jerusalem! See, your king comes to you, righteous and victorious, lowly and riding on a donkey, on a colt, the foal of a donkey.

ZECHARIAH 9:9

The Book of Zechariah is toward the end of the Old Testament and was written by someone who had seen some tough times. After King David, the nation of Israel started dabbling with the religions of their neighboring countries instead of worshipping God alone.

God chose to turn the people's hearts back to himself by allowing them to experience life without his help. It didn't take long for Israel to fall apart. The nation split and was conquered by various enemies, but then God gave them another chance.

In the days of the prophet Zechariah, the people of Israel were allowed to rebuild the temple in Jerusalem and Zechariah predicted the countries who conquered Israel would be conquered in return. Then Israel's true king would come, not in strength with an army, but in peace while riding on a donkey.

Who was this true king? Jesus! Check out John 12:14–15, "Jesus found a young donkey and sat on it, . . . see, your king is coming, seated on a donkey's colt.'"

That's the fifth ridge of the fingerprint pointing to Jesus being the Messiah.

> **What are some tough times God has allowed so you turn back to him?**
>
> **If you could ride any animal into Jerusalem, what would you choose and why?**

Lord, keep me close so I don't need tough times to turn my heart back to you.

27

Betrayed by a Friend

> *Even my close friend, someone I trusted, one who shared my bread, has turned against me.*
>
> **PSALM 41:9**

When it's time for lunch at school, who are we most likely to sit near? Our friends! Sharing meals is a great way to spend quality time with the people we value most. We don't typically eat with people we don't like or don't trust. What if they spit in our food?

Eating together has always been important, even in the Old Testament. When King David wrote Psalm 41, he was going through a tough time. David was sick and he felt like his enemies were happy about his illness. He was even feeling betrayed by the people closest to him, the people who he ate with. Still, David trusted God and asked him to take care of his needs.

When Jesus was eating with his disciples right before he was crucified, he quoted Psalm 41 to them. Jesus was going through a tough time. While he wasn't physically sick like David, he was facing death on the cross and he knew one of the people closest to him, Judas, was going to betray him.

As uncomfortable as it would be to eat with people who aren't our friends, it is so much worse to be betrayed by people who are. When that happens to us, we can trust Jesus to know how we feel. Judas's betrayal is the sixth ridge of the fingerprint pointing to Jesus being the Messiah.

How would it feel to eat with people who aren't your friends?

Have you ever been betrayed by one of your friends?

Lord, help me be faithful to my friends.

David's Crucifixion Prediction

> *I am poured out like water, and all my*
> *bones are out of joint. My heart has turned*
> *to wax; it has melted within me.*
> *... a pack of villains encircles me; they*
> *pierce[b] my hands and my feet.*

PSALM 22:14–16

As Jesus looked down from the cross, he quoted Psalm 22 which was written by King David about one thousand years before, "My God, my God, why have you forsaken me?"

When David wrote Psalm 22, he wrote how he was feeling. He didn't know how accurate his description would be when it came to Jesus's crucifixion. It wasn't just that Jesus felt forsaken by God (v. 1). He was mocked (v. 7), his bones were pulled out of joint (v. 14), his hands and feet were pierced (v. 16), and the soldiers divided up his clothes by casting lots (v. 18). When we read through Matthew 27 in the New Testament, we see how specific David's prediction was.

What's really amazing is when David was alive and describing this scene, crucifixion hadn't even been invented yet.

Even though David didn't know what would happen to Jesus, God did. He chose to get on the cross and endure the punishment for us, knowing exactly what to expect. That's the seventh ridge of the fingerprint pointing toward Jesus being the Messiah.

Have you ever felt forsaken by God?

How does it feel to know that Jesus endured the cross to pay the punishment for your sins?

> *Amazing God, the cross didn't surprise you.*
> *Thank you for taking my punishment for sin.*

The Risen Messiah

*Because you will not abandon me to
the realm of the dead, nor will you
let your faithful one see decay.*

PSALM 16:10

There are a few things everyone has in common. Everyone was born. Everyone breathes. Everyone eats. Eventually, everyone dies. After that, everyone decays.

When King David wrote Psalm 16, people may have scratched their heads about the end of David's song. Psalm 16:9–11 says, "Therefore my heart is glad and my tongue rejoices; my body also will rest secure, because you will not abandon me to the realm of the dead, nor will you let your faithful one see decay. You make known to me the path of life; you will fill me with joy in your presence, with eternal pleasures at your right hand."

Was David really saying God would show him the path back to life after his death? That his body wouldn't decay? That he'd rule at God's right hand? Sure, he was a king after God's own heart, but that would still be a bold claim for David to make.

No. David knew his body would decay. He was predicting the Messiah who would rule at God's right hand, would die, and come back to life. When Jesus died then rose again three days later, David's prophecy came true. His resurrection is the final ridge of the fingerprint pointing to Jesus being the Messiah.

What are some things everyone has in common?

How would you react if someone you knew claimed they'd rise from the dead?

*Risen Lord, help me live in your power
that even death couldn't stop.*

30

The Coincidence Argument

> *But this is how God fulfilled what he had foretold through all the prophets, saying that his Messiah would suffer.*
>
> **ACTS 3:18**

Some people think making a correct prediction is a coincidence. By correctly predicting a coin flip, we may feel like we're good at guessing. If we make a few guesses that come true, we might be considered lucky. So was it just by lucky coincidence Jesus's fingerprint matched the Old Testament prophecies about the Messiah?

Mathematician Peter W. Stoner figured out the probability of one person fulfilling just eight prophecies is one chance in one hundred million billion.

Let's imagine we marked a silver dollar coin then mixed it in with one hundred million billion others. Then we filled the state of Texas two feet high with all these coins. What are the chances of a blindfolded person grabbing one coin, and it being the one we marked?

Those are the odds of "accidentally" fulfilling the prophecy. Statistically speaking, it couldn't happen. But Jesus didn't fulfill just eight Old Testament prophecies; his life matches up with dozens of others.

The odds reveal it's impossible for anyone to fulfill all of the Old Testament prophecies. Yet Jesus—and only Jesus, throughout all of history—managed to do it.

How is Jesus fulfilling the Old Testament prophecies different from flipping a coin?

Do you think it's a coincidence that Jesus fulfilled all those prophecies?

> *Lord, there are no accidents or coincidences with you. Thank you for loving me on purpose.*

31

The Intentional Fulfillment Argument

Many are the plans in a person's heart, but it is the LORD's purpose that prevails.

PROVERBS 19:21

Let's say someone made a prediction we would have a peanut butter and jelly sandwich for lunch. They may or may not be right. If we knew about the prediction, we could make sure it came true by making a peanut butter and jelly sandwich.

Some people think that's what Jesus and his disciples did with the Old Testament prophecies. If one of the prophecies said the Messiah rode into Jerusalem on a donkey, they would go find a donkey for Jesus to ride in on. Not too impressive, right?

But Jesus fulfilled lots of prophecies no one could control. Could he have made Mary give birth in Bethlehem? Could he arrange for his ancestors to include Abraham and David? Why would he intentionally make one of his disciples betray him, or choose to be executed on a cross? Could he have prevented his legs from being broken (compare Numbers 9:12 with John 19:31–37)?

Either these things happened because Jesus was the prophesied Messiah or he somehow made them happen because he is the God who controls all things. In any case, no one could say Jesus intentionally fulfilled the prophecies as a normal human being.

Which prophecy do you think would be hardest to fulfill?

How would you answer someone who said Jesus and his disciples made the prophecies come true?

Lord, help me answer people who doubt you with kindness and wisdom.

32

The Altered Gospels Argument

*For we are taking pains to do what is
right, not only in the eyes of the Lord
but also in the eyes of man.*

2 CORINTHIANS 8:21

People who don't believe Jesus was the Messiah sometimes say the gospel writers left out parts of the truth to make it seem like Jesus fulfilled prophecies when he actually didn't. For instance, did the apostle John just leave out the part where Roman soldiers broke Jesus's legs?

Pastor Louis S. Lapides, who grew up Jewish and converted to Christianity, says no. Lapides has spent years studying the Old Testament prophecies about Jesus.

"When the gospels were being circulated, there were people living who had been around when all these things happened," he explains. "If someone had seen a mistake, they would've said, 'John, you know it didn't happen that way. We're trying to communicate a life of righteousness and truth, so don't taint it with a lie.'"

Not only would Christians have made sure the gospel accounts were accurate, opponents of Christianity would have jumped on any opportunity to discredit the gospels. But no evidence exists to suggest Jesus's fulfillment of the prophecies were falsified.

Honesty is truly the best policy, and everyone knew the gospel writers were being honest when they claimed Jesus was the Messiah.

How would you feel if accused of lying when you were telling the truth?

Would other people believe your story based on your past truthfulness?

*Lord, keep me from lying, so people
believe when I tell the truth about you.*

33

The Context Argument

Whoever walks in integrity walks securely, but whoever takes crooked paths will be found out.

PROVERBS 10:9

The final argument people use to deny Jesus is the Messiah is to say the Old Testament prophecies are taken out of context when applied to Jesus in the New Testament. What if the verses Christians use as evidence are just misunderstood?

That idea makes Bible scholar and pastor Louis S. Lapides sigh. "You know, I go through the books that people write to try to tear down what we believe. That's not fun to do, but I spend the time to look at each objection individually and then to research the context and wording in the original language," he says. "And every single time, the prophecies have stood up and shown themselves to be true."

For anyone who still doesn't believe Jesus is the Messiah, Lapides makes this challenge: "Sincerely ask God to show you whether or not Jesus is the Messiah. That's what I did—and without any coaching it became clear to me who fit the fingerprint of the Messiah."

If we aren't sure Jesus is the Anointed One who came to rescue mankind from our sins, we should definitely ask God to guide us to the truth. Psalm 145:18-19 says "The LORD is near to all who call on him, to all who call on him in truth. He fulfills the desires of those who fear him; he hears their cry and saves them."

> How would you answer someone who says the Old Testament prophecies are misunderstood?
>
> What do you think it means that God is near to all who call on him?

Lord, may I always be near to you and trust the truths you show me.

Of Penguins & Messiahs

> *For prophecy never had its origin in the human*
> *will, but prophets, though human, spoke from God*
> *as they were carried along by the Holy Spirit.*
>
> **2 PETER 1:21**

Let's imagine we were assigned a group project to write a research paper about penguins. Our group would probably go to the library or look up penguin facts on the internet. We'd want to make sure our facts lined up and we didn't all say the same thing. In the end, our paper would be graded on whether we told the truth about penguins.

The Bible is like a group project, but it isn't about penguins. It's about God's rescue plan for humanity, and it features the Messiah all over the place. God used lots of different people throughout history to write the Bible, but they couldn't proofread each other's work. They wrote all kinds of different things about what the Messiah would do or be like.

When Jesus came and fulfilled hundreds of prophecies about the Messiah, the Bible proved it was telling the truth. But how did a group of prophets writing different things about the Messiah across history write such accurate predictions about who Jesus was and what he did?

What do you think it means to be "inspired" by the Holy Spirit?

What is God's rescue plan for humanity?

Although the Bible was written by lots of different people, it was all inspired by the same Holy Spirit. God told the writers what to write, and they wrote it down. Wouldn't it be nice if the teacher told us what to write in every research paper?

> *Lord, help me listen to your Spirit like*
> *the prophets who wrote the Bible.*

God's New Deal

> *"The days are coming," declares the LORD,*
> *"when I will make a new covenant with the*
> *people of Israel and with the people of Judah."*
>
> **JEREMIAH 31:31**

In looking at the prophecies about the Messiah, we've seen how Jesus fits the fingerprint by his ancestry, by his miraculous birth in Bethlehem, by his entrance into Jerusalem on a donkey, by Judas's betrayal, by his death on the cross, and by his resurrection.

But how about prophecies about what the Messiah would do? Let's look at Jeremiah 31:33–34:

"This is the covenant I will make with the people of Israel after that time," declares the LORD. "I will put my law in their minds and write it on their hearts. I will be their God, and they will be my people. No longer will they teach their neighbor, or say to one another, 'Know the LORD,' because they will all know me, from the least of them to the greatest," declares the LORD. "For I will forgive their wickedness and will remember their sins no more."

In the original covenant, God made with the nation of Israel, the people offered sacrifices to God to pay for their sins and God communicated through his prophets and priests. In the new covenant, God is promising a personal relationship and removing the need for more sacrifices. Why? Because Jesus was the perfect sacrifice to cover the sins of the world, making it possible for God to live inside us through the Holy Spirit!

How did Jesus fulfill this prophecy about a new covenant with God's people?

Why is this good news for us?

> *God, thank you for including me in your*
> *new deal and forgiving my sins.*

36

Water in the Desert

And the Lord's servant must not be quarrelsome but must be kind to everyone, . . . God will grant them repentance leading them to a knowledge of the truth.

2 TIMOTHY 2:24–25

Imagine being in the desert. The sun is hot. Water is scarce. Suddenly, a figure appears in the distance. As he gets closer, we can hear him yelling, "Follow me to cold water and refreshing shade! Everyone is welcome!" We'd probably follow him.

But if he came up and yelled, "Why are you dummies out here where it's hot instead of over there where the water is? Everyone knows you need water in the desert! I think it was back that way." We'd probably ignore him and look for water away from where he was pointing.

Even though we've seen enough fingerprint evidence to know Jesus was the promised Messiah, there are a lot of people who don't believe in him. As Christians, it's our job to spread the good news about how Jesus came to rescue the world from sin.

If we want people to follow us to the life-giving message of Jesus, we need to be kind and knowledgeable. People without a relationship may not know how much they need him. First, we should pray for those people to be able to hear our message, then we should present them the good news with kindness.

Who is someone you know who might not know the good news about Jesus?

How can you present them the message in kindness?

Lord, may I tell others the good news in a kind way.

Eyewitness Evidence

> *For we did not follow cleverly devised stories when we told you about the coming of our Lord Jesus Christ in power, but we were eyewitnesses of his majesty.*
>
> **2 PETER 1:16**

In criminal investigations, eyewitness testimony can make the difference between the conviction of a guilty person or that person going free. Before fingerprints and DNA evidence became part of the criminal justice system, eyewitnesses were considered the best way to convince a jury of someone's guilt.

Eyewitnesses aren't just important in criminal investigations. When siblings fight, parents regularly ask each kid for their side of the story. Classroom disruptions often require teachers to ask, "Who saw what happened?" Eyewitness testimony can even be used to see whether Jesus Christ is the Son of God.

But what eyewitness accounts do we possess? Do we have the testimony of anyone who personally interacted with Jesus, who saw his miracles, who witnessed his death, and who perhaps even encountered him after his resurrection?

Why is eyewitness evidence important to determine what happened?

Do you think we'll be able to trust the eyewitness accounts in the Gospels?

The answer is yes. The first four books of the New Testament, called the Gospels, were all written from eyewitness accounts of Jesus's life and work. In the coming days, we'll look at each account and see whether these eyewitnesses can be trusted.

> *Lord, show me the truth about the eyewitnesses who saw your ministry.*

38

Dig Deeper–Papias & Irenaeus

Can we really trust the gospels as eyewitness accounts of history? The early leaders of the church believed so. Let's take a closer look at two of them: Papias and Irenaeus.

Papias was born nearly sixty years after Jesus was. He was a writer and church leader who studied under the apostle John, the son of Zebedee, the "apostle Jesus loved." While Papias would naturally be able to attest to the accuracy of John's gospel, he also supported the gospel of Mark as being an eyewitness account.

In about AD 125, Papias said Mark had carefully and accurately recorded Peter's eyewitness observations. His exact words were that Mark "made no mistake" and did not include "any false statement." Papias also noted how Matthew had preserved the teachings of Jesus as well.

Iranaeus was born around one hundred years after Jesus. He was raised in a Christian household and grew up in the town where Polycarp—another church father and disciple of John, like Papias—had his church.

About sixty years after Papias wrote about the gospel of Mark, Irenaeus wrote:

Matthew published his own Gospel among the Hebrews in their own tongue, when Peter and Paul were preaching the Gospel in Rome and founding the church there. After their departure, Mark, the disciple and interpreter of Peter, himself handed down to us in writing the substance of Peter's preaching. Luke, the follower of Paul, set down in a book the Gospel preached by his teacher. Then John, the disciple of the Lord, who also leaned on his breast, himself produced his Gospel while he was living at Ephesus in Asia.

From reading the words of these early church leaders, it was obvious that people in Jesus's day knew who wrote the Gospels and they believed the writers' words.

Differences in the Gospels

*Many have undertaken to draw up an account
of the things that have been fulfilled[a] . . .
eyewitnesses and servants of the word.*

LUKE 1:1–2

Some people say the Bible isn't true because of differences in the same stories. For example, Luke 9 and Mark 9 tell similar stories. In Luke 9:50 Jesus is quoted as saying, "For whoever is not against you is for you." Jesus's quote in Mark 9:39–40 is a sentence longer and from a different point of view. Does that prove the Bible is full of errors? Not at all.

Bible scholar Daniel B. Wallace once had a young woman approach him with six handwritten pages of supposed discrepancies in the Gospels. "You're going to have to answer every single one of these before I can believe anything about Christianity," she said.

"Don't you think this list proves that the writers didn't conspire and collude when they wrote their Gospels?" Wallace answered.

Wallace went on to point out that the core message of the Gospels—Jesus performed miracles, healed people, forgave sins, prophesied his own death and resurrection, died on a cross, and rose from the dead—is exactly the same in all accounts.

Two weeks later, this young woman gave her life to Christ.

Do you think differences in the eyewitness accounts make the stories stronger?

Have you ever remembered an event differently from someone in your family?

*Lord, don't let differences in the Gospels
stop me from believing in your love.*

Who Really Wrote Them?

> *... I too decided to write an orderly account for you, ... so that you may know the certainty of the things you have been taught.*
>
> **LUKE 1:3–4**

While some people get tripped up on the differences in the Bible, others have trouble believing the Gospel writers actually wrote the books which bear their names. If the Bible wasn't written by the people it claims, is the content trustworthy?

"Strictly speaking, the gospels are anonymous," admits Dr. Craig Blomberg, a seminary professor and author of many books. "But the uniform testimony of the early church was that Matthew, the tax collector and one of the twelve disciples, was the author of the first gospel in the New Testament; that John Mark, was the author of the gospel we call Mark; and that Luke, wrote both the gospel of Luke and the Acts of the Apostles."

When later writings emerged pretending to be authentic gospels, their writers used the names of famous Jesus followers like Philip, Peter, and Mary to trick people into believing them. The Synoptic Gospels, a special name for Matthew, Mark, and Luke, didn't claim to be written by famous disciples.

According to Dr. Blomberg, "There would not have been any reason to attribute authorship to these three less-respected people if it weren't true."

> **Do you believe the Gospels are trustworthy records of Jesus's life?**
>
> **How would you answer someone who doubted the authors' identities?**

Lord, I believe you are trustworthy and the accounts about you are too.

41

Who was Matthew?

As Jesus went on from there, he saw a man named Matthew sitting at the tax collector's booth. "Follow me," he told him, and Matthew got up and followed him.

MATTHEW 9:9

Of the Synoptic Gospels, only the book of Matthew was written by one of Jesus's twelve disciples. Prior to being called by Jesus, Matthew, also known as Levi, was a tax collector.

Jewish tax collectors in Jesus's day were considered by many to be traitors to the nation of Israel. It was their job to collect taxes for the Roman empire, and many tax collectors used their positions of authority to take more money than they should have. If people complained about them, the tax collectors could accuse them of not paying their taxes and turn them over to the Roman soldiers.

Matthew would have been a very unlikely choice for Jesus to call as a disciple. But Jesus doesn't see people the way the rest of society sees them. With the skills of record-keeping and writing he acquired through his previous profession, Matthew was a perfect choice to write down his eyewitness account of Jesus's life and ministry.

When we feel like we aren't good enough, we can think of Matthew and remember how Jesus can use anyone from any background to do great things for him!

If you were calling disciples, would you have picked someone like Matthew? Why or why not?

How do you think Jesus could use your skills to do great things?

Lord, thank you for choosing me, regardless of how other people feel about it.

42

What was Important to Matthew?

"Enter through the narrow gate. For wide is the gate and broad is the road that leads to destruction, ... But small is the gate and narrow the road that leads to life, and only a few find it."

MATTHEW 7:13–14

Matthew, Mark, and Luke are called the Synoptic Gospels because they deal with a lot of the same events and stories.

The word *synoptic* is related to the word *synopsis*, which is a mash-up of the Greek words *syn*, which means "together," and *opsis*, which means "sight." The idea is that the Synoptic Gospels offer the same kind of pictures of Jesus.

Still, the way Matthew tells Jesus's biography shows what things are important to him. As a former tax collector, Matthew was in a unique position to interact with both Jews and Gentiles. The details he included in his gospel show how Jesus was the Messiah the Jews were waiting for, and also how salvation was available to Gentiles.

Although it is available to everyone, salvation isn't always easy to accept. It means leaving our lives and former priorities behind. But following Jesus is worth more than anything this world can offer.

Matthew knew it doesn't matter what people think of us if Jesus has accepted us. Whether we grew up hoping for the Messiah to come or not, the important thing is our response to Jesus's acceptance.

What things would be important for you to tell others about Jesus?

Why would it be hard to accept God's gift of salvation?

Lord, keep my feet from the broad road that leads to destruction.

Matthew's Exclusive: Fulfilling the Law

"Do not think that I have come to abolish the Law or the Prophets; I have not come to abolish them but to fulfill them."

MATTHEW 5:17

When Jesus stepped into his ministry on earth as a rabbi, healing and teaching with God's power, the pharisees didn't like it. They had hundreds of years of tradition behind them to keep life predictable. They thought this Rabbi Jesus was doing new things and getting rid of the old. By keeping life predictable with their traditions, the pharisees missed the Messiah predicted in the Old Testament.

In a passage exclusive to Matthew's gospel, Jesus addresses the controversy with his disciples. Matthew 5:17–18 says, "Do not think that I have come to abolish the Law or the Prophets; I have not come to abolish them but to fulfill them. For truly I tell you, until heaven and earth disappear, not the smallest letter, not the least stroke of a pen, will by any means disappear from the Law until everything is accomplished."

When we believe Jesus is the promised Messiah and we accept his gift of salvation, we recognize the fulfillment of an ancient promise. In the process, we become a new creation.

"Therefore, if anyone is in Christ, the new creation has come: The old has gone, the new is here!" (2 Corinthians 5:17)

Do you like trying new things or do you like life being predictable?

What do you think it means to be a new creation?

Lord Jesus, don't let my relationship with you become just a tradition. Keep it fresh and new.

Matthew's Exclusive: The Rest Giver

> *"Come to me, all you who are weary and burdened, and I will give you rest."*
>
> **MATTHEW 11:28**

There's a difference between going to a fast food restaurant and attending a formal dinner. Formal dinners include fancy invitations, dress codes (tuxedos for guys and elegant clothes for ladies), multiple courses, and more silverware than anyone knows what to do with. Eating fast food usually requires us to avoid getting ketchup on the car seats.

When Jesus walked the earth, the pharisees had more rules and traditions than formal dinners had silverware. There were complicated handwashing rituals, strict social guidelines for who they would hang out with, and public prayers to draw attention to their "holiness." They took pride in having more rules to follow than anyone else, even if they didn't follow all the rules themselves.

Jesus knew how tiresome it would be to remember and keep all those rules. When one of the pharisees asked him which was the most important law, "Jesus replied: 'Love the Lord your God with all your heart and with all your soul and with all your mind.' This is the first and greatest commandment. And the second is like it: 'Love your neighbor as yourself.' All the Law and the Prophets hang on these two commandments." (Matthew 22:37–40)

If we are hungry for Jesus and loving to others, we will be following the rules well.

> **What are some rules you struggle to keep?**
>
> **How would loving God and others make keeping the rules easier?**

Lord, help me love you and love others.

45

DAY 39

Matthew's Exclusive: Hidden Treasure

"The kingdom of heaven is like treasure hidden in a field. When a man found it, he hid it again, and then in his joy went and sold all he had and bought that field."

MATTHEW 13:44

Banks weren't really around in Jesus's day. If people wanted to keep their money safe, they buried it in a secret place. If they died without sharing the secret, the location of their money died with them.

One of Jesus's shortest parables talks about just such a story. He compares the kingdom of heaven to a treasure hidden in a field. The owner of the treasure must be out of the picture because the man is able to buy the field where it is buried. If the treasure's owner was alive, he wouldn't have sold the field, right?

But there's still a catch. The field isn't free. The man has to sell everything he owns to buy it. Considering the hidden treasure he's about to get, it's a wise investment. How is this like the kingdom of heaven?

Jesus isn't saying people need to get rid of all their stuff in order to be saved. He's saying the short-term joys of this world don't compare to the long-term joys of heaven. Discovering Jesus's gift of salvation should change our priorities, just like the man's priorities changed when he found the hidden treasure. He was willing to give up everything. Are we?

> **What would you do if you found hidden treasure?**
>
> **Is there anything you own that would be hard to give up, even if you could get a treasure for doing so?**

Dear Jesus, change my priorities so your kingdom is the most important thing to me.

Matthew's Exclusive: The Net and the Fish

> *... The kingdom of heaven is like a net that was let down into the lake and caught all kinds of fish.... Then they sat down and collected the good fish in baskets, but threw the bad away."*

MATTHEW 13:47–48

Jesus knew fishing. He taught from fishing boats. At least four out of the twelve disciples were fishermen. And he convinced Peter of his miraculous powers by telling him where to drop his fishing nets for a catch so big it almost sank Peter's boat! (Seriously, check out Luke 5:1–11.)

In one of the parables only found in Matthew's Gospel, Jesus compares the kingdom of heaven to a fishing expedition. Fishing with a net catches all kinds of fish, but not all of them are good to eat. In fact, Old Testament laws said Jews weren't allowed to eat some kinds of fish:

"Of all the creatures living in the water of the seas and the streams you may eat any that have fins and scales. Anything living in the water that does not have fins and scales is to be regarded as unclean by you" (Leviticus 11:9, 12).

The sorting process of good fish from bad fish isn't something that's happened yet. We'll all keep swimming along until the net is full. In the end, Jesus will decide who goes in the baskets and who gets tossed aside. We just need to be the best fish we can and keep swimming toward Jesus!

Are you ever tempted to judge whether someone is a "good fish" or a "bad fish?"

How would you feel if someone labeled you a "bad fish?"

> *Lord, you are the one who will judge us in the end. Keep me from taking your job.*

47

Matthew's Exclusive: Vineyard Workers

> ... *"For the kingdom of heaven is like a landowner who went out early in the morning to hire workers for his vineyard."*
>
> **MATTHEW 20:1**

Ancient Israel was big on farming. The country grew all kinds of crops, but they were famous for their grapes. Working for a whole day at a vineyard, where grapes grow on vines, a person could earn one *denarius* (a Roman coin similar to the dime).

In the parable of the vineyard workers in Matthew 20:1–16, Jesus told the story of a vineyard owner who hired some workers to work all day. After a few hours, he found some more workers and sent them to the vineyard. Every few hours, the owner hired a few more workers. At the end of the day, the owner paid everyone a denarius.

The workers who picked grapes all day were furious they were paid the same as the ones who only worked an hour. The vineyard owner simply replied, "Take your pay and go. I want to give the one who was hired last the same as I gave you. Don't I have the right to do what I want with my own money? Or are you envious because I am generous?" (Matthew 20:14–15)

This parable was aimed at the Jews. They didn't think it was fair how they waited for the Messiah, and when he came, he offered salvation to the Gentiles too. But God is never unfair to us when he is generous. None of us deserve the gifts he gives.

Do you ever feel like God is unfair?

How can you be thankful instead of jealous?

God, may I never accuse you of being unfair.

Who was Mark?

> *... When this had dawned on him, he went to the house of Mary the mother of John, also called Mark, where many people had gathered and were praying.*
>
> **ACTS 12:11–12**

Mark is the second of the Synoptic Gospels, and early leaders of the Christian church attribute it to John Mark.

John Mark was not one of Jesus's twelve disciples, but his name pops up throughout the New Testament as a loyal believer of Jesus Christ. After Peter miraculously escaped prison, he went to the home of John Mark's mom, which was known to be a gathering place for Christians (Acts 12: 11–12). John Mark was the cousin of Barnabas (Colossians 4:10), who helped Paul on his first missionary journey. Later on, he helped Peter in Rome (1 Peter 5:13).

John Mark wrote his gospel from Peter's eyewitness account around thirty or forty years after Jesus rose from the grave. If he wrote it while in Rome with Peter, the original readers of the gospel would have been Roman Christians with a Gentile background.

John Mark's gospel was the first biography of Jesus. Both Matthew and Luke used it as a resource in writing their own gospels. The most amazing thing about John Mark isn't what *he did* in writing the gospel, but what *God was able to do* because John Mark was willing.

Are you willing to let God do things through you?

How can you let others know about Jesus?

Lord, let my life be a testimony for you.

49

What was Important to Mark?

"Whoever wants to be my disciple must deny themselves and take up their cross and follow me. For whoever wants to save their life will lose it, but whoever loses their life for me and for the gospel will save it.

MARK 8:34–35

As the first writer of the Synoptic Gospels, Mark had a unique opportunity to write down Peter's eyewitness accounts of Jesus's life and ministry. While Matthew used his gospel to show Jews how the Messiah had come and to tell Gentiles salvation was available, Mark used his gospel to show Jesus as both the Son of God and the suffering servant.

Not only did God open heaven at Jesus's baptism to tell everyone Jesus is his Son (Mark 1:11), Jesus does things only God can do. He forgives sins (Mark 2:10) and nature obeys his commands (Mark 4:35–41).

But Jesus was fully human too. He got angry (Mark 3:5), sleepy (Mark 4:38), hungry (Mark 11:12), and felt deep sorrow (Mark 14:34). When he died, he died a human being (Mark 15:37).

Fortunately for all of us, Jesus didn't stay dead. Mark wanted Christians to know who Jesus is so they could follow in his footsteps, relying on his strength through trials, even when those trials end in death. The Christian life isn't always easy, but it is worthwhile.

Why is it important that Jesus is fully God and fully human?

How can you relate to Jesus through suffering?

Lord, I may not understand how you could be both God and man, but I trust you anyway.

Mark's Exclusive: The Sons of Thunder

These are the twelve he appointed: Simon . . .
James son of Zebedee and his brother John
(to them he gave the name Boanerges, which
means "sons of thunder") . . . who betrayed him.

MARK 3:16–19

How great would it be if Jesus gave us nicknames? In Mark's list of the twelve disciples, we get to see Jesus rename some of his followers. Simon became Peter, which means "rock." James and John earned the name Boanerges, which means "sons of thunder."

Peter's name change gets a lot of attention because he became the leader of the group after Jesus ascended to heaven.

But what about Boanerges? Mark is the only one to mention how Jesus called James and John the "sons of thunder." While Peter's name change probably relates to Jesus building his church on the rock, no explanations are given for Jesus's nickname for James and John.

What we *do* know is that Jesus does give new names to people when they come to faith in him.

Jesus gives us a new name to go with our new identity in him! Not only that, but we get to have his name too. That's why we call ourselves "*Christ*ians."

What nickname would you want Jesus to call you?

Why do you think Jesus called James and John the "sons of thunder?"

Lord, thank you for giving me
a new identity in you.

Mark's Exclusive: The Growing Seed

*All by itself the soil produces grain—
first the stalk, then the head, then
the full kernel in the head.*

MARK 4:28

Why shouldn't you tell a secret on a farm? Because the corn has ears.

That is a a corny joke, but isn't corn cool? It's delicious by itself, but it can be made into tortilla chips, breakfast cereals, and even fuel for cars! And the best part is how it grows by itself.

In Mark's Gospel, Jesus compares the kingdom to a farmer who plants a seed. "Night and day, whether he sleeps or gets up, the seed sprouts and grows, though he does not know how. All by itself the soil produces grain—first the stalk, then the head, then the full kernel in the head. As soon as the grain is ripe, he puts the sickle to it, because the harvest has come." (Mark 4:27–29)

The farmer plants the seed, but he can't make it grow. And seeds take time to develop into plants.

First Corinthians 3:7 says, "So neither the one who plants nor the one who waters is anything, but only God, who makes things grow." Growth happens because God makes it happen, and it happens on his schedule, not ours.

If things aren't happening as quickly as we'd like them to, we need to trust God. We don't need to be in control. We need to trust the one who is!

Are you ever frustrated because things take too long?

How can you show God you trust him, even when waiting is hard?

Lord, grow patience in me. Help me trust your timing.

52

Mark's Exclusive: The Deaf and Mute Man

> *He looked up to heaven and with a deep sigh said to him, "Ephphatha!" (which means "Be opened!"). At this, the man's ears were opened, his tongue was loosened and he began to speak plainly.*
>
> **MARK 7:33–35**

Jesus healed a lot of people throughout his ministry, but only Mark recorded the healing of the deaf and mute man from the Decapolis. The special description given to the man's condition is only used in one other place in the Bible.

Isaiah 35:5–6 says, "Then will the eyes of the blind be opened and the ears of the deaf unstopped. Then will the lame leap like a deer, and the mute tongue shout for joy.

The passage from Isaiah describes the joy in Lebanon when they see the glory of God in person. Actually, the Old Testament location for Lebanon is the same as the New Testament Decapolis, so Jesus isn't just healing a man in need, he's fulfilling one of the prophecies about the Messiah!

Even though Jesus isn't sticking his fingers in people's ears anymore, he still has the power to heal and save. We just need to pray and ask.

How do you think the deaf and mute man felt when Jesus stuck his fingers in his ears?

What do you think the man's first words were?

Lord, when I need healing, help me trust your process, no matter how strange it seems.

Mark's Exclusive: The Two-Stage Healing

When he had spit on the man's eyes and put his hands on him, Jesus asked, "Do you see anything?" He looked up and said, "I see people; they look like trees walking around."

MARK 8:23–24

Most of the time when Jesus healed people, they were immediately made whole. In fact, Mark 5 records the story of a woman in a crowd of people who was instantly healed when she just touched Jesus's robes. He just felt his power go out and heal the woman because of her faith. The healing of the blind man of Bethsaida was unique because Jesus healed him in two stages.

Mark 8:23–25 says, "He took the blind man by the hand and led him outside the village. When he had spit on the man's eyes and put his hands on him, Jesus asked, 'Do you see anything?'

"He looked up and said, 'I see people; they look like trees walking around.'

"Once more Jesus put his hands on the man's eyes. Then his eyes were opened, his sight was restored, and he saw everything clearly."

When we ask God for healing, it doesn't always happen immediately. The blind man of Bethsaida required the repeated touch of Jesus to be made whole. For our physical needs—and especially for our spiritual needs—we need to keep coming back to Jesus.

Why do you think the man required two touches for Jesus to heal him?

What are some ways you can keep in touch with Jesus?

Lord, when I can only see you through blurry eyes, heal my spiritual sight.

Mark's Exclusive: The Naked Guy at Gethsemane

A young man, wearing nothing but a linen garment, was following Jesus. When they seized him, he fled naked, leaving his garment behind.

MARK 14:51–52

After Jesus finished praying in the garden of Gethsemane, Judas approached with a group of soldiers. At first, the disciples stood by Jesus, refusing to allow the soldiers to arrest him. Peter even cut off a guy's ear (which Jesus immediately healed). In the end, the soldiers seized Jesus and the disciples fled for their lives.

This scene is repeated in each of the gospels, but Mark adds a detail the others left out. There was another man following behind, but when he got too close, the soldiers seized him too. He only got away by wriggling out of his clothes and fleeing naked.

The man was so scared, he would rather face embarrassment than suffer the same fate as Jesus.

Jesus warned his disciples what would happen. "Everyone will hate you because of me," he said in Mark 13:13, "but the one who stands firm to the end will be saved." Unfortunately, as the young man proved, no one stood firm when Jesus was arrested.

But we have something the disciples didn't have that night: The Holy Spirit living inside us. With God's help, we can stand firm.

> **Have you ever been as scared as the young man who followed Jesus?**
>
> **How can you fight those fears to stand firm?**

Lord Jesus, help me stand firm, even when I'm scared.

Who was Luke?

> *Our dear friend Luke, the doctor,*
> *and Demas send greetings.*
>
> **COLOSSIANS 4:14**

Luke is the third Synoptic Gospel and is attributed to this doctor and steadfast companion of the apostle Paul. Like each of the gospels, Luke was published anonymously. To figure out who wrote it, we need to look for clues in the text of the gospel.

Luke and Acts were both written to someone named Theophilus, so we can assume they share an author. Since the author includes himself in passages of Acts referring to travels with Paul, we can assume that he was one of Paul's missionary companions.

We know the author wasn't an eyewitness to the life of Jesus from Luke 1:1–2: "Many have undertaken to draw up an account of the things that have been fulfilled among us, just as they were handed down to us by those who from the first were eyewitnesses and servants of the word."

When we put those clues together, they point to Luke, who Paul counts as a dear friend in Colossians 4:14. Luke probably wrote his gospel, using Mark's gospel as a guide and adding in details from eyewitnesses and trustworthy sources.

What clues about you would lead people to know you're a Christian?

Why do you think Luke wrote his gospel?

The end result is the most complete biography of Jesus's life available. By reading this gospel we can see how from hated tax collectors—like Matthew—to respected doctors—like Luke—to people like us, Jesus is for everyone.

> *Lord, let my life be full of clues*
> *that I'm your follower.*

What was Important to Luke?

"But when you give a banquet, invite the poor, the crippled, the lame, the blind, and you will be blessed. Although they cannot repay you, you will be repaid at the resurrection of the righteous."

LUKE 14:13–14

Luke's reason for writing his gospel is in his introduction.

"With this in mind, since I myself have carefully investigated everything from the beginning, I too decided to write an orderly account for you, most excellent Theophilus . . ." (Luke 1:3–4)

In addition to being a doctor, Luke was a historian. He wanted people to know that Jesus was God's Son. As the other gospel writers highlighted different aspects of Jesus's ministry, Luke's gospel reveals a deep love for the poor and oppressed.

Luke set the tone for Jesus's ministry with this story. Jesus was handed a scroll from Isaiah, and he read, "'The Spirit of the Lord is on me, because he has anointed me to proclaim good news to the poor. He has sent me to proclaim freedom for the prisoners and recovery of sight for the blind, to set the oppressed free, to proclaim the year of the Lord's favor.'

"Then he rolled up the scroll, gave it back to the attendant and sat down. The eyes of everyone in the synagogue were fastened on him. He began by saying to them, 'Today this scripture is fulfilled in your hearing'" (Luke 4:18–21).

Who would you consider to be poor and oppressed today?

How can you show them some love?

Lord, may I love the poor and oppressed like you do.

Luke's Exclusive: The Widow's Son

... He said, "Young man, I say to you, get up!" The dead man sat up and began to talk, and Jesus gave him back to his mother.

LUKE 7:14–15

Luke 7:12 says, "As he approached the town gate, a dead person was being carried out—the only son of his mother, and she was a widow. And a large crowd from the town was with her."

Jesus then commanded the dead man to get up, and he did. Jesus called the son back to life so he could save the boy's mother from life on the streets.

As cool as his miracle was, Jesus wasn't the only one in history to perform it. In 1 Kings 17, Elijah did the same thing for a widow from Zarephath, not too far from Nain. Elijah's miracle would have been especially fresh in the minds of Jesus's disciples because he talked about it in Luke 4:26.

Jesus proved his power like a prophet of old and his compassion as a loving savior. Since we share his power through the Holy Spirit, we can show compassion like him too.

Why do you think Jesus raised the young man?

How can you help someone who doesn't have a voice in society?

Lord, give me compassion for others like you showed to the widow and her son.

58

Luke's Exclusive: The Good Samaritan

> *"Which of these three do you think was a neighbor to the man who fell into the hands of robbers?"*
> *... "The one who had mercy on him."*
> *Jesus told him, "Go and do likewise."*
>
> **LUKE 10:36–37**

The parable of the good Samaritan, found only in Luke's gospel, is famous throughout the world. When an expert in religious law tries to stump Jesus by asking what's required to have eternal life, Jesus answered that he must love God and love his neighbor. Instead of asking how he can love his neighbor well, the expert asked, "And who is my neighbor?"

Jesus answered with the now-famous parable about an Israelite attacked by robbers and left for dead. After two fellow Israelites passed him without helping, a Samaritan came along and nursed him back to health.

After telling this story, Jesus asked the expert who the wounded man's neighbor was. Jesus answered both the question the expert asked ("Who is my neighbor?") and the question he didn't ("How can I love my neighbor well?").

Jesus doesn't allow us to exclude people from God's love just because we don't like them. It isn't enough to love them in our hearts or pray for them as we pass by. Jesus wants us to love each other with our actions too.

Do you ever feel like excluding people because they are different from you?

How would you feel if God treated you like you treat your neighbors?

Lord, everyone is my neighbor. Help me love them with my heart and my actions.

59

Luke's Exclusive: The Prodigal Son

*"For this son of mine was dead and is
alive again; he was lost and is found."*
So they began to celebrate.

LUKE 15:24

Even more famous than the parable of the good Samaritan is the parable of the prodigal (lost) son, also only found in Luke's gospel.

While Jesus taught, the pharisees listened to catch him teaching untruths to his disciples. Knowing this, Jesus told the story of the prodigal son. It's worth rereading the whole story in Luke 15:11–31.

Everyone remembers the younger son who demanded his inheritance while his father was still alive. Upon receiving the inheritance, the young man squandered it and eventually crawled back to his father. The father was delighted with his son's return and threw a feast in his honor.

Jesus could have ended the story there, but he didn't. The older brother refused to go into the feast. He wouldn't acknowledge his brother's welcome back into the family. He was jealous. The father pleaded with the older brother, but we never know if he joined the feast or not.

Jesus told the parable for the pharisees. They were the older brother in his story. But he also told it for us, because we have been welcomed back into the family (like the younger son) and we shouldn't be mean to our spiritual siblings (like the older son).

How have you been like the younger brother?

How have you been like the older brother?

*Lord, help me be like the father
who loved both of his sons.*

60

Luke's Exclusive: The Ten Lepers

*They stood at a distance and called out in a
loud voice, "Jesus, Master, have pity on us!"
When he saw them, he said, "Go, show yourselves to
the priests." And as they went, they were cleansed.*

LUKE 17:12–14

People with skin diseases weren't allowed to live near other people, because they might be contagious. That's why the ten mentioned in Luke 17:11–19 shouted to Jesus from a distance. They were desperate for his help.

There are a couple of lessons we could learn from Jesus's healing. First, the lepers were cleansed *as they went*. If they heard Jesus's instructions, but didn't act on them, they wouldn't have been healed.

Second, and most shocking, the only one who showed Jesus appreciation for his help was someone who normally would have shunned a Jew like Jesus. Luke 17:16–19 says, "He threw himself at Jesus's feet and thanked him—and he was a Samaritan. Jesus asked, "Were not all ten cleansed? Where are the other nine? Has no one returned to give praise to God except this foreigner?" Then he said to him, "Rise and go; your faith has made you well."

As sinners, we all need to be cleansed by Jesus. It isn't enough to ask for healing if we then keep on sinning. We'll show we're healed *as we go*. After we're forgiven and cleansed, we should be thankful and praise God.

When is a time you've needed to ask Jesus for cleansing?

How can you show your thankfulness for God's help in your life?

*God, cleanse me from my sin
and help me live for you.*

Luke's Exclusive: The Persistent Widow

> *"And will not God bring about justice for his chosen ones, who cry out to him day and night? Will he keep putting them off?"*
>
> **LUKE 18:7**

In the parable of the persistent widow (Luke 18:1-8), we see a widow in distress. Unlike the widow of Nain from Luke 7, the widow in Jesus's parable has no son to ensure she's treated fairly.

In the parable, the widow took matters into her own hands. The judge in the story isn't a good man. He doesn't care about God or people, and he couldn't care less about the widow. But she won't be put off. She demands justice again and again.

Luke 18:4-5 says, "For some time he refused. But finally he said to himself, 'Even though I don't fear God or care what people think, yet because this widow keeps bothering me, I will see that she gets justice, so that she won't eventually come and attack me!'"

The story is almost funny. And although it features a widow demanding justice, it isn't about unjust judges or unfairness at all. This is a story about prayer.

Since God is the perfect example of fairness and justice, how much more loving and giving will he be when we ask for good things from him? We are welcome to come to him again and again and he'll answer us fairly each time, not because he's afraid we'll attack him, but because he loves us as his children!

When you ask for something from God, do you believe he'll answer you?

What is something you need from God?

Lord, you are always just and fair.

62

Who was John?

This is the disciple who testifies to these things and who wrote them down. We know that his testimony is true.

JOHN 21:24

Like the other gospel biographies of Jesus, the gospel of John's author is technically anonymous. Early church leaders have affirmed John's gospel was written by John, the son of Zebedee. When we add up the clues within the text, we can come to the same conclusion. But who was John?

Prior to following Jesus, John was a fisherman with his father Zebedee. Jesus called John and his brother James the "sons of thunder," but no one really knows why. Throughout his gospel, John refers to himself as "the disciple whom Jesus loved" (John 13:23, 19:26, and 20:2, to name a few). He is recognized as being one of the inner circle of Jesus's twelve disciples, along with Peter and James.

John was the only disciple to avoid a violent death. Following imprisonment on the Isle of Patmos, where he wrote the book of Revelation, *Foxe's Book of Martyrs* says, "John was ordered to be sent to Rome, where it is affirmed he was cast into a cauldron of boiling oil. He escaped by miracle, without injury." He probably died of old age in the city of Ephesus.

What are some things you'd ask John if you could?

Why do you think he called himself "the disciple whom Jesus loved"?

Like John, we can confidently claim to be disciples whom Jesus loves, because we know he died for our sins so we could join him in everlasting glory!

Lord, thank you for inviting me into your inner circle as a believer.

63

What was Important to John?

> *In the beginning was the Word, and the Word was with God, and the Word was God. He was with God in the beginning.*
>
> **JOHN 1:1–2**

Like the other gospel writers, John wrote so people would know Jesus.

John 20:31 says, "But these are written that you may believe that Jesus is the Messiah, the Son of God, and that by believing you may have life in his name."

Like his fellow disciple Matthew, John wanted his readers to know that Jesus was the Messiah. Unlike Matthew, John was more direct. After John the Baptist pointed out Jesus to Andrew, John wrote in John 1:41, "The first thing Andrew did was to find his brother Simon and tell him, 'We have found the Messiah' (that is, the Christ)."

John also wanted his readers to know Jesus was more than just the Anointed One who had come to claim his kingdom. Jesus was the Son of God. John 5:17–18 says, "Jesus said to them, 'My Father is always at his work to this very day, and I, too, am working.' For this reason the Jews tried all the harder to kill him; not only because he was breaking the Sabbath, but he was even calling God his own Father, making himself equal with God."

By knowing Jesus is the Son of God and the promised Messiah, we can have eternal life by placing our faith in him.

How can you know Jesus is the Messiah?

How can you know Jesus is the Son of God?

> *Lord Jesus, thank you for being God and offering me salvation.*

64

John's Exclusive: Nathanael's Nazareth Insult

> Philip found Nathanael and told him, "We have found the one Moses wrote about … Jesus of Nazareth, the son of Joseph." "Nazareth! Can anything good come from there?" Nathanael asked.
>
> **JOHN 1:45–46**

Some towns are known for certain things. Chicago has deep dish pizza. New Orleans is the home of Dixieland jazz. But some towns are not known for much of anything.

In Jesus's day, Nazareth was a tiny town which fell into the second category. Josephus, a historian, never mentioned it in a list of forty-five other towns in Galilee. It isn't mentioned in the Old Testament either.

That's why when Nathanael heard where the Messiah had come from, he said, "Nazareth! Can anything good come from there?" (John 1:46)

But that's where the best thing in history grew up. Before it was known for anything else, Nazareth became known as the hometown of Jesus Christ. And at Jesus's crucifixion, John 19:19 says, "Pilate had a notice prepared and fastened to the cross. It read: JESUS OF NAZARETH, THE KING OF THE JEWS."

As we grow, most of us want to make a name for ourselves. We want to be famous for something. Really, we should want to be famous for the same reason Nazareth was. Our hearts should be the hometown of Jesus.

Is your hometown known for anything?

How could you make it known that your heart is the home for Jesus?

> Lord, I don't need to make a name for myself. I just want to make you more famous.

John's Exclusive: Jesus & Nicodemus

> *For God so loved the world that he gave his one and only Son, that whoever believes in him shall not perish but have eternal life.*
>
> **JOHN 3:16**

The story behind this famous verse starts with Nicodemus.

Nicodemus was a Pharisee and member of the Sanhedrin. Word about Jesus had probably reached him through people who saw him performing miracles. John 2:23 says, "Now while he was in Jerusalem at the Passover Festival, many people saw the signs he was performing and believed in his name."

As someone familiar with the Old Testament prophecies about the Messiah, Nicodemus suspected Jesus had come to claim Israel's throne and overthrow their Roman oppressors.

Nicodemus guessed correctly. Jesus was the Messiah. But their conversation revealed how he misunderstood what that meant. Jesus wasn't interested in an earthly kingdom. For someone to enter into Jesus's kingdom, they needed to be born again.

"How can someone be born when they are old?" Nicodemus asked.

Jesus told him belief was the key to being born again. When we believe Jesus is the Son of God, that he died in our place, and that he rose from the dead, we are born again!

Have you been born again?

If you have been, who can you tell about your experience?

Lord, I believe you are who you say you are.

John's Exclusive: The Healing at the Pool

*When Jesus saw him lying there and learned
that he had been in this condition for a long
time, he asked him, "Do you want to get well?"
Pick up your mat and walk."*

JOHN 5:6, 8

When Jesus was in Jerusalem for one of the Jewish feasts, he visited a pool by the Sheep's Gate just north of the temple. The pool had once been used by temple officials to clean and prepare sheep for sacrifice in the temple. Over time, the pool earned a reputation for healing powers.

As he walked around the pool, Jesus saw a man who had been waiting a long time to be healed—thirty-eight years! When Jesus asked the man whether he wanted to get well, the injured man may have wondered if Jesus was making fun of him. That's why he was at the pool in the first place! The man was basing his hope on a pool used for sacrificial sheep instead of placing his hope in the sacrificial Lamb of God, Jesus.

When we need help, we would be wise to remember where our help comes from. Sure, we should visit doctors and take medicine when we get sick, but our hope shouldn't be in man alone. Our hope is in Christ.

Where is your hope?

If God doesn't heal us physically, why should we still trust him?

Lord, be my hope. Help me not trust only in the things of this world.

67

John's Exclusive: Jesus's Most Audacious Claim

"Very truly I tell you," Jesus answered, "before Abraham was born, I am!"

JOHN 8:58

To the Jews expecting a Messiah to overthrow the Roman empire, Jesus was a disappointment. He wasn't interested in an earthly kingdom. To those who recognized him as a teacher, he was confusing. Jesus didn't just teach God's truths through stories; he claimed to be the Son of God.

In John 8, the Jews just wanted Jesus to be clear. Who was he really? So Jesus told them.

"I am."

While it might sound like Jesus was avoiding the answer, he was actually being very clear. Jesus was claiming to be God himself.

When Moses stood before the burning bush in the wilderness and asked God how he could prove to the Israelites who sent him, God told Moses his name. "God said to Moses, "I AM WHO I AM. This is what you are to say to the Israelites: 'I AM has sent me to you.'" (Exodus 3:14)

Jesus wasn't just claiming to be older than Abraham, founder of the Israelite nation. He was claiming to be the God who called Abraham in the first place.

Why does it matter if Jesus is God?

What do you think God means when he says his name is "I am"?

For people today who are still asking who Jesus really is, the answer stands the same: Jesus is God. We may not like the answer, but it doesn't change the truth. Now what are we going to do with that truth?

God, help me know you more, so I question your existence less.

John's Exclusive: Doubting Thomas

*Then he said to Thomas, "Put your finger here;
see my hands. Reach out your hand and put
it into my side. Stop doubting and believe."*

JOHN 20:27

When Jesus appeared to his disciples after the resurrection, Thomas wasn't with them. The rest of the disciples could talk and laugh about how amazing it was. Jesus really did rise from the dead, but to Thomas, the whole thing might have felt like an inside joke.

John 20:25 records his reaction: "So the other disciples told him, 'We have seen the Lord!'

"But he said to them, 'Unless I see the nail marks in his hands and put my finger where the nails were, and put my hand into his side, I will not believe.'"

One week later, Jesus visited again. This time, Thomas was with them. Jesus took Thomas's words and used them to prove not only was he with Thomas right then in the flesh, but he was present when Thomas voiced his doubts to the other disciples before.

We may not see Jesus like Thomas and the other disciples did, but that doesn't mean we shouldn't believe. We can trust in Jesus as God. He sacrificed himself for us. He rose victorious over death and sin, and we will be blessed for our belief with eternal life.

Have you ever felt left out by your friends?

How can you bring others inside of your experiences with Jesus?

Lord, help me believe, even though I can't see you.

John v the Synoptic Gospels

Sanctify them by the truth; your word is truth.

JOHN 17:17

Some people have noticed how different John's gospel is to the Synoptic Gospels. How do we know John's Jesus is the same one from the other gospels?

"Well, it's true that John is more different than similar to the Synoptics," says Bible expert, Craig L. Blomberg. "Only a handful of the major stories that appear in the other three gospels reappear in John, although that changes noticeably when one comes to Jesus's last week. From that point forward the parallels are much closer."

Still, John's gospel shows a more talkative Jesus who openly claims to be God. The other gospels don't.

"No question," answers Blomberg, "but do they deserve to be called contradictions? I think the answer is no, and here's why: for almost every major theme or distinctive in John, you can find parallels in Matthew, Mark, and Luke, even if they're not as plentiful."

Even though the book of John doesn't read like the other gospels, we can trust in John's Jesus as the real deal. Whether John saw the Synoptic Gospels and chose not to duplicate them or whether he never saw them at all, his testimony to Jesus's miracles, teachings, death, and resurrection can help us find our Savior. God's word is true in all four gospels, and should be used to make us more like Jesus.

Do you think John is less trustworthy than the other Gospels?

How would you answer someone who didn't think the gospel of John belonged in the Bible?

Lord, help me defend your Word with my actions.

Jesus, Son of Man

*"For the Son of Man came to
seek and to save the lost."*

LUKE 19:10

One of the terms for Jesus found in all four gospels is the Son of Man. Here are just a few places to find it: Matthew 8:10, Mark 14:62, Luke 5:24, and John 3:13. Some people think he uses this term to suggest he wasn't really the Son of God, but just a normal human guy. That thought couldn't be further from the truth.

When Jesus claims to be the Son of Man, he's actually claiming an Old Testament title found in the book of Daniel.

"In my vision at night I looked, and there before me was one like a son of man, coming with the clouds of heaven. He approached the Ancient of Days and was led into his presence. He was given authority, glory and sovereign power; all nations and peoples of every language worshiped him. His dominion is an everlasting dominion that will not pass away, and his kingdom is one that will never be destroyed." (Daniel 7:13–14)

By referring to himself as the Son of Man, Jesus was saying he could approach God face-to-face, that he's been given God's authority over the earth forever. That's a lot different from suggesting he's just a normal human guy!

How does Jesus fit the description of Daniel's "son of man"?

If God gave you authority over the earth, what would you do?

Lord, you are holy and in charge. Help me obey your leadership in my life.

Jesus, Forgiver of Sins

When Jesus saw their faith, he said to the paralyzed man, "Son, your sins are forgiven."

MARK 2:5

In addition to his title Son of Man, Jesus claims to have the authority to forgive people's sins in all four gospels.

In the Synoptic Gospels, Jesus healed people by telling them their sins are forgiven. In Mark 2, some religious officials overheard him and thought he was telling lies about God's truth. Jesus knew their thoughts and said, "Which is easier: to say to this paralyzed man, 'Your sins are forgiven,' or to say, 'Get up, take your mat and walk'? But I want you to know that the Son of Man has authority on earth to forgive sins." (Mark 2:9–10)

The gospel of John is less direct, but "Moreover, the Father judges no one, but has entrusted all judgment to the Son, that all may honor the Son just as they honor the Father. Whoever does not honor the Son does not honor the Father, who sent him. Very truly I tell you, whoever hears my word and believes him who sent me has eternal life and will not be judged but has crossed over from death to life." (John 5:22–24)

Jesus has authority to forgive sins because he's the Son of God. As if that wasn't enough, he paid for the right to forgive us by taking the punishment for our sins on the cross. By hanging onto sin, we are trying to take something God has paid for. It's better to let it go and be forgiven.

What do you need to be forgiven for today?

What gives Jesus the right to forgive sins?

Lord, help me let go of my sins.

72

Jesus, Accepter of Worship

> *Then those who were in the boat worshiped him, saying, "Truly you are the Son of God."*
>
> **MATTHEW 14:33**

The word *worship* started out as the word *worth-ship*. It refers to something which has value or deserves praise. In the Bible, worship is reserved for God alone.

God said in the Ten Commandments, "You shall have no other gods before me. You shall not make for yourself an image in the form of anything in heaven above or on the earth beneath or in the waters below. You shall not bow down to them or worship them; for I, the LORD your God, am a jealous God, punishing the children for the sin of the parents to the third and fourth generation of those who hate me, but showing love to a thousand generations of those who love me and keep my commandments." (Exodus 20:3–6)

Not even angels are allowed to be worshiped. The apostle John tried to worship one in Revelation, "But he said to me, 'Don't do that! I am a fellow servant with you and with your fellow prophets and with all who keep the words of this scroll. Worship God!'" (Revelation 22:9)

But Jesus accepted worship. Why? Because he is God.

One day, everyone will worship Jesus in heaven, but we don't need to wait until then. We can, and should worship him now!

What are some ways you can worship Jesus?

What are some things you can worship him for?

Jesus, you are worthy to be praised!

73

Hot News from History

*The grass withers and the flowers fall, but
the word of our God endures forever.*

ISAIAH 40:8

If someone wrote a story about our life, would we want them to write it right after we lived or 400 years later? If an author waited too long, details about our life could get mixed up or forgotten.

Alexander the Great ruled Greece about 300 years before Jesus was born. Alexander earned his name "the Great" by winning many battles and creating a massive empire that stretched from Greece to India. The two earliest biographies about him were written by Arrian and Plutarch more than four hundred years after the leader's death. Still, historians have studied them and consider these biographies to be generally trustworthy.

Let's compare that to the Bible.

Luke wrote Acts, which ends with Paul in Rome sometime before AD 64. Since Acts is the second of a two-part work, the first part—the Gospel of Luke—must have been written before AD 64. And because Luke incorporates parts of the Gospel of Mark, that means Mark was written even earlier than that.

"If you allow maybe a year for each of those," says Bible expert Craig Blomberg, "you end up with Mark written no later than about AD 60. And if Jesus was put to death in AD 30 or 33, we're talking about a maximum gap of thirty years."

Do you find God's word trustworthy?

What is something you'd want included in a biography about you?

Lord, I believe the Bible is true and trustworthy.

Dig Deeper—The Mystery of Q

In addition to the four gospels, scholars often refer to what they call Q, which stands for the German word *Quelle*, or "source." Because of similarities between Matthew and Luke, scholars assume their authors drew upon Mark's earlier gospel in writing their own. But scholars also believe Matthew and Luke brought in some material from this mysterious Q, material which isn't from Mark.

Dr. Craig Blomberg says, "It's nothing more than a hypothesis. With few exceptions, Q is just sayings or teachings of Jesus, which once may have formed an independent, separate document."

So what would Q tell us about Jesus if we didn't have the gospels?

"Well, you have to keep in mind that Q was a collection of sayings," continues Blomberg. "Even so, you find Jesus making some very strong claims—for instance, that he was wisdom personified and that he was the one by whom God will judge all humanity, whether they confess him or disavow him."

One significant scholarly book argues if we isolate all the Q sayings from Matthew and Luke, we would actually get the same kind of picture of Jesus as we find in the gospels more generally.

They even mention Jesus's miracles.

"For example," says Blomberg, "Luke 7:18–23 and Matthew 11:2–6 say that John the Baptist sent his messengers to ask Jesus if he really was the Christ, the Messiah they were waiting for. Jesus replied in essence, 'Tell him to consider my miracles. Tell him what you've seen: the blind see, the deaf hear, the lame walk, the poor have good news preached to them.'"

Although there are no copies of Q laying around for us to look at, we can see how even in their absence, we have been given evidence the claims about Jesus are true.

Reordering the New Testament

> *I, Paul, write this greeting in my own hand,*
> *which is the distinguishing mark in all my*
> *letters. This is how I write. The grace of*
> *our Lord Jesus Christ be with you all.*
>
> **2 THESSALONIANS 3:17**

We're probably familiar with the order of books in the New Testament. But this order didn't exist until a few hundred years after the original letters and gospels had been written.

"The Gospels were written after almost all of the letters of Paul, whose writing ministry probably began in the late 40s AD," says Craig Blomberg.

The apostle Paul had traveled much of the known world, preaching the gospel and starting churches. Then he wrote letters to those churches. Most of his major letters appear to be written during the 50s AD.

By using the earliest accepted date of the crucifixion at AD 30, Paul met the risen Lord and believed in Jesus (see Acts 9) in about AD 32. Immediately, Paul was blinded and ushered into Damascus where he met with a Christian named Ananias. That puts his first meeting with the apostles in Jerusalem in about AD 35.

"This is enormously significant," says Craig. "Now you're not comparing thirty to sixty years—you're talking about two!"

Do you remember things that happened to you two years ago?

What are some things that you wouldn't forget no matter how much time has passed?

Lord, help me remember the
love you've shown me.

DAY 69

What Was the Early Church Like?

"For where two or three gather in my name, there am I with them."

MATTHEW 18:20

While the gospels were written to share Jesus's biography with unbelievers, most of the New Testament was written to encourage the early church to live confidently as believers in Christ. The book of Acts, by the same writer as Luke's gospel, gives an account of how the good news of Jesus was spread by missionaries who started churches. It also shows us what life was like in those churches.

"All the believers were together and had everything in common. They sold property and possessions to give to anyone who had need. Every day they continued to meet together in the temple courts. They broke bread in their homes and ate together with glad and sincere hearts, praising God and enjoying the favor of all the people. And the Lord added to their number daily those who were being saved." (Acts 2:44–47)

When God's people gather together, God shows up.

Some people think attending church isn't needed in this day and age because we have so many other ways of connecting. But church is more than going to a building once a week to hear someone preach. It is connecting with the body of Christ, meeting others' needs, and allowing them to meet ours. It is continuing a practice that's been going on for thousands of years. And God is still showing up.

> **Why is it important to go to church?**
>
> **How could you help a church grow?**

Lord, give me a desire to connect to you through the church.

79

Dig Deeper—Modern vs. Ancient Biographies

The gospels were written to be biographies of Jesus's life on earth. But when we go into a bookstore and look in the biography section, we don't see the same kind of writing we see in the gospels. What kind of literature are the gospels anyway?

Modern biographies tell the whole story of a person's life. But the gospel of Mark, for instance, doesn't talk about Jesus's birth or really anything through Jesus's early adult years. Instead, he focuses on a three-year period and spends half his gospel on the events leading up to, and resulting in, Jesus's last week.

Dr. Craig Blomberg explains what's going on. "Basically," he says, "this is how people wrote biographies in the ancient world. They did not have the sense, as we do today, that it was important to give equal proportion to all periods of an individual's life or that it was necessary to tell the story in strictly chronological order or even to quote people [word for word], as long as the essence of what they said was preserved.

"The only purpose," continues Blomberg, "for which they thought history was worth recording was because there were some lessons to be learned from the characters described. Therefore the biographer wanted to dwell at length on those portions of the person's life that were exemplary, that were illustrative, that could help other people, that gave meaning to a period of history.

"So Mark in particular, as the writer of probably the earliest gospel, devotes roughly half his narrative to the events leading up to and including one week's period of time and culminating in Christ's death and resurrection.

"Given the significance of the crucifixion," he concludes, "this makes perfect sense in ancient literature."

Letters from Paul: Thessalonica

You should mind your own business and work with your hands, just as we told you, so that your daily life may win the respect of outsiders and so that you will not be dependent on anybody.

1 THESSALONIANS 4:11B–12

Thessalonica, the capital of Macedonia, was a bustling port city. We know from Luke's book of Acts the apostle Paul planted a church there, but he had to leave before he wanted to.

"When Paul and his companions had passed through Amphipolis and Apollonia, they came to Thessalonica, where there was a Jewish synagogue. As was his custom, Paul went into the synagogue, and on three Sabbath days he reasoned with them from the Scriptures, explaining and proving that the Messiah had to suffer and rise from the dead. 'This Jesus I am proclaiming to you is the Messiah,' he said." (Acts 17:1–3)

In his letter to the church at Thessalonica, Paul encouraged believers to work hard and let their daily lives be a testimony to their Christianity.

It is important to work hard and not be lazy. When Christians are hard workers, we win the respect of the world and make them wonder why we're different. Plus, our hard work leads us to greater skills, which leads to reaching more people in our community. Proverbs 22:29 says, "Do you see a man skillful in his work? He will stand before kings; he will not stand before obscure men."

> **Do you consider yourself a hard worker?**
>
> **How does your work ethic (commitment to hard work) reflect on Jesus?**

Lord, may my hard work be motivated by a desire to bring more people to you.

Letters from Paul: Galatia

*It is for freedom that Christ has set us free.
Stand firm, then, and do not let yourselves
be burdened again by a yoke of slavery.*

GALATIANS 5:1

Acts 14 tells all about Paul's missionary journeys with Barnabas. They preached in the synagogues, performed a few miracles, were mistaken for Greek gods, and were either run out of town or stoned until people thought they were dead. Somehow along the way they planted churches with strong believers.

But after Paul and Barnabas left, the churches of Galatia were led astray by false teachers. These leaders said since Christianity was started as a Jewish religion (Jesus *was* Jewish), Christians needed to be following some of the Jewish laws. Paul sets them straight.

"You foolish Galatians! Who has bewitched you? Before your very eyes Jesus Christ was clearly portrayed as crucified. I would like to learn just one thing from you: Did you receive the Spirit by the works of the law, or by believing what you heard?" (Galatians 3:1–2)

Paul is clear. If we are saved by faith, Jesus has set us free! But why did Jesus set us free?

Galatians 5:13 says, "You, my brothers and sisters, were called to be free. But do not use your freedom to indulge the flesh; rather, serve one another humbly in love."

Do you believe you've been saved by faith or by keeping the rules well?

How are you using the freedoms Jesus gives you?

*Lord, help me use my freedoms
to be a loving neighbor.*

Letters from Paul: Corinth

"I have the right to do anything," you say—but not everything is beneficial. "I have the right to do anything"—but not everything is constructive. No one should seek their own good, but the good of others.

1 CORINTHIANS 10:23–24

In his missionary journeys, Paul stayed in Corinth for a year and half to establish a church there. Corinth was known for a lot of things, and almost none of them were good. The people lived for their own pleasure and worshipped a lot of different gods.

Like the churches in Galatia, the Corinthian church struggled with their freedoms in Christ. They didn't struggle with having too many rules to follow though. The believers in Corinth were using their freedoms as an excuse to live for themselves. In doing so, they were becoming selfish and looking too much like the culture around them.

Selfishness, is a problem for a lot of us. Companies who want us to buy their stuff use our selfishness against us. *Have it your way. Just do it.* We could probably think of other slogans, right?

But selfishness isn't what Christians are called to. Jesus set us free to be able to follow his example. Jesus said in Luke 9:23, "Whoever wants to be my disciple must deny themselves and take up their cross daily and follow me."

As followers of Jesus, we should look for ways to put the things we want aside so we can take care of the needs of other people.

> **Are your wants getting ahead of other people's needs?**
>
> **What's something unselfish you can do for someone else?**

God, keep me from living only for myself.

81

Letters from Paul: Rome

*First, I thank my God through Jesus
Christ for all of you, because your faith
is being reported all over the world.*

ROMANS 1:8

Paul's letter to the Roman church is unique because Paul didn't start the church at Rome. The book of Romans is Paul's introduction to the church, both to encourage them to live like Jesus and to be encouraged by them.

When he wrote his letter, the church in Rome was having some serious connection issues. The church was originally started by Jewish believers, it attracted Gentiles too. Then in AD 49, the Roman emperor Claudius kicked all the Jews—including the Jewish Christians who started the church—out of Rome because of problems caused by "Chrestus" (which probably refers to Jesus *Christ*).

Over the next few years, the Gentile Christians carried the church alone, but when the Jewish Christians returned, disagreements threatened to break the church apart. Unity was a common theme for Paul. First Corinthians 1:10 says, "I appeal to you, brothers and sisters, in the name of our Lord Jesus Christ, that all of you agree with one another in what you say and that there be no divisions among you, but that you be perfectly united in mind and thought."

How do you handle disagreements with people?

How can you have unity, even when you disagree with someone?

Paul's message is still good for us today. Even when we disagree about opinions, we can be united in our knowledge and worship of Jesus.

Lord, give me unity with other Christians.

Letters from Paul: Philippi

Do everything without grumbling or arguing.

PHILIPPIANS 2:14

The apostle Paul wrote to the church at Philippi while he was imprisoned at Rome around AD 62. The city of Philippi was a wealthy town because of gold and silver mines there. It was also home to the first church Paul planted in Europe.

Unlike his letters to Galatia or Corinth, Paul didn't write to the church at Philippi to correct them on something they did wrong. He wrote to encourage them to keep doing things well.

Philippians 1:4–6 says, "In all my prayers for all of you, I always pray with joy because of your partnership in the gospel from the first day until now, being confident of this, that he who began a good work in you will carry it on to completion until the day of Christ Jesus."

Paul prayed with joy in spite of his imprisonment because of what God was doing in people's lives. He didn't grumble or argue and he encouraged the Philippians to follow his example.

When we are tempted to grumble, we should ask God to shift our focus. For the many things we could grumble about, we have more to rejoice over. Rejoicing doesn't need to wait until we don't feel like grumbling. It is often the best way to stop.

Philippians 4:4 says, "Rejoice in the Lord always. I will say it again: Rejoice!"

What is something you grumble about often?

What is something you are thankful for?

Lord, change my attitude from grumbling to praise.

Letters from Paul: Colosse

See to it that no one takes you captive through hollow and deceptive philosophy, which depends on human tradition and the elemental spiritual forces of this world rather than on Christ.

COLOSSIANS 2:8

Although Paul didn't start the church of Colosse, he wrote to help them fight against false teaching. Paul learned of some people in the church who were adding rules to Christianity and worshipping angels alongside God.

Paul responded by reminding the church they were saved through faith in Jesus and extra rules and worshipping angels was only going to lead them away from God.

"Therefore, as God's chosen people, holy and dearly loved, clothe yourselves with compassion, kindness, humility, gentleness and patience. Bear with each other and forgive one another if any of you has a grievance against someone. Forgive as the Lord forgave you. And over all these virtues put on love, which binds them all together in perfect unity." (Colossians 3:12–14)

The world is still trying to lead Christians astray. Faith in Jesus alone has the power to save, not keeping the rules or worshipping angels or giving a lot of money or dressing a certain way. Once we are saved by faith alone, we will *want* to be compassionate, patient, forgiving, and loving.

How do you think the world is leading Christians astray?

What can you do to clothe yourself with compassion, kindness, humility, gentleness and patience?

God, don't let me fall for the world's false teaching.

Letters from Paul: Ephesus

Finally, be strong in the Lord and in his mighty power. Put on the full armor of God, so that you can take your stand against the devil's schemes.

EPHESIANS 6:10–11

Paul wrote to the Ephesians to encourage them more than to address problems within the church.

Ephesus was steeped in magical interest and idol worship. Acts 19:19 records when Paul first spread the gospel in Ephesus, "A number who had practiced sorcery brought their scrolls together and burned them publicly. When they calculated the value of the scrolls, the total came to fifty thousand drachmas." Since a drachma was about a day's wage, that would be about six million dollars today!

Given this background, Paul told church members to prepare for spiritual battle. The church at Ephesus wasn't fighting against flesh and blood, but against the unseen powers of Satan. It is a battle still raging today and we need to put on our armor!

"Stand firm then, with the belt of truth buckled around your waist, with the breastplate of righteousness in place, and with your feet fitted with the readiness that comes from the gospel of peace. In addition to all this, take up the shield of faith, with which you can extinguish all the flaming arrows of the evil one. Take the helmet of salvation and the sword of the Spirit, which is the word of God." (Ephesians 6:14–17)

Are you dressed for battle in the armor of God?

Why do you think the early believers burned their scrolls?

Lord, help me stand firm in your armor.

85

The Gospel of Paul?

*By this gospel you are saved, if you hold
firmly to the word I preached to you.
Otherwise, you have believed in vain.*

1 CORINTHIANS 15:2

What does the fact that many of Paul's letters to the early churches pre-date the four Gospels tell us about the case for Christ?

"When we more closely examine Paul's letters, we see signs that he used even earlier sources in writing them," says Bible expert Craig Blomberg. "Paul incorporated some creeds, confessions of faith, or hymns from the earliest Christian church. These go way back to the dawning of the church soon after Jesus's resurrection."

First Corinthians 15:3–7 is a great example.

"For what I received I passed on to you as of first importance: that Christ died for our sins according to the Scriptures, that he was buried, that he was raised on the third day according to the Scriptures, and that he appeared to Cephas, and then to the Twelve. After that, he appeared to more than five hundred of the brothers and sisters at the same time, most of whom are still living, though some have fallen asleep. Then he appeared to James, then to all the apostles."

How much does the creed from 1 Corinthians sound like the Gospel accounts of Jesus?

What is the gospel that Paul preached?

"Notice that Paul used language that he was passing on what he had received," Craig emphasizes. "The earliest Christians were convinced that Jesus died, was buried, was raised from the dead, and appeared to hundreds of people."

*Lord, may I pass on the knowledge of
you that I receive from your word.*

Testing the Eyewitness Accounts

*Dear friends, do not believe every spirit,
but test the spirits to see whether they
are from God, because many false
prophets have gone out into the world.*

1 JOHN 4:1

Let's go back to the Gospels of Matthew, Mark, Luke, and John. In order to accept these biographies of Jesus as true eyewitness accounts, we need to put them to the test.

In a courtroom, there are two sides of each criminal case. The prosecutor's job is to make a case against an accused criminal and back it up with evidence. The defense attorney's job is to defend the accused criminal by either explaining how their client couldn't have committed the crime or by explaining how there was some kind of misunderstanding.

Defense attorneys have a challenging job: to raise questions, to generate doubts, to probe the soft and vulnerable spots of a witness's story. They do this by subjecting the testimony to a variety of tests.

If the eyewitness testimony of the Gospels is true, it should have no problem passing each of the eight different tests defense attorneys use in the courtroom. And since God is the ultimate authority on truth, he doesn't have much to worry about.

First John 5:20 says, "We know also that the Son of God has come and has given us understanding, so that we may know him who is true. And we are in him who is true by being in his Son Jesus Christ. He is the true God and eternal life."

> **How well do you think the Gospels will hold up to scrutiny?**
>
> **Who do you think has the hardest job in a courtroom?**

Lord, show me whether I can trust the eyewitness accounts of Jesus.

The Intention Test

> *. . . It is sharper than any sword that has two edges.*
> *It cuts deep enough to separate soul from spirit. . . .*
> *It judges the thoughts and purposes of the heart.*
>
> **HEBREWS 4:12 (NIRV)**

The first test for eyewitness testimony is the intention test. Some people think the gospels are just made-up stories to inspire people to be nicer to each other. So we have to ask, "Were these first-century writers even interested in recording what actually happened?"

"Yes, they were," answers Craig Blomberg. "You can see that at the beginning of the gospel of Luke, which reads very much like prefaces to other generally trusted historical and biographical works of antiquity."

Luke 1:1–4 says, "Many have undertaken to draw up an account of the things that have been fulfilled among us, just as they were handed down to us by those who from the first were eyewitnesses and servants of the word. With this in mind, since I myself have carefully investigated everything from the beginning, I too decided to write an orderly account for you, most excellent Theophilus, so that you may know the certainty of the things you have been taught."

Since the Synoptic Gospels are so similar to Luke, we can assume Matthew and Mark wrote with the same intention, and John makes his intentions clear in John 20:31.

What does John 20:31 say about John's intentions?

Do you think the gospel writers meant to tell the truth about Jesus?

> *Lord, be my purpose both in sharing*
> *about you and living for you.*

88

Objection! Didn't Jesus Say He'd Come Back Soon?

"Therefore keep watch, because you do not know on what day your Lord will come."

MATTHEW 24:42

Critics of Christianity have said early Christians were convinced Jesus was going to return during their lifetime so they didn't think it was necessary to preserve any historical records about his life or teachings. After all, why bother if he's going to come and end the world at any moment?

To these critics, Craig Blomberg answers, "The truth is that the majority of Jesus's teachings presuppose a significant span of time before the end of the world. But second, even if some of Jesus's followers did think he might come back fairly quickly, remember that Christianity was born out of Judaism."

What does that have to do with this? The Jews waited for eight centuries while their prophets proclaimed that the Day of the Lord was at hand.

"And still the followers of these prophets recorded, valued, and preserved the words of the prophets," points out Blomberg. "Given that Jesus's followers looked upon him as being even greater than a prophet, it seems very reasonable that they would have done the same thing."

We still believe Jesus is coming back soon, but that doesn't stop us from carrying on with our lives and spreading the gospel while there's time. If anything, we should be working harder because we expect Jesus's return, not being lazy about doing good works.

> How well do you handle waiting for things you want?
>
> How should you live while waiting for Jesus to return?

Lord, may I be found working hard for you when you come back for me.

89

The Ability Test

*These commandments that I give you today are to be on
your hearts. Impress them on your children. Talk about
them when you sit at home and when you walk along
the road, when you lie down and when you get up.*

DEUTERONOMY 6:6–7

The second test for eyewitness testimony is the ability test. How can we be sure the material about Jesus's life and teaching was well preserved for thirty years before it was finally written down in the gospels?

To find out, let's look at the context of first-century life. "We have to remember that we're in a foreign land in a distant time and place and in a culture that has not yet invented computers or even the printing press," says Craig Blomberg. "Books—or actually, scrolls of papyrus—were relatively rare. Therefore education, learning, worship, teaching in religious communities—all this was done by word of mouth."

This type of teaching and learning is known as an oral tradition.

"In studies of cultures with oral traditions, there was freedom to vary how much of the story was told on any given occasion. One study suggested that in the ancient Middle East, anywhere from ten to forty percent of any given retelling of sacred tradition could vary from one occasion to the next. However, there were always fixed points that were unalterable, and the community had the right to intervene and correct the storyteller if he erred on those important aspects of the story."

Does your family have any stories they retell regularly?

Could you tell someone else the story and cover all the main points?

*Lord, help me remember all the
main points of your word.*

90

Amazing Memory Capacity

> *Jesus did many other things as well. If every one of them were written down, I suppose that even the whole world would not have room for the books that would be written.*
>
> **JOHN 21:25**

When Jewish boys were six years old, they'd go to school and begin memorizing the first five books of the Scriptures—Genesis, Exodus, Leviticus, Numbers, and Deuteronomy. By age ten, they'd know every word. The best students continued memorizing all the way to Malachi.

Some critics of the Bible say the Gospels contain legends and exaggerations, because nobody could accurately memorize everything Jesus did. New Testament expert Craig Blomberg wholeheartedly disagrees. "Rabbis became famous for having the entire Old Testament committed to memory," he said. "So it would have been well within the capability of Jesus's disciples to have committed much more to memory than appears in all four Gospels put together—and to have passed it along accurately."

The stories of Jesus are accurate. They give us a glimpse of everything Jesus did on earth. In fact, he did a lot more. The disciple John wrote, "Jesus did many other things as well. If every one of them were written down, I suppose that even the whole world would not have room for the books that would be written" (John 21:25).

What is the longest verse you have memorized?

What are some different ways you could use to memorize scripture?

Lord, help me hide your word in my heart and in my head.

Objection! Isn't the Bible like the Telephone Game?

"Every word of God is flawless; he is a shield to those who take refuge in him."

PROVERBS 30:5

We've all played the telephone game. A phrase is whispered into someone's ear, who whispers it into the ear of the next person, and so on.

Critics of the Bible say the four Gospels were written so many years after Jesus's death, they can't be accurate. Just like with the telephone game, the message probably got garbled.

Biblical scholar Craig A. Evans disagrees. "Unlike the telephone game, this is a community effort," he says about the writing of the Gospels. "It's not one guy who tells it to one other guy, who weeks later tells it to one other person, so that with the passage of time there would be distortion." Instead, the stories of Jesus's life were a living tradition the community discussed. People constantly talked about what Jesus did because it was precious to them.

Because the Christian community guarded and cherished the stories of Jesus's life, many scholars agree that the Gospels accurately report the essential elements of his teaching, life, death, and resurrection. During the years when many New Testament books were written, people were still alive who heard Jesus speak and watched his miracles. They knew the original material and made sure it was recorded properly.

Do you ever talk about what Jesus did for you?

What is Jesus doing for you today?

Lord, help me keep your message clear.

The Character Test

The integrity of the upright guides them, but the unfaithful are destroyed by their duplicity.

PROVERBS 11:3

Remember the story of the boy who cried wolf? Three times he ran to the village crying that a wolf was eating his sheep. Each time, the boy had been joking. When the wolf actually did come to eat the sheep, the boy cried for help, but no one came to help because the boy was known to be a liar.

The third test for eyewitness testimony is the character test. This test looks at whether it was in the character of these writers to be truthful. Was there any evidence of dishonesty or immorality?

Craig Blomberg says. "We simply do not have any reasonable evidence to suggest they were anything but people of great integrity."

"We see them reporting the words and actions of a man who called them to as exacting a level of integrity as any religion has ever known. In addition, they were willing to live out their beliefs despite persecution, deprivation, and suffering, which shows great character.

"In terms of honesty, in terms of truthfulness, in terms of virtue and morality, these people had a track record that should be envied."

We should strive to be like the authors of the Gospel. It's good to be believed when we have something important to say, and nothing is more important than telling others about Jesus.

Is it in your character to be truthful?

How can you help others trust what you say to be true?

Lord, keep me from telling lies, no matter the reason.

The Consistency Test

*He is before all things, and in him
all things hold together.*

COLOSSIANS 1:17

The fourth test for eyewitness testimony is the consistency test. When two eyewitnesses tell stories that disagree, it is hard to believe they're both telling the truth.

Skeptics often say the gospels fail the consistency test. After all, aren't there irreconcilable differences among the various gospel accounts?

As Craig Blomberg pointed out in regard to the nature of oral histories, the differences between the gospels fall well within what was acceptable for consistency by ancient standards.

Simon Greenleaf of Harvard Law School, an expert on legal evidence, says this: "There is enough of a discrepancy to show that there could have been no previous concert among them; and at the same time such substantial agreement as to show that they all were independent narrators of the same great transaction."

That's some fancy language which says the gospels are different enough to show they are independent, but they agree enough to show they can be trusted.

Still, what about all those contradictions? In the coming days, we'll look at a few of the specific objections people make about the gospels' lack of agreement. We'll find out how God holds all the gospels together in truth.

> **Have the differences between the gospels ever made you doubt they were true?**
>
> **How would you try to explain some of those differences?**

*Lord, show me how the differences
between the gospels can help
strengthen their trustworthiness.*

94

The Flip Side of Consistency

Live in harmony with one another.
ROMANS 12:16A

While some critics point to differences in the gospels as contradictions, too much consistency leads to other problems.

If a teacher sees two tests with identical answers, they would immediately assume two students cheated on the test. The same is true with courtroom eyewitness testimonies. Too many of the same exact answers are bad for credibility.

If the gospels had been identical to each other, word for word, this would have raised charges that the authors had planned to coordinate their stories in advance, and that would have cast doubt on them.

"That's right," agrees Craig Blomberg. "If the gospels were too consistent, that in itself would invalidate them as independent witnesses. People would then say we really only have one testimony that everybody else is just parroting."

Hans Stier, a classical German scholar, suggests that agreement over basic data and divergence of details actually increases credibility. "Every historian," he wrote, "is especially skeptical at that moment when an extraordinary happening is only reported in accounts which are completely free of contradictions."

What we see in the gospels is a harmony of information. We see tests with different answers which are nonetheless all correct.

> **How do the same exact details hurt eyewitness testimonies?**
>
> **What are some ways the gospels harmonize with each other?**

Lord Jesus, help me defend the credibility of your word.

Objection! What About the Centurion's Servant?

When Jesus heard this, he was amazed and said to those following him, "Truly I tell you, I have not found anyone in Israel with such great faith."

MATTHEW 8:10

There's a well-known story of healing found in both Matthew and Luke about a Roman centurion whose servant was ill. While Jesus was nearby, a centurion requested help from Jesus to heal his servant. Instead of asking Jesus to come to his home, the centurion believed Jesus could do it from where he was. Jesus marveled at the man's words and, praised him as showing more faith than anyone in Israel.

Here's the issue: In Matthew 8:5–13, the centurion comes to make the request of Jesus. In Luke 7:1–10, the centurion enlists some elders of the Jews to make the request on his behalf. That's an obvious contradiction, right?

"No, I don't think so," answers Craig Blomberg. "Think about it this way: in our world today, we may hear a new report that says, 'The president today announced that . . .' when in fact the speech was written by a speechwriter and delivered by the press secretary—and with a little luck, the president might have glanced at it somewhere in between."

> What's the most important part of the story of Jesus healing the centurion's servant?
>
> How does your faith in God compare to the centurion's?

Lord, I don't need to see you to know you can help me.

Objection! Was it Gerasa or Gadara?

When the demons came out of the man, they went into the pigs, and the herd rushed down the steep bank into the lake and was drowned.

LUKE 8:33

Another famous healing by Jesus involves a man living among the tombs who is inhabited by a host of demons. Jesus heals the man, but sends the demons into a herd of pigs, who then run off a cliff into the Sea of Galilee.

The problem is that Mark and Luke say Jesus sent the demons into pigs at Gerasa, while Matthew says it was in Gadara (Matthew 8:23). Those are two completely different places. Case closed!

Not quite. One was a town; the other was a province. But even this explanation has problems since the town of Gerasa wasn't anywhere near the Sea of Galilee. Let's look closer.

"There have been ruins of a town that have been excavated at exactly the right point on the eastern shore of the Sea of Galilee," says Craig Blomberg. "The English form of the town's name often gets pronounced, 'Khersa,' but as a Hebrew word translated into Greek, it could have come out sounding something very much like 'Gerasa.' So it may very well have been in Khersa—whose spelling in Greek was rendered as Gerasa—in the province of Gadara."

What's the important part of the story of Jesus casting demons out of the man?

How does faith in Jesus lead to thinking clearly?

Lord, keep me away from influences that try to separate me from you.

Objection! Whose Genealogy of Jesus is Right?

*This is the genealogy of Jesus the Messiah
the son of David, the son of Abraham.*

MATTHEW 1:1

The next objection is the two different genealogies of Jesus that are found in Matthew and Luke.

"This is another case of multiple options," Blomberg says. "The two most common have been that Matthew reflects Joseph's lineage, because most of his opening chapter is told from Joseph's perspective, and Joseph, as the adoptive father, would have been the legal ancestor through whom Jesus's royal lineage would have been traced. These are themes that are important for Matthew.

"Luke, then, would have traced the genealogy through Mary's lineage. And since both are from the ancestry of David, once you get that far back the lines converge."

"A second option is that both genealogies reflect Joseph's lineage in order to create the necessary legalities. But one is Joseph's human lineage—the gospel of Luke—and the other is Joseph's legal lineage, with the two diverging at the points where somebody in the line did not have a direct offspring. They had to raise up legal heirs through various Old Testament practices.

"The problem is made greater because some names are omitted, which was perfectly acceptable by standards of the ancient world."

Which explanation makes the most sense to you?

How would you answer someone who didn't believe in Jesus because of these genealogies?

Lord, thank you for adopting me into your family!

The Bias Test

My brothers and sisters, believers in our glorious Lord Jesus Christ must not show favoritism.

JAMES 2:1

The term *bias* is related to an old English game played by King James. The balls in this game are made heavier on one side so they don't roll straight.

Today, we use the word to describe how our feelings affect how straight we roll with other people. If we like someone, we are biased toward them and speak well of them. If we are biased against someone, we treat them poorly.

We can't underestimate how much the gospel writers loved Jesus. They weren't neutral observers; they were his devoted followers. Wouldn't it be likely for them to change things to make Jesus look good?

Even Craig Blomberg admits the potential exists. "On the other hand," he adds, "people can so honor and respect someone that it prompts them to record his life with great integrity. That's the way they would show their love for him. And I think that's what happened here."

Even if we liked someone, would we allow our bias to lead to our torture and death? That's what happened to the disciples and members of the early church. If they were willing to be killed for how they felt, we can trust the gospels are likely true.

What are some biases you have?

How can you correct the negative biases you have?

Lord, help me treat all people fairly and well. Let my love for you make me kinder to everyone.

99

The Cover-up Test

Not only so, but we also glory in our sufferings, because we know that suffering produces perseverance; perseverance, character; and character, hope.

ROMANS 5:3–4

The sixth test for eyewitness testimony is the cover-up test. When people tell a story, they'll often leave out embarrassing details or things which are hard to explain. If a story sounds too good to be true, something must be missing. But nothing's missing from the gospels.

All the gospel writers detail how Peter denied Christ three times on the night of his arrest. Matthew shows Peter nearly drowning when he takes his eyes off Jesus as he walks on water. He also records Peter trying to set up tents for Elijah and Moses at Jesus's transfiguration.

"Here's the point," explains Craig Blomberg. "If they didn't feel free to leave out stuff when it would have been convenient and helpful to do so, is it really plausible to believe that they outright added and fabricated material with no historical basis? I'd say not."

The gospel writers were men of great integrity. Their integrity guided them, along with the inspiration of the Holy Spirit, as they recorded the events of Jesus's life. The gospels reflect their honesty in telling the whole story, even when it made them look bad. That's why we can trust the gospels and why they've stood the test of time.

What are some embarrassing moments you wouldn't want to share with others?

How would you react if someone shared their embarrassing moment with you?

Lord, if the disciples were willing to be real with us in the gospels, help me be willing to be real with my friends and family.

100

Embarrassing Moments: Ignorant Jesus

"But about that day or hour no one knows, not even the angels in heaven, nor the Son, but only the Father."

MARK 13:32

Matthew and Mark both include passages where Jesus talks about the end of the world (Matthew 24:36–44 and Mark 13:32–37). Jesus warns his disciples to keep watch, because not even he knows when the end will come.

God is omniscient, or all-knowing. Jesus is God. Shouldn't Jesus know when the end of the world will happen?

Jesus could have said, "The end will come when you least expect it."

Or he could have said, "I know when the end will be, but I want you to keep watch, so I'm not going to tell you."

Instead, the Bible says Jesus didn't know. Fortunately, it also talks about Jesus laying aside some of his power in Philippians 2:6–8:

"Who, being in very nature God, did not consider equality with God something to be used to his own advantage; rather, he made himself nothing by taking the very nature of a servant, being made in human likeness. And being found in appearance as a man, he humbled himself by becoming obedient to death—even death on a cross!"

Jesus *is* God, but he was also fully human. So is it possible he limited his knowledge in the same way he allowed his body to be killed? Sure! It may be hard to understand, but that's also why we can trust it to be true.

> Since you don't know when the world will end, how should you act right now?
>
> Why do you think the Gospels added this detail in?

Lord, help me live well all the time.

101

Embarrassing Moments: Mark's Account of Peter

But when Jesus turned and looked at his disciples, he rebuked Peter. "Get behind me, Satan!" he said. "You do not have in mind the concerns of God, but merely human concerns."

MARK 8:33

As we learned earlier, the Gospel of Mark was written by John Mark, one of Peter's companions. In many of Mark's stories, we see Jesus through Peter's eyes. So if any of the gospels had a reason to show Peter in a positive light, the gospel of Mark should have been it. Instead, we see Peter in a negative light time after time.

Mark 4:35-41 shows Peter and the disciples scared and faithless during a storm on the Sea of Galilee. Mark 8:1-10 shows the disciples doubting Jesus's ability to feed a large crowd after he already performed a similar miracle in Mark 6:30-44. After proclaiming Jesus to be the Messiah in Mark 8:29, Jesus turns around and calls Peter "Satan" in Mark 8:33. And in Mark 14:27-31, Peter swears he'll stand by Jesus only to find himself denying him three times that night.

If Peter wanted Mark to paint him in a positive light, he should have left out some of these details. But that's not what happened. Mark recorded the gospel just like it happened.

When we do embarrassing things (like Peter did), we can know Jesus still loves us and can work through us (like he did with Peter).

> **Have you ever failed to keep a promise like Peter did?**
>
> **How can Peter's embarrassments encourage you to live boldly for Jesus?**

Jesus, if you could use Peter, you can use me.

Embarrassing Moments: The Dense Disciples

*The disciples did not understand any of this.
Its meaning was hidden from them, and they
did not know what he was talking about.*

LUKE 18:34

With Jesus being such a gifted teacher, it might be surprising how many times in the gospels he asks his disciples, "Do you have eyes but fail to see, and ears but fail to hear? And don't you remember?" (Mark 8:18). Or how many times the gospels say they did not understand.

Want to look them up? Check out:

- Matthew 16:9
- Mark 8:17
- Mark 8:21
- Mark 9:32
- Luke 9:45
- Luke 18:34
- John 12:16
- John 20:9

Jesus could have chosen anyone as disciples. He picked fishermen and tax collectors who were well over the age most disciples would begin learning under a rabbi. Sometimes, it showed. The disciples were constantly misunderstanding Jesus's parables and prophecies. It took the Holy Spirit's arrival for them to clearly understand things as they wrote them down for us in the gospels.

In giving their eyewitness accounts of Jesus, the disciples could easily have made themselves look better by not including so many instances of misunderstandings. But they didn't. They weren't concerned with making themselves look good. They were concerned with presenting reality and telling people about Jesus.

Do you ever feel bad for not understanding the Bible?

How do you feel knowing Jesus's disciples didn't always understand things either?

*Lord, teach me your truths
through the Holy Spirit.*

The Corroboration Test

Remember the days of old; consider the generations long past. Ask your father and he will tell you, your elders, and they will explain to you.

DEUTERONOMY 32:7

The seventh test for eyewitness testimony is the corroboration test. Are the details given by an eyewitness able to be checked and verified? When the gospels mention people, places, and events, do they check out to be correct?

"Yes, they do," says Craig Blomberg. "The longer people explore this, the more the details get confirmed. Within the last hundred years archaeology has repeatedly unearthed discoveries that have confirmed specific references in the gospels."

But does Jesus pop up in any historical sources aside from the Bible?

Craig Blomberg says we can actually learn a lot of facts about Jesus through non-Christian sources. "And when you stop to think that ancient historians for the most part dealt only with political rulers, emperors, kings, military battles, official religious people, and major philosophical movements, it's remarkable how much we can learn about Jesus and his followers even though they fit none of those categories at the time these historians were writing."

We'll take a closer look at some of the archaeological and historical proofs later. For now, we have enough to say the gospels pass the corroboration test.

> How could you use corroboration to see if someone was telling the truth?
>
> What kind of evidence do you think we'll find in support of Jesus's existence?

God, may the fact that I'm your child be corroborated by the way I live my life.

The Adverse Witness Test

For there is nothing hidden that will not be disclosed, and nothing concealed that will not be known or brought out into the open.

LUKE 8:17

The eighth and final test for eyewitness testimony is the adverse witness test. Were others present who would have contradicted or corrected the gospels if they had been proven to be false?

Craig Blomberg says although many wanted to discredit the Christian movement, they couldn't.

"Look at what his opponents did say," says Blomberg. "In later Jewish writings Jesus is called a sorcerer who led Israel astray—which acknowledges that he really did work marvelous wonders, although his writers dispute the source of his power.

"This would have been a perfect opportunity to say something like, 'The Christians will tell you he worked miracles, but we're here to tell you he didn't.' Yet that's the one thing we never see his opponents saying. Instead they implicitly acknowledge that what the gospels wrote—that Jesus performed miracles—is true."

If Jesus's opponents said he performed miracles—which is one of the more unbelievable parts of Jesus's ministry—should we doubt the gospel accounts of the less fantastic parts of his life?

> Why does it mean more to someone's credibility if an opponent agrees they're telling the truth?
>
> Why did his Jewish opponents call Jesus a sorcerer?

Lord, if even your opponents admit you did amazing things, I believe you can do them too.

God vs. Lies

The LORD detests lying lips, but he delights in people who are trustworthy.

PROVERBS 12:22

As Christians, we have a responsibility to speak the truth. God loves the truth and he hates lies. As the ultimate authority for justice and truth, he takes it seriously when people lie.

Proverbs 6:16–19 says, "There are six things the LORD hates, seven that are detestable to him: haughty eyes, a lying tongue, hands that shed innocent blood, a heart that devises wicked schemes, feet that are quick to rush into evil, a false witness who pours out lies and a person who stirs up conflict in the community."

Notice how God lists lies twice? He hates "a lying tongue" and "a false witness who pours out lies." Lies go against his very nature. Deuteronomy 32:4 says, "He is the Rock, his works are perfect, and all his ways are just. A faithful God who does no wrong, upright and just is he."

Since justice is so important to God, and lies are detestable to him, as his followers, we should make sure we're people who tell the truth. When we are trustworthy with the people around us, we resemble God, which makes him happy. When we are untrustworthy, unfortunately, that reflects on God too, and might cause people not to trust in him. That doesn't just make God sad; it should make us sad too.

> **How does it reflect on God when we tell lies?**
>
> **Why does God delight in people who are trustworthy?**

God, keep my lips from speaking lies. Make me trustworthy so I resemble you.

106

Documentary Evidence

This is what the LORD, the God of Israel, says: "Write in a book all the words I have spoken to you."

JEREMIAH 30:2

We've looked at how the Old Testament prophecies about the Messiah make a fingerprint that fits Jesus in the New Testament. We've proven the biographies of Jesus presented in the gospels to be accurate eyewitness testimonies by his followers. But to make the case for Christ, we're going to need more evidence. Let's take a look at the documents involved in the case.

Documentary evidence is made up of written material in a case. Before any document can be admitted into a court case, they must be verified to be real. If the documents are on the official company letter-head, how do we know they haven't been forged? Are the signatures real?

In the case for Christ, we need to make sure the Bible fits the standards for documentary evidence. How do we know the gospels and letters in our Bibles today look anything like they did in the first century? The originals must have crumbled into dust ages ago. How do we know the documents are telling the whole story?

It's good to ask questions when we're willing to seek answers. In the coming days, we'll find what our faith already knows: God's word is reliable, whole, and verifiably true, even after all these years!

> **How could you make a case that your family went grocery shopping with documentary evidence?**
>
> **Why is it important to make sure all documentary evidence is genuine?**

Lord, help me see and trust the documentary evidence that is your word.

107

What is Legendary Corruption?

You are the God who performs miracles; you display your power among the peoples.

PSALM 77:14

Nicholas of Myra was born in the third century. Very little historical evidence of his life remains, but he was reputed to be generous.

The earliest complete account of Nicholas' life we have today was written in the early ninth century by Michael the Archimandrite, nearly five hundred years after Nicholas' probable death. In that time, legends had grown up about Nicholas which may have their roots in history, but are too fantastical to be real.

Fast forward to today and we see Nicholas as a jolly white-bearded fellow who puts toys in stockings, lives at the North Pole, and flies around the world in a single night in a sleigh. Over the course of hundreds of years, the legend changed drastically.

Some critics say the same thing happened with Jesus. They may agree Jesus was a Jewish rabbi who got into trouble with the leaders of his day and was killed by the Romans, but they say his miracles fall into the same category as Santa and his elves.

How can we know legendary corruption—false stories attached to real people—hasn't crept into the gospels? We have documentary evidence dating back, not five hundred years afterward, but within a few years after Jesus's death and resurrection!

How is Jesus's story different from the Santa Claus story?

Do you know of any stories that got bigger each time they were told?

Lord, may I trust your miracles aren't legends, but truth.

108

Copies of Copies

For truly I tell you, until heaven and earth disappear, not the smallest letter, not the least stroke of a pen, will by any means disappear from the Law until everything is accomplished.

MATTHEW 5:18

When Jesus lived, there were no computers or printers. Stories about Jesus were told orally before they were eventually written down. For another copy to exist someone had to carefully copy it by hand.

Today's Bible is the product of countless copies of ancient documents.. If the New Testament is a copy of a copy of a copy, how can we be sure the biographies of Jesus are still reliable?

"This isn't an issue that's unique to the Bible," says Bruce Metzger, a leading authority on New Testament issues. "It's a question we should ask of other historical manuscripts as well. What the New Testament has in its favor, especially when compared with other ancient writings, is the unprecedented multiplicity of copies that have survived."

Multiplicity means a lot, and Bruce Metzger wasn't kidding. The New Testament has more early copies than any other ancient manuscript. Because Christians took their time and recognized the importance of the Bible, they were careful; so careful, in fact, that the earliest copies still sound like the Bibles of today.

> Choose a verse to copy from the Bible today! Write it carefully and take your time.
>
> How long do you think it would take to copy the whole Bible?

Lord, thank you for preserving the Bible through all these years.

109

The Value of Multiplicity

For, "All people are like grass, and all their glory is like the flowers of the field; the grass withers and the flowers fall, but the word of the Lord endures forever." And this is the word that was preached to you.

1 PETER 1:24–25

Ancient Greek copies of the New Testament have popped up from a variety of geographical locations.

"In addition to Greek manuscripts," says New Testament expert Bruce Metzger, "we have translation of the gospels into other languages at a relatively early time—into Latin, Syriac, and Coptic. And beyond that, we have what may be called secondary translations made a little later, like Armenian and Gothic. And a lot of others—Georgian, Ethiopic, a great variety."

Why is that important?

"Because even if we had no Greek manuscripts today, by piecing together the information from these translations from a relatively early date, we could actually reproduce the contents of the New Testament."

The multiplicity of documents available shows how God's Word spread quickly after Jesus died and rose again. And with so many copies in so many languages, experts have confidence the essential message has stayed the same over time.

How does having so many copies help us know the New Testament is accurate?

Why would earlier copies of the New Testament be more trusted than later copies?

Jesus, your word stands strong and your love never changes.

Jarring Truths

But the plans of the Lord stand firm forever, the
purposes of his heart through all generations.

PSALM 33:11

There are many stories about how the Dead Sea Scrolls were discovered in 1947. Some say Bedouin herders were searching the caves in Israel for a lost goat. Others claim they were looking for treasure when they came across nearly a dozen caves that contained large pottery jars with ancient scrolls inside. Many mysteries still surround the Dead Sea Scrolls. But one thing is no mystery—these ancient documents contain the words of God.

More than 800 scrolls were found, written on parchment, papyrus, and leather. Some dated back more than 250 years before Jesus was born. They were so brittle some scrolls took years to unroll. Others were in pieces and had to be put together like a puzzle. Biblical scholars joined archaeologists to piece the scrolls together. Soon they had identified sections of every Old Testament book of the Bible except one. Many of the books had multiple copies.

The Dead Sea Scrolls were an amazing discovery. And when scholars compared the words on the scrolls with the same books in modern Bibles, they discovered our modern versions have been transmitted with 99.99 percent accuracy!

Just as God does not change, his Word has remained the same throughout history. His truths and his plans stand firm forever.

What would you leave in a jar for future generations to discover?

How do the Dead Sea Scrolls support the accuracy of the Bible?

Lord, may your unchanging word
change me to look more like you.

A Mountain of Manuscripts

For you have been born again, not of perishable seed, but of imperishable, through the living and enduring word of God.

1 PETER 1:23

It's important to have multiple copies of ancient documents to help us test for accuracy. Now, let's put the gospels into context.

Tacitus wrote *Annals of Imperial Rome* in about AD 116. Today, his first six books exist in only one ancient manuscript, and it was copied in about AD 850. Books eleven through sixteen are in another manuscript dating from the eleventh century. Books seven through ten are lost. That means more than 700 years have passed between when Tacitus originally recorded his history and when the only existing copy was made. Yet, this one copy is considered accurate.

There are nine Greek manuscripts of Josephus's work *The Jewish War*. These copies were made in the tenth, eleventh, and twelfth centuries. There is also a Latin translation from the fourth century. Again, historians consider the modern version of *The Jewish War* to be true.

So how many Greek New Testament manuscripts exist today? According to Bruce Metzger, more than five thousand have been cataloged!

"The quantity of New Testament material is almost embarrassing in comparison with other works of antiquity," he adds.

Why do you think the Annals of Imperial Rome is considered accurate, but the New Testament is questioned?

How does the mountain of manuscripts encourage your faith?

Lord, in addition to all these manuscripts, let my life speak truth to the people around me.

The New Testament vs. Homer's *Iliad*

> *"The gods have come down to us in human form!"*
> *Barnabas they called Zeus, and Paul they called*
> *Hermes because he was the chief speaker.*
>
> **ACTS 14:11–12**

Comparing the single manuscript of Tacitus' *Annals of Imperial Rome* and the nine manuscripts of Josephus's *The Jewish War* to the over five thousand New Testament Greek manuscripts may not feel like a fair comparison. So after the New Testament, what is the runner-up for "most Greek manuscripts"?

"Next to the New Testament," says Bruce Metzger, "the greatest amount of manuscript testimony is of Homer's *Iliad*, which was the bible of the ancient Greeks."

"There are fewer than 650 Greek manuscripts of [the *Iliad*] today. Some are quite fragmentary. They come down to us from the second and third century AD and following. When you consider that Homer composed his epic about 800 BC, you can see there's a very lengthy gap."

Since we have thousands more manuscripts of the New Testament, verifiably uncorrupted by time, we can be confident God's word isn't a myth. It's the truth!

How do you think the Iliad compares to the New Testament?

What would you tell someone who said Jesus is just another myth?

Lord, help me be bold in defending your name.

113

A Strong Foundation

". . . is like a man who built a house on the ground without a foundation. The moment the torrent struck that house, it collapsed and its destruction was complete."

LUKE 6:49

We've seen the outstanding numbers in support of the New Testament's reliability, but let's take a closer look at the manuscripts themselves. How does Bible expert Bruce Metzger describe the manuscripts we have? "There are now ninety-nine fragmentary pieces of papyrus that contain one or more passages or books of the New Testament."

"The most significant to come to light are the Chester Beatty Biblical Papyri, discovered about 1930. Of these, Beatty Biblical Papyrus number one contains portions of the four gospels and the book of Acts, and it dates from the third century. Papyrus number two contains large portions of eight letters of Paul, plus portions of Hebrews, dating to about the year 200. Papyrus number three has a sizable section of the book of Revelation, dating from the third century."

There are other papyrus manuscripts too. The collection of M. Martin Bodmer contains about two-thirds of the gospel of John and dates back to about 200, as well as portions of Luke and John, dating from the third century.

Both papyri collections contain the story of the wise and foolish builder. When we build our lives on Jesus's teaching, others will see the foundation Jesus laid and know his words are true.

Is hearing God's word enough to build a strong foundation?

How can you put the Bible into practice today?

Lord, help me hear your words and live them out today.

112

King of the Fragments

> *"You are a king, then!" said Pilate.*
> *Jesus answered, "You say that I am a king. In fact, the*
> *reason I was born and came into the world is to testify*
> *to the truth. Everyone on the side of truth listens to me."*
>
> **JOHN 18:37**

So, what is the earliest portion of the New Testament we possess today?

"That would be the fragment of the gospel of John containing material from chapter eighteen," answers Bruce Metzger. "It has five verses—three on one side, two on the other—and it measures about two and a half by three and a half inches."

This tiny fragment is huge! It contains John 18:34–38, where Pontius Pilate asked Jesus if he was King of the Jews.

"It was purchased in Egypt as early as 1920, but it sat unnoticed for years among similar fragments of papyri. Then in 1934 C. H. Roberts of Saint John's College, Oxford, was sorting through papyri at the John Rylands Library in Manchester, England. He immediately recognized this as preserving a portion of John's gospel. He was able to date it from the style of the script."

Just how far back does it go?

"He concluded it originated between AD 100 to 150. Lots of other prominent paleographers . . . have agreed with his assessment."

Since the apostle John died around AD 98, this fragment dates back within a few years of when he lived!

Are you on the side of truth?

How can you show others you listen to Jesus?

Lord, be the king of my life.

115

Dog Bites Man vs. Man Bites Dog

> But the Advocate, the Holy Spirit, whom the Father
> will send in my name, will teach you all things and
> will remind you of everything I have said to you.
>
> **JOHN 14:26**

It is hard to believe copying errors didn't happen in manuscripts over the years. Aren't there literally tens of thousands of variations among the ancient manuscripts we have?

"Quite so," agrees Bruce Metzger, "Although for the most part scribes were scrupulously careful, errors did creep in.

"But," he is quick to add, "there are factors counteracting that. For example, sometimes the scribe's memory would play tricks on him. Between the time it took for him to look at the text and then to write down the words, the order of words might get shifted. He may write down the right words but in the wrong sequence. This is nothing to be alarmed at, because Greek, unlike English, is an inflected language."

Bruce says: "[It] makes a whale of a difference in English if you say, 'Dog bites man' or 'Man bites dog.' But in Greek it doesn't. One word functions as the subject of the sentence regardless of where it stands in the sequence; consequently, the meaning of the sentence isn't distorted if the words are out of what we consider to be the right order. So yes, some variations among manuscripts exist, but generally they're inconsequential variations like that."

Why wouldn't the order of the words matter in Greek?

Has your memory ever played tricks on you?

> Lord, thank you for preserving the
> meaning of your word through the
> years and across languages.

116

Get the Message?

Man does not live on bread alone but on every
word that comes from the mouth of the LORD.

DEUTERONOMY 8:3B

Cna yuo raed tihs? Jsut a fwe wrods aer spllede corcrtoly, yet yuo cna aulaclty uesdnatnrd waht you aer rdanieg. Rchearch sohws yuor mnid cna unsrcamlbe jmubedl wrods, btu it maeks yuo raed muhc mroe slwoly. It hlpes to hvae teh frsit and lsat ltteers in the rghit pclae. The rset can be a taotl mses. Tihs is bcuseae the huamn mnid deos not raed ervey lteter by istlef, but the wrod as a wlohe. Azanmig, huh?

Textual critics are experts who get at the truth of God's Word. Looking at ancient biblical manuscripts and fragments, they work hard to make sure every word in the Bible is correct, as they seek to determine the writer's original message. Bible expert Daniel B. Wallace says, "The quantity and quality of the New Testament manuscripts are unequalled in the ancient Greco-Roman world."

Wallace points out the New Testament has more than 5,800 of the earliest Greek copies in existence—in fact, about 24,000 manuscripts in all.

God left a lot of evidence so we'd believe in his miracles and mighty power. And he trusted specific people with his words so they wouldn't get mixed up. The Bible is more than a history book. It nourishes us (Deuteronomy 8:3). Adn wehn we raed it, taht mesasge is claer.

> **Were you able to read the first paragraph quickly?**
>
> **Do you think it's true your brain craves understanding?**

Lord, help me read and understand the Bible.

Marvelously Correct

The Sovereign LORD has given me a well-instructed tongue, to know the word that sustains the weary. He wakens me morning by morning, wakens my ear to listen like one being instructed.

ISAIAH 50:4

The modern printing press was invented around AD 1440. Before then, God's Word was painstakingly written down on scrolls. If a mistake was made, the scroll would be destroyed.

And even when a spelling mistake or the order of the words slipped through, the changes over the years would be minor. Still we must ask, "How many fundamental beliefs of the church have been altered because of these copying errors?"

"None," answers Bruce Metzger, our Bible expert friend.

The New Testament's text has been reliably preserved for us through the centuries. Benjamin Warfield, a professor who held four doctorates and taught at Princeton Theological Seminary nearly a hundred years ago, put it this way:

"If we compare the present state of the New Testament text with that of any other ancient writing, we must ... declare it to be marvelously correct. Such has been the care with which the New Testament has been copied—a care which has doubtless grown out of true reverence for its holy words. ... The New Testament [is] unrivaled among ancient writings in the purity of its text as actually transmitted and kept in use."

> Why were scribes so careful when copying God's Word?
>
> How can you show "true reverence for its holy words"?

God, may I treat your Word with the respect it deserves.

118

Questioning the Bible

If any of you lacks wisdom, you should ask God, who gives generously to all without finding fault, and it will be given to you.

JAMES 1:5

Our modern Bible is made up of sixty-six books. The thirty-nine books of the Old Testament make up the Bible of Judaism. The twenty-seven books of the New Testament tell us the story of Jesus.

The New Testament books we see today were recognized as the inspired word of God in AD 367 by church father Athanasius. Critics of the Bible ask a lot of questions about the selection of these books:

- Why the gap of years between when they were written and when they were accepted?
- Did church councils squelch equally legitimate documents because they didn't like the picture of Jesus they portrayed?
- Do the twenty-seven books of the New Testament represent the best and most reliable information?
- Why is it that our Bibles contain Matthew, Mark, Luke, and John, but many other ancient gospels were excluded?

These questions, along with any others we can think of, are welcome to the God of truth.

What are some questions you'd like to ask to God?

In what ways do you think he'll answer you?

Father, when I have big questions for and about you, help me find my answers in you.

119

Of Cannons & Canons

*See that you do all I command you; do
not add to it or take away from it.*

DEUTERONOMY 12:32

A cannon is a type of gun made of a large tube which fires a projectile over a long distance. Although they have fallen out of use in modern warfare, they can still occasionally be seen at a circus, firing a stunt person into a net. And while cannons may be interesting, we don't want to confuse them with the biblical *canon*.

The term *canon* comes from a Greek word meaning "rule," "norm," "or "standard." The biblical canon describes the books that have become accepted as official in the church and included in the New Testament. Our guide, Bruce Metzger, is considered a leading authority in the field.

With so many books claiming to be written by New Testament characters, how did the early church leaders decide which would be considered authoritative and which would be discarded?

"You have to understand," says Bruce, "that the canon was not the result of a series of contests involving church politics. The canon is rather the separation that came about because of the intuitive insight of Christian believers.... [It] is a list of authoritative books more than it is an authoritative list of books. These documents didn't derive their authority from being selected; each one was authoritative before anyone gathered them together."

How does your family come up with the rules for your home?

Do you think the church left out any legitimate books of the Bible?

Lord, show me why the books we have in the New Testament pass the test for being from You.

120

The Inspired Word of God

> *But when he, the Spirit of truth, comes, he will guide you into all the truth. He will not speak on his own; he will speak only what he hears, and he will tell you what is yet to come.*
>
> **JOHN 16:13**

When people feel especially motivated to do something, they might say they were *inspired* to do it. Inspire has become a term to describe a feeling, but the original meaning was deeply spiritual.

The word *inspire* comes from the Latin word *inspirare*, which means to "blow into or breathe upon," and it's related to the word *spirit* (*spirare* or *spiritus* in Latin). Inspiration, then, is something that has been breathed into life by God.

A literal example can be found in Genesis 2:7, "Then the Lord God formed a man from the dust of the ground and breathed into his nostrils the breath of life, and the man became a living being."

The same idea is found in 2 Timothy 3:16–17, "All Scripture is God-breathed and is useful for teaching, rebuking, correcting and training in righteousness, so that the servant of God may be thoroughly equipped for every good work."

The people who wrote the Bible were inspired by the Holy Spirit and given the words to say. God breathed life into his Word just like he breathed life into Adam in the beginning.

What would happen if you stopped breathing?

How is the Bible useful for equipping Christians to do good works?

Lord, may I breathe deep from your inspired Word.

121

Canon Test #1: Apostolic Authority

*I will instruct you and teach you in
the way you should go; I will counsel
you with my loving eye on you.*

PSALM 32:8

Early church leaders needed to test and decide which documents were truly inspired by God and which were just written by man.

First John 4:1 says, "Dear friends, do not believe every spirit, but test the spirits to see whether they are from God, because many false prophets have gone out into the world."

What were the tests?

"Basically, the early church had three criteria," says Bruce Metzger. "First, the books must have apostolic authority—that is, they must have been written either by apostles themselves, who were eyewitnesses to what they wrote about, or by followers of apostles. So in the case of Mark and Luke, while they weren't among the twelve disciples, early tradition has it that Mark was a helper of Peter, and Luke was an associate of Paul."

In a classroom, a teacher has the authority to teach. The principal would surely kick out a random person who came in, trying to teach.

In the same way, the early church recognized the authority of the eyewitnesses and their associates and trusted their words to be inspired by God.

Why does it matter whether the instructions come from a recognized authority or not?

Who has the authority to instruct you in your home?

Lord Jesus, help me follow the instructions that I know are from you.

Canon Test #2: The Rule of Faith

*I am writing these things to you about
those who are trying to lead you astray.*

1 JOHN 2:26

Just as John warned against heresy, 2 Peter 2:1 says, "But there were also false prophets among the people, just as there will be false teachers among you. They will secretly introduce destructive heresies, even denying the sovereign Lord who bought them—bringing swift destruction on themselves."

The second test is called the rule of faith. Does it fit with the basic Christian teachings already recognized by the church?

If a document claimed to be written by Peter, but it said lying was allowed on Fridays and children didn't have to obey their parents, it wouldn't pass the rule of faith.

Remember Proverbs 12:22? "The LORD detests lying lips, but he delights in people who are trustworthy."

And Exodus 12:20? "Honor your father and your mother."

Since these verses are commonly known to be from God, New Testament books should support them. That's exactly what happens in Colossians 3:9, which says, "Do not lie to each other, since you have taken off your old self with its practices," and Ephesians 6:1, which says, "Children, obey your parents in the Lord, for this is right."

What would the rule of faith say about murder?

Can you back up your thoughts with verses from the Old and New Testaments?

Lord, help me recognize when someone is trying to lead me astray.

Canon Test #3: Widely Used & Approved

*They devoted themselves to the apostles'
teaching and to fellowship, to the
breaking of bread and to prayer.*

ACTS 2:42

God's Word was written by people inspired by the Holy Spirit. It only took one person at a time to write down what the Spirit said, but figuring out whether someone's document was inspired by the Spirit requires a community.

The final test to determine the New Testament canon asked whether a document had continuous acceptance and usage by the church at large, or in all the churches across the world.

Since the church is made up of such a diverse population in many different places, it is amazing they were able to agree on anything.

"There were certainly different opinions about which criterion should be given the most weight," agrees Bruce Metzger. "But what's remarkable is that even though the fringes of the canon remained unsettled for a while, there was actually a high degree of unanimity concerning the greater part of the New Testament within the first two centuries."

So if someone came forward with a "new gospel" claiming previously hidden instructions from God, it needed to be tested. Does its teaching agree with what we know to be true? Is it widely agreed upon by the church to be genuine?

> **What are some truths that are widely accepted and used by the church?**
>
> **What would you say to someone who claimed to have new teachings about Jesus?**

*Lord, may my beliefs be based on the
recognized wisdom of your church.*

124

The Best Roads in Europe

Your word is a lamp for my
feet, a light on my path.

PSALM 119:105

The gospels in our New Testament are recognized to be part of biblical canon based on the three tests we just read. What happened to the rest of the "gospels" out there?

"It was, if I may put it this way, an example of 'survival of the fittest.'" answers Bruce Metzger. "In talking about the canon, Arthur Darby Nock used to tell his students at Harvard, 'The most traveled roads in Europe are the best roads; that's why they're so heavily traveled.' That's a good analogy. British commentator William Barclay said it this way: 'It is the simple truth to say that the New Testament books became canonical because no one could stop them doing so.'

"We can be confident that no other ancient books can compare with the New Testament in terms of importance for Christian history or doctrine. When one studies the early history of the canon, one walks away convinced that the New Testament contains the best sources for the history of Jesus."

And what do the canonical gospels say about Jesus? He is the Son of God (Matthew 14:33). He was human like us (Luke 2:40). He is the sacrifice for our sins (Mark 10:45). He is the way, the truth, and the life (John 14:6).

The road to Jesus is well established in the Bible. The only way to keep on that road is to stay in his Word.

Why would the best roads be the most traveled?

Who would you bring along with you on the road to Jesus?

Lord, light my way with your word.

What About the Gospel of Thomas?

Turn away from godless chatter and the opposing ideas of what is falsely called knowledge, which some have professed and in so doing have departed from the faith. Grace be with you all.

1 TIMOTHY 6:20–21

In 1945, a trove of ancient documents was found near Nag Hammadi, Egypt. Among them was the Gospel of Thomas, which claimed to contain "the secret words which the living Jesus spoke and Didymus Judas Thomas wrote down." Why was it excluded by the church?

Bruce Metzger says: "The Gospel of Thomas came to light in a fifth-century copy in Coptic, which I've translated into English. It contains 114 sayings attributed to Jesus but no narrative of what he did, and seems to have been written in Greek in Syria about AD 140. In some cases I think this gospel correctly reports what Jesus said, with slight modifications.

"For instance," continues Bruce, "in the Gospel of Thomas Jesus says 'A city built on a high hill cannot be hidden.' Here the adjective *high* is added, but the rest reads like Matthew's gospel. Or Jesus says, 'Render to Caesar the things that are Caesar's, render to God the things that are God's, render to me the things that are mine.' In this case the later phrase had been added."

Before we embrace the Gospel of Thomas, let's remember Paul's warning in 1 Timothy 6:20–21.

Why should we be wary of the Gospel of Thomas?

How would you answer someone who claimed the Gospel of Thomas was right and the other gospels were wrong?

Lord, when I hear things opposed to your word, help me know what is true.

The Gospel of Thomas: Pantheism vs. Christianity

> *They exchanged the truth about God for a lie,*
> *and worshiped and served created things rather*
> *than the Creator—who is forever praised. Amen.*
>
> **ROMANS 1:25**

The Gospel of Thomas claims to have the secret sayings of Jesus. How do these sayings compare to our Bible?

"There are some things in Thomas that are totally alien to the canonical gospels," says Bruce Metzger. "Jesus says, 'Split wood; I am there. Lift up a stone, and you will find me there.' That's pantheism, the idea that Jesus is coterminous with the substance of this world. That's contrary to anything in the canonical gospels."

We believe God created the world, and the Bible shows each member of the Trinity present in creation.

Genesis 1:1 says, "In the beginning God created the heavens and the earth." That's God the Father.

Genesis 1:2 says, "Now the earth was formless and empty, darkness was over the surface of the deep, and the Spirit of God was hovering over the waters." That's the Holy Spirit.

John 1:14 says, "The Word became flesh and made his dwelling among us." That's Jesus.

The Bible *doesn't* say God *is* the rock and the tree he created. We must worship the Creator, not his creation.

What does Romans 1:25 say about worship?

Why does it make a difference whether you worship creation vs. the Creator?

> *Lord, your creation is amazing, but you*
> *are the only one worthy of praise.*

The Gospel of Thomas: A Woman's Worth

Charm is deceptive, and beauty is fleeting; but a woman who fears the LORD is to be praised.

PROVERBS 31:30

John 6:53–55 says, "Jesus said to them, "Very truly I tell you, unless you eat the flesh of the Son of Man and drink his blood, you have no life in you. Whoever eats my flesh and drinks my blood has eternal life, and I will raise them up at the last day. For my flesh is real food and my blood is real drink."

Is Jesus talking about cannibalism? No. In the surrounding verses, we see people asking Jesus for free bread to eat. Jesus is trying to get their minds off their stomachs and onto their souls. He is saying faith in him will sustain a person spiritually, which is more important than physical hunger.

But the Gospel of Thomas had Jesus saying crazy things that can't be understood in *any* context. Bruce Metzger says this: "The Gospel of Thomas ends with a note saying, 'Let Mary go away from us, because women are not worthy of life.' Now, this is *not* the Jesus we know from the four canonical gospels!"

In the Bible, Jesus praised the faith of the Canaanite woman in Matthew 15:28. Paul praised his female coworkers in Philippians 4:3.

God loves women and men equally and wants us all to put our faith in him!

Does the Gospel of Thomas accurately capture Jesus's feeling toward women?

How do you treat people of the opposite gender?

God, help me value all people equally.

Are Christians Close-Minded?

"You shall have no other gods before me."

EXODUS 20:3

The God of Christianity is the one true God. The first commandment says, "You shall have no other gods before me" (Exodus 20:3). Our God is the only God deserving of our trust and worship.

At the same time, as we defend our beliefs, we should try not to come across as close-minded know-it-alls. That only turns off other people from accepting Jesus as the Savior. Many of the people we meet will value tolerance above honesty, integrity, and conviction. That's a sad statement about society, but it's true. This tolerance has seeped into the belief systems of many Christians. A survey of people who said they were Christians found 70 percent of them thought many religions could lead to eternal life. That's just not the case!

Jesus said, "I am the way and the truth and the life. No one comes to the Father except through me" (John 14:6). We need to live with confidence, knowing God is the only way to eternal life. As we interact with people, we should strive to show love and respect. We can't bully or argue anybody into believing the truth about God. But our words and actions can demonstrate God's love, which could lead people to understand his way is the only way to go.

How can you pray for people who don't believe in Jesus?

How can you live so people will know that you do believe in Jesus?

Lord, help me show love to people with honesty, integrity, and conviction.

129

Use It or Lose It

> *Keep this Book of the Law always on your lips; meditate on it day and night, so that you may be careful to do everything written in it. Then you will be prosperous and successful.*
>
> **JOSHUA 1:8**

For more than 100 years, researchers have studied the effects of summer break on students. While summer means no homework, and fewer responsibilities, it also means learning loss.

The solution? We must exercise our brains. Just putting away video games, turning off the TV, and reading a book can make a huge difference. We could play strategy games with family members or friends or put together a puzzle. Our minds are like muscles. We have to use them to strengthen them.

Learning loss doesn't only hinder our academic abilities. It can affect our walk with Christ. If we "take a break" from God, our relationship will suffer. But by engaging with God through reading the Bible and going to church, we'll know what he expects and grow closer to him.

Remember what it says in Joshua 1:8. Joshua wanted God's people to talk about, think about, and follow God's Word. If they did that, the results would take care of themselves.

What are your favorite ways to engage your brain?

How will you engage with Christ this week?

The same thing is true for us today. Make a plan to get into the Bible on a regular basis. When we keep learning about God, we'll never be at a loss.

Lord, keep me from "taking a break" from you.

Corroborating Evidence

"They will be like a tree planted by the water that sends out its roots by the stream. It does not fear when heat comes; its leaves are always green. It has no worries in a year of drought and never fails to bear fruit."

JEREMIAH 17:8

No tree stands taller than the coastal redwood. And not only do these trees grow to gigantic proportions, but they also live a long time. Scientists estimate redwoods can survive more than 2,000 years.

We might think such a massive tree would have roots plunging hundreds of feet into the ground. But Redwood roots go down only about four to six feet. The roots do, however, spread out more than 125 feet. By intertwining their roots with those of neighboring trees, redwoods strengthen and hold each other up.

When it comes to examining the validity of the Bible, it's important to look for corroborating evidence written by other historians. Several historians and other ancient writers did write about Jesus in a way that intertwines and strengthens the stories found in the Gospels.

"The fact is that we have better historical documentation for Jesus than for the founder of any other ancient religion," says Bible scholar and professor Edwin Yamauchi.

Over the next few days, we'll be digging into these documents to see the truth of gospels' accounts of Jesus.

> How would intertwined roots help the redwoods stand tall?
>
> How could you help fellow Christians stand tall?

Jesus, help me be rooted in your word with fellow believers.

Who Was Josephus?

> *For everything that was written in the past was written to teach us, so that through the endurance taught in the Scriptures and the encouragement they provide we might have hope.*
>
> **ROMANS 15:4**

Josephus was a very important Jewish historian during the time of the early Christian church.

"In his autobiography," says Bible expert and historian Edwin Yamauchi, "he defended his behavior in the Jewish-Roman War, which took place from AD 66 to 74. You see, he had surrendered to the Roman general Vespasian during the siege of Jotapata."

Josephus was a priest and a Pharisee. His most ambitious work, called *The Antiquities*, was a history of the Jewish people from Creation until the time he lived.

"As you can imagine from his collaboration with the hated Romans," says Yamauchi. "Josephus was extremely disliked by his fellow Jews. But he became very popular among Christians, because in his writings he refers to James, the brother of Jesus, and to Jesus himself."

Josephus wasn't a gospel writer or a Christian. His words weren't the inspired word of God, but his writings as a historian helps us corroborate what we know about Jesus already: he really lived and died and his followers believe he rose again!

If you were to write a history of your family, what stories would you include?

Why is it significant that Josephus wasn't a Christian, but he wrote about Jesus?

> *Lord, help me know that you really lived and died and rose again for me.*

Josephus & James

> *Blessed is the one who perseveres under trial because, having stood the test, that person will receive the crown of life that the Lord has promised to those who love him.*
>
> **JAMES 1:12**

James the son of Mary and brother of Jesus (Matthew 13:55). After initially discounting Jesus as a crazy person (Mark 3:21), James became a follower of Christ, eventually leading the church in Jerusalem (Acts 15:13). James's existence is talked about by Josephus.

Edwin Yamauchi, Bible scholar and historian, says this about Josephus's mention of James, "In *The Antiquities* he describes how a high priest named Ananias took advantage of the death of the Roman governor Festus—who is also mentioned in the New Testament—in order to have James killed.

"'He convened a meeting of the Sanhedrin,'" quotes Yamauchi from Josephus's book, "'and brought before them a man named James, the brother of Jesus, who was called the Christ, and certain others. He accused them of having transgressed the law and delivered them up to be stoned.'"

"I know of no scholar," says Yamauchi confidently, "who has successfully disputed this passage."

Since James's death—and Jesus's life—has historical documentation, we can be confident our faith will get us a crown of life too.

> Why do you think James changed his mind about Jesus being the Messiah?
>
> What are some trials you need perseverance to get through?

> *Lord, give me the faith I need to persevere through trials.*

Josephus & the *Testimonium Flavianum*

> *I have been crucified with Christ and I no longer live, but Christ lives in me. The life I now live in the body, I live by faith in the Son of God, who loved me and gave himself for me.*
>
> **GALATIANS 2:20**

We've seen how Josephus mentioned Jesus in *The Antiquities*. But Josephus also mentioned Jesus in the *Testimonium Flavianum*.

This second work is controversial though. Some historians believe well-meaning but misguided Christians added some parts, called *interpolations*, to Josephus's original passage.

Edwin Yamauchi explains: "For instance, the first line says, 'About this time there lived Jesus, a wise man.' It seems authentic for Josephus. But the next phrase says, 'if indeed one ought to call him a man.' This appears to be an interpolation.

"It goes on to say, 'For he was one who wrought surprising feats and was a teacher of such people as accept the truth gladly. He won over many Jews and many of the Greeks.' That seems to be quite in accord with the vocabulary Josephus uses elsewhere, and it's generally considered authentic."

Also considered authentic are Josephus's mentions of Jesus's trial, his crucifixion, and how his followers loved him. Even without the interpolations, Josephus corroborated many details included in the gospels.

Why were the additions to Josephus's Testimonium Flavianum a bad idea?

How can you show Jesus alive in you?

> *Jesus, be alive in me so others will know you are real.*

Who Was Tacitus?

No one can hold back his hand. No one can say to him, "What have you done?"

DANIEL 4:35 (NIRV)

Tacitus is considered to be the most important Roman historian of the first century. We know a lot about the history of Rome because of his work.

Tacitus wrote the *Annals* and the *Historiae (Histories)*, which told the history of the Roman Empire from AD 14 to 96. He was a skillful writer and his histories have been corroborated by other accounts and by archaeological excavations.

Since most of his writing was concerned with Roman politics and Rome's leaders, it is surprising Tacitus had anything to say about Jesus or Christianity. But according to expert Edwin Yamauchi, Tacitus recorded probably the most important reference to Jesus outside the New Testament.

Tacitus wasn't a Christian. In fact, he was quite opposed to Christianity, but that doesn't stop God from using his works to testify to the reality of Jesus.

Romans 8:28 says, "And we know that in all things God works for the good of those who love him, who have been called according to his purpose." As Christians, we know God loves us and will do what is best for us, even using people who are opposed to him to accomplish his will.

> **How do you feel about the fact that God can use anyone to do his will?**
>
> **How can you best serve God's purposes today?**

Lord, you can use anyone, but you like when we are willing to be used. Use me today.

135

Tacitus & the Fire of Rome

> *For it is better, if it is God's will, to suffer*
> *for doing good than for doing evil.*
>
> **1 PETER 3:17**

What exactly did the Roman historian Tacitus have to say about Jesus?

"In AD 115," says Edwin Yamauchi, "he explicitly states that Nero persecuted the Christians as scapegoats to divert suspicion away from himself for the great fire that had devastated Rome in AD 64."

The exact passage reads:

> *Nero fastened the guilt and inflicted the most exquisite tortures on a class hated for their abominations, called Christians by the populace. Christus, from whom the name had its origin, suffered the extreme penalty during the reign of Tiberius at the hands of one of our procurators, Pontius Pilatus, . . . then, upon their information, an immense multitude was convicted, not so much of the crime of firing the city, as of hatred against mankind.*

Nero's persecution didn't stop Christianity any more than Jesus's crucifixion stopped him from saving the world. Persecution may be unfair, but it shouldn't scare us away from standing by Jesus.

First Peter 3:17–18 says, "For it is better, if it is God's will, to suffer for doing good than for doing evil. For Christ also suffered once for sins, the righteous for the unrighteous, to bring you to God. He was put to death in the body but made alive in the Spirit."

Have you ever suffered for doing good?

Would you do it again?

> *Lord, give me strength to stand*
> *by you no matter what.*

Tacitus & a Most Mischievous Superstition

*But I tell you, love your enemies and
pray for those who persecute you.*

MATTHEW 5:44

As we've seen from Tacitus's account of Nero's persecution of Christians, he isn't very supportive of Christianity. He specifically refers to it as "a most mischievous superstition."

"How can you explain the spread of a religion based on the worship of a man who had suffered the most ignominious death possible?" asks Edwin Yamauchi. "Of course, the Christian answer is that he was resurrected. Others have to come up with some alternative theory if they don't believe that. But none of the alternative views, to my mind, are very persuasive."

Just how important is what Tacitus wrote about Jesus?

"This is an important testimony by an unsympathetic witness to the success and spread of Christianity, based on a historical figure—Jesus—who was crucified under Pontius Pilate," says Yamauchi. "And it's significant that Tacitus reported that an 'immense multitude' held so strongly to their beliefs that they were willing to die rather than recant."

People may not understand why Christians are so committed to Jesus, but Christians can't fully understand why Jesus would die for our sins.

**What sets
Christianity apart
from other religions?**

**How do you show your
commitment to Christ?**

*Jesus, thank you for loving me when I
don't understand how you could.*

Who Was Pliny the Younger?

That is why, for Christ's sake, I delight in weaknesses, in insults, in hardships, in persecutions, in difficulties. For when I am weak, then I am strong.

2 CORINTHIANS 12:10

Pliny the Younger was younger than Pliny the Elder, but that doesn't clear things up, does it? Pliny the Elder was a famous encyclopedist who died in the eruption of Vesuvius in AD 79. Upon his death, he left everything to his nephew, Pliny the Younger.

The younger Pliny became governor of Bithynia in northwestern Turkey. Many of his letters to the Roman emperor Trajan, as well as the historian Tacitus, have been preserved to the present time.

In book 10 of his letters to Trajan, he specifically refers to the Christians he has arrested.

Like Tacitus, Pliny the Younger was clearly not a fan of Christians. He didn't understand how a Christian's strength is in his weakness. When we are weak, we allow Christ to prove his strength in us.

Second Corinthians 12:10 says, "That is why, for Christ's sake, I delight in weaknesses, in insults, in hardships, in persecutions, in difficulties. For when I am weak, then I am strong."

In what way is Christ strong when you are weak?

How would you answer Pliny the Younger's question?

Lord, be strong in my weakness.

138

Pliny & the Worshipers

Yet a time is coming and has now come when the true worshipers will worship the Father in the Spirit and in truth, for they are the kind of worshipers the Father seeks.

JOHN 4:23

Church attendance in the United States has been on the decline for decades. It doesn't seem as important to people. In fact, according to some research, only around 40% of Christians have attended church in the last seven days.

In the year AD 111, Pliny the Younger wrote to Roman Emperor Trajan about the Christians he arrested and his reasons for doing so:

> They had met regularly before dawn on a fixed day to chant verses alternately amongst themselves in honor of Christ as if to a god . . .

Pliny is describing a church service! Knowing they could be executed for doing so, these prisoners self-identified as Christians, then pleaded guilty to worshiping Jesus. Pliny's letter testifies to the church's belief that Jesus was worthy of worship. Not only that, but they were willing to face severe punishment to meet weekly so they could honor him.

Does your family make church attendance a priority?

Why do you think it was important to the early church to gather and worship Jesus?

When we compare the early church to today's church, what we find is a bit sad. What does it say about our priorities when less than half of all Christians have attended church in the last week?

Lord, help me worship you in church and on my own.

Pliny & Christian Morals

> *Love does no harm to a neighbor. Therefore love is the fulfillment of the law.*
>
> **ROMANS 13:9–10**

No one likes to have their faults pointed out. If we did poorly on a math test, it wouldn't help if the smartest kid in class bragged about his perfect grade. And when Pliny the Younger was confronted with a group of prisoners who had better morals than he did, it didn't make him happy.

In his letter to Emperor Trajan about arresting Christians, he described how they met weekly to worship Jesus, and:

> ...also to bind themselves by oath, not for any criminal purpose, but to abstain from theft, robbery, adultery....

The early church was a group of Christians committed to worshiping Jesus and holding themselves to his standards, which were much higher than the Roman standards around them.

Pliny the Younger's letter is valuable evidence of the spread of the early church across the world and its appeal to people at all levels of society, the rich and poor, free and slave alike.

How do you feel when someone points out one of your faults?

How can you help others feel loved instead of judged for their faults?

Lord, help me love my neighbors well.

The Day the Earth Went Dark

*From noon until three in the afternoon
darkness came over all the land.*

MATTHEW 27:45

One of the most unbelievable claims in the gospels is how the world went dark as Jesus hung on the cross. If the world really did go dark, wouldn't there be some mention of this extraordinary event outside the Bible?

Scholar Edwin Yamauchi points to a footnote in historian Paul Maier's 1968 book *Pontius Pilate*:

> This phenomenon, evidently, was visible in Rome, Athens, and other Mediterranean cities. According to Tertullian . . . it was a "cosmic" or "world event." Plegon, a Greek author from Caria writing a chronology soon after 137 AD, reported that in the fourth year of the 202nd Olympiad (i.e., 33 AD) there was "the greatest eclipse of the sun" and that "it became night in the sixth hour of the day [i.e., noon] so that stars even appeared in the heavens. There was a great earthquake in Bithynia, and many things were overturned in Nicaea.

"So there is," says Yamauchi, "as Paul Maier points out, nonbiblical attestation of the darkness that occurred at the time of Jesus' crucifixion. Apparently, some found the need to try to give it a natural explanation by saying it was an eclipse."

Is anything unbelievable with God?

What would you say to someone who doubted the world really went dark at Jesus's crucifixion?

*Lord, your Word is true, even when
it seems unbelievable.*

Pontius Pilate the Inflexible?

> *The crowd came up and asked Pilate to do for them what he usually did. "Do you want me to release to you the king of the Jews?" asked Pilate.*
>
> **MARK 15:8–9**

Critics of the Bible sometimes question the gospels because of the way they portray Pontius Pilate. While the New Testament paints him as weak and willing to yield to the pressures of a Jewish mob by executing Jesus, other historical accounts picture him as being obstinate and inflexible. Doesn't this show the Bible got it wrong?

"No, it really doesn't," says Edwin Yamauchi. Pontius Pilate was closely associated with a man named Sejanus, an influential leader in the Roman government who fell from power in AD 31 for plotting against the emperor. Why does that matter?

"Well," continues Yamauchi, "this loss would have made Pilate's position very weak in AD 33, which is most likely when Jesus was crucified. So it would certainly be understandable that Pilate would have been reluctant to offend the Jews at that time and to get into further trouble with the emperor. That means the biblical description is most likely correct."

In order to fulfill the Old Testament prophecies about the Messiah, Jesus needed to be crucified. God orchestrated things in just such a way for Pilate, a normally inflexible ruler, to bend to the will of the Jewish mob. Nothing is beyond God's control.

Does it ever feel like God has lost control of a situation?

How does Pilate's situation tell us that God is always in control?

Lord, help me trust you when I feel lost.

Jesus in the Talmud

"Whoever acknowledges me before others, I will also acknowledge before my Father in heaven."

MATTHEW 10:32

We've seen a number of examples from the Roman world to support the gospels' version of Jesus, but is there anything available in Jewish literature? Jesus was Jewish after all.

Actually, Jesus is mentioned in the Talmud finished about AD 500 that incorporates the Mishnah, compiled around AD 200.

"Jews, as a whole, did not go into great detail about heretics," says scholar Edwin Yamauchi. "There are a few passages in the Talmud that mention Jesus, calling him a false messiah who practiced magic and who was justly condemned to death."

Professor M. Wilcox put it in this way:

> The Jewish traditional literature . . . supports the gospel claim that he was a healer and miracle-worker, even though it ascribes these activities to sorcery. In addition, it preserves the recollection that he was a teacher, and that he had disciples (five of them), and that at least in the earlier Rabbinnic period not all of the sages had finally made up their minds that he was a "heretic" or a "deceiver."

How confident are you in Jesus being a real person?

Why do you think Jewish literature would call him a false messiah?

Although these are negative views of Jesus, they do corroborate his existence and his reputation.

Jesus, keep me from denying you when I know you are real.

143

Jesus Among Rival Religions

... and there is but one Lord, Jesus Christ, through whom all things came and through whom we live.

1 CORINTHIANS 8:5–6

Between the different first century accounts of Josephus, Tacitus, and Pliny the Elder, as well as Jewish literature, we have quite a bit of historical evidence to know Jesus lived. But since Jesus is God, wouldn't there be more about him in ancient writings outside the Bible?

"When people begin religious movements," says Edwin Yamauchi, "it's often not until many generations later that people record things about them. But the fact is that we have better historical documentation for Jesus than for the founder of any other ancient religion."

"The scriptures of Buddha, who lived in the sixth century BC, were not put into writing until after the Christian era, and the first biography of Buddha was written in the first century AD. Although we have the sayings of Muhammad, who lived from AD 570 to 632, in the Qur'an, his biography was not written until 767—more than a full century after his death.

"So the situation with Jesus is unique—and quite impressive in terms of how much we can learn about him aside from the New Testament."

Of course, there is no comparison when it comes to different gods, because there is only one true God and one true Lord.

> Do you remember how long the gap was between Jesus' death and the gospels being written?
>
> How do you know if Jesus lives in you?

Lord, you alone are God.

144

Reconstructing Jesus Outside of the Bible

But in your hearts revere Christ as Lord. Always be prepared to give an answer to everyone who asks you to give the reason for the hope that you have. But do this with gentleness and respect.

1 PETER 3:15

Let's pretend for a minute we didn't have the New Testament. It's a sad thought because the New Testament is filled with wisdom for life and stories about Jesus. But let's just pretend Christians never wrote anything down. What would we be able to know about Jesus from ancient non-Christian sources?

According to Edwin Yamauchi, just by looking at the non-Christian historical evidence, we would have an outline for the life of Jesus.

"We would know that first, Jesus was a Jewish teacher; second, many people believed that he performed healings and exorcisms; third, some people believed he was the Messiah; fourth, he was rejected by the Jewish leaders; fifth, he was crucified under Pontius Pilate in the reign of Tiberius; sixth, despite this shameful death, his followers, who believed that he was still alive, spread beyond Palestine so that there were multitudes of them in Rome by AD 64; and seventh, all kinds of people worshiped him as God."

That's an impressive amount of independent corroboration! And that's not even all of it.

> **Without the New Testament, would you still know enough about Jesus to believe in him?**
>
> **Why do you think people don't believe, even with all the evidence?**

Lord, help me remember what I learn so I can answer critics or those with doubts with confidence.

Paul's Corroboration

Then make my joy complete by being like-minded, having the same love, being one in spirit and of one mind.

PHILIPPIANS 2:1–2

The apostle Paul never met Jesus prior to Jesus's death, but he said he did encounter the resurrected Christ and later talked with some eyewitnesses to make sure he was preaching the same message they were. Because he began writing his New Testament letters years before the gospels were written down, they contain extremely early reports about Jesus.

Paul saw Christianity as a threat to Judaism, so he was actively trying to shut it down. His unexpected conversion to Christianity is evidence of Paul's encounter with Jesus. And it makes what Paul says about Jesus significant.

He focuses on Jesus's death and resurrection, as well as how we are made new in him.

"Paul also corroborates some important aspects of the character of Jesus . . ." says Edwin Yamauchi, Bible scholar. "Paul's letters are an important witness to the deity of Christ—he calls Jesus 'the Son of God' and 'the image of God.'"

Just like with Paul, encountering the real Jesus has the power to turn our lives upside down, or rather, right side up. Paul's testimony is backed up by his life change. And the early letters he wrote corroborate Jesus really lived, died, and rose again.

How does your life back up your encounter with Jesus?

What about Jesus did Paul focus on most?

Lord, may others see a change in me because of you.

The Letters of Ignatius

> *Jesus said to her, "I am the resurrection and the life. The one who believes in me will live, even though they die."*
>
> **JOHN 11:25**

In addition to the gospels, Paul's letters in the Bible, and the non-Christian historical documents we've seen, we also have a lot of writings by the "apostolic fathers," who were the earliest Christian writers after the New Testament. Among the most important of these writings are those of Ignatius, the bishop of Antioch in Syria who was martyred before AD 117.

"What is significant about Ignatius," says Edwin Yamauchi, "is that he emphasized both the deity of Jesus and the humanity of Jesus, as against the Docetic heresy, which denied that Jesus was really human. He also stressed the historical underpinnings of Christianity; he wrote in one letter, on his way to be executed, that Jesus was truly persecuted under Pilate, was truly crucified, was truly raised from the dead, and that those who believe in him would be raised, too."

Ignatius believed Jesus was fully human and fully God, less than one hundred years after Jesus was crucified. And he was willing to testify to those truths even as his own life was in danger.

beliefs?

Do you believe Jesus was fully man and fully God?

The writings of Ignatius, added to all the rest, give us a large pile of persuasive documentary evidence corroborating all the essentials found in the biographies of Jesus.

Why was Ignatius willing to be martyred, or killed, for his

> *Jesus, I believe in you and I trust I'll be alive with you after I die.*

147

Scientific Evidence

The simple believe anything, but the prudent give thought to their steps.

PROVERBS 14:15

The scientific method has been around for a long time. As people made in the image of God, we value understanding because God values understanding. Any fear Christians experience over developments in science shows a lack of faith in the God who created the universe according to his own glorious design. And God encourages us to understand it!

Proverbs 14:15 says, "The simple believe anything, but the prudent give thought to their steps."

How can we better believe in God?

- Collect information, make observations, and ask questions.
- Formulate a hypothesis.
- Design an experiment to test our hypothesis.
- Conduct the experiment.
- Compare the results.
- Draw conclusions.
- Report our findings.

In making the case for Christ, we are using the scientific method to gather information in order to test our hypothesis that Jesus is real. But the scientific method can be applied to other biblical truths as well.

We'll see God isn't opposed to science at all. In fact, he created it as a way for us to know him better!

Do you feel like faith in God is opposed to science?

What are some ways you've been prudent instead of simple?

Lord, give me the wisdom to see your truth, both in the Bible and in the universe you've created.

The Limits of Science

By faith we understand that the universe was formed at God's command, so that what is seen was not made out of what was visible.

HEBREWS 11:3

In order to understand how the universe works, scientists look at the clues they can see. Even with invisible things like the wind, scientists can see the effects those things cause and make hypotheses based on the effects.

Since God is both unseen and immeasurable, it's easier for some scientists to say he doesn't exist. But the inability to measure something doesn't mean it isn't there.

Some scientists say God was thought up by people who didn't know how to explain things found in nature. Since some cultures believed the gods were responsible for moving the sun across the sky, once scientists proved that the earth rotates as it orbits the sun, those gods didn't make sense anymore.

While that's one hundred percent true about lesser gods, it is not true about our God. In fact, as scientists study the universe, it becomes *more* evident it was created at a specific point in time and ruled over by something outside of its existence. What could that something be aside from God?

Science can show us how the universe works; it cannot say God doesn't exist.

> **What are some things you can't see, but you know exist?**
>
> **What are some things you can see that are worth thanking God for?**

God, give me faith to understand you better.

How We Tick

*For every house is built by someone, but
God is the builder of everything.*

HEBREWS 3:4

Imagine we were out for a walk in the woods. Birds are chirping. Sunlight is filtering through the trees. We feel the rocks and roots of trees under our feet as we walk. Looking down, we see a pocket watch on the trail. Would we assume the watch was there naturally like the rocks and roots? No, the complexity of the watch's machinery would suggest it was dropped there by someone and was made by a watchmaker.

William Paley first published the clockmaker analogy described above as evidence of a creator in 1802. Just over two hundred years later in 2011, two scientists would publish an article about how human red blood cells have built-in clocks to flip enzymes from one form to another regularly within a 24-hour cycle.

We don't need to discover a pocket watch in the woods to understand Paley's analogy. The cells in our body are complex clocks pointing to the evidence of a clockmaker.

Hebrews 3:4 says, "For every house is built by someone, but God is the builder of everything." Just like complex clocks don't happen naturally, for a house to exist it needs a builder. And the author of Hebrews tells us that God is the builder of all things.

> **Do you think complex things like houses (or universes) happen naturally?**
>
> **How are people like houses?**

Lord, I am evidence that you make complex things.

150

A Work of Art

The heavens declare the glory of God; the skies proclaim the work of his hands.

PSALM 19:1

The creation of the universe is a disagreement which continues to pop up between science and belief in God. But not all scientists see creation the same way.

In an article on DesiringGod.com, professor and scientist John Bloom says, "The trend I see over time is that the more we study and understand the creation through science, the more clearly we see that it must be the handiwork of God.

"No good art critic can say that a masterpiece like the Mona Lisa is just 'random splotches on canvas' or 'somehow painted itself.' Similarly, our growing awareness that nature is a masterpiece makes it increasingly hard for a scientist today to shrug and say that 'it just happened somehow' or 'it's always been here.'"

This world we live in, the heavens above us, and even our own bodies are evidence, not only of a creator, but of an artist who pays attention to detail and makes things beautiful. Why? For God's enjoyment. Genesis 1:31 says, "God saw all that he had made, and it was very good."

> **What are some things in nature you find especially beautiful?**
>
> **Why does God enjoy adding something to our enjoyment?**

When God is pleased, he shares his pleasure with his children. We get to enjoy the beauty of creation, recognizing it as his handiwork, and giving him the glory he deserves.

> *God, thank you for making beautiful things for everyone to enjoy.*

151

Expansion & New Beginnings

> *He determines the number of the stars and calls them each by name. Great is our LORD and mighty in power; his understanding has no limit.*
>
> **PSALM 147:4–5**

Standing under a clear night sky, we can't see the stars moving. But with today's technology, scientists are able to see how the distance between galaxies has been increasing over time. The universe, say scientists, is expanding.

An expanding universe is no problem for Christianity. Our God is both omnipresent (everywhere at the same time) and omnipotent (all powerful).

In addition, if the universe is expanding, it used to be smaller, which means it started at some point. While scientists theorize this is due to some Big Bang theory, we know our start actually began when the infinite God spoke the heavens into existence and spun the planets and stars into motion.

Just as the Bible told us how the universe began in Genesis 1:1, it tells us how it will end in 2 Peter 3:10–13: "But the day of the Lord will come like a thief. The heavens will disappear with a roar; the elements will be destroyed by fire, and the earth and everything done in it will be laid bare."

What do you think about when you look at the stars?

How should we live since we don't know when the end will be?

The Bible also tells us God has promised us a new beginning. "But in keeping with his promise we are looking forward to a new heaven and a new earth, where righteousness dwells." (2 Peter 3:13)

> *Lord, you are bigger than the universe. Thank you for loving someone as small as me.*

Truth Below, Holiness Above

His truth springs up from the earth. His holiness looks down from heaven.

PSALM 85:11 (NIRV)

The scientific evidence for God isn't only found among the stars. It is also buried beneath our feet, just waiting for an archaeologist to dig it up.

Archaeologists are the scientists who fact-check ancient events. Archaeology involves careful digging to uncover artifacts, architecture, art, coins, monuments, documents, and other remains of ancient cultures. Experts study relics from biblical times to learn what life was like in the days when Jesus walked the dusty roads of ancient Israel.

"Archaeology has made some important contributions," says archaeologist, author and professor, John McRay, "but it certainly can't prove whether the New Testament is the Word of God. If we dig in Israel and find ancient sites that are consistent with where the Bible said we'd find them, that shows that its history and geography are accurate. However, it doesn't confirm that what Jesus Christ said is right. Spiritual truths cannot be proved or disproved by archaeological discoveries."

That may be true, but if the details of an ancient historian's story can be proven through archaeology, this increases our confidence in other material written by that historian. In the case for Christ, is there enough verifiable evidence in the gospels supported by archaeological findings to support the credibility of their authors?

> If you were to bury something for future archaeologists to find, what would it be?
>
> Why can't spiritual truths be proved or disproved by archaeological discoveries?

Lord, surround me with your truth from below and your holiness from above.

Digging for the Truth

They will rebuild the ancient ruins and restore the places long devastated; they will renew the ruined cities that have been devastated for generations.

ISAIAH 61:4

Our quest for the historical truth about Jesus brings us to John McRay, an archaeologist who took part in some digs in Caesarea on the coast of Israel, where he and others excavated the harbor of Herod the Great.

"For a long time people questioned the validity of a statement by Josephus," says McRay, "the first-century historian, that this harbor was as large as the one at Piraeus, which is a major harbor of Athens. People thought Josephus was wrong, because when you see the stones above the surface of the water in the contemporary harbor, it's not very big.

"But when we began to do underwater excavation, we found that the harbor extended far out into the water underground, that it had fallen down, and that its total dimensions were indeed comparable to the harbor of Piraeus. So it turns out Josephus was right after all. This was one more bit of evidence that Josephus knew what he was talking about."

With his experience in the field verifying Josephus' claim, will John McRay be able to help us with the New Testament writers? Did *they* really know what they were talking about?

What do you remember about what Josephus said about Jesus?

Have you ever doubted someone's story only to have them prove they were right?

Jesus, when I have questions about the Bible, help me dig in and look for answers instead of burying them.

Luke the Historian

> *In my former book, Theophilus, I wrote about all that Jesus began to do and to teach until the day he was taken up to heaven, after giving instructions through the Holy Spirit to the apostles he had chosen.*
>
> **ACTS 1:1–2**

Luke authored both the Gospel bearing his name and the book of Acts. Together, these two books make up about one-quarter of the New Testament. Given the quantity of his writing, it's a big deal whether Luke could be trusted to get things right.

As one of the apostle Paul's traveling companions, Luke traveled far and wide throughout the Roman empire to spread the gospel. His detailed reports in Acts read like a travel diary or some kind of road trip.

We see a repeating pattern of the gospel being given, people joining the church, opponents persecuting the Christian leaders, and then God's intervention to protect his people. Along the road, Luke wrote details about the places he went allowing us to investigate his accuracy.

Luke says he "carefully investigated everything from the beginning," but did science agree?

"The general consensus of scholars is that Luke is very accurate as a historian," says John McRay. "He's eloquent in his writing. His Greek, the language he wrote in, approaches classical quality. And archaeological discoveries are showing over and over again that Luke is accurate in what he has to say."

What would it mean if Luke lied about small details in his books?

If you wrote a road trip journal, where would you want to go and what would you write about?

> *Lord, keep me truthful in the small things and the big things.*

Luke's Accuracy: Lysanias

In the fifteenth year of the reign of Tiberius Caesar—when Pontius Pilate was governor of Judea, Herod tetrarch of Galilee, his brother Philip tetrarch of Iturea and Traconitis, and Lysanias tetrarch of Abilene—

LUKE 3:1

Luke was a detailed historian who placed names and dates into his books. These details allow modern historians to fact check his work. As an example, John McRay brought up Luke 3:1, where Luke refers to Lysanias as a tetrarch.

What is a tetrarch? After Herod the Great died, his kingdom was divided four ways. A tetrarch was the governor or ruler of one of those four areas. Luke named Lysanias as the one in charge of the region of Abilene in about AD 27.

For years, scholars pointed to this as evidence Luke didn't know what he was talking about. History showed Lysanias was not a tetrarch, but rather the ruler of Chalcis fifty years earlier. If Luke couldn't get this basic fact right, nothing he wrote could be trusted.

About 150 years ago, an inscription was found on a temple in the city of Abila, near Damascus, that names Lysanias as tetrarch. This inscription dated back to the time of Tiberius, from AD 14 to 37. Archaeologists had proven Luke was exactly right. There had been two government officials named Lysanias who served fifty years apart from each other.

Do you know anyone who has the same first name as you?

How could you pray for that person today?

Lord, the details in your Bible are nice, but the fact it says you love me is most important.

Luke's Accuracy: The Politarchs

But when they did not find them, they dragged Jason and some other believers before the city officials, shouting: "These men who have caused trouble all over the world have now come here."

ACTS 17:6

Getting someone's job title right is a big deal. The president of the United States may take offense if we refer to them as a cook, or a prince, or an assistant manager.

In his travels around the Roman world, Luke encountered a number of different officials with different job titles, and he carefully recorded them in his gospel and in the book of Acts. We've already seen how his mention of Lysanias as the tetrarch of Abilene was supported by archaeology.

Another example of his commitment to accuracy is Luke's reference in Acts 17:6 to "politarchs" in the city of Thessalonica. The NIV Bible translated this word as "city officials." For a long time people thought Luke was mistaken because no evidence of the term "politarchs" had been found in any ancient Roman documents.

As it turns out, Luke was correct again. In 1960, Carl Schuler published a list of thirty-two inscriptions found at archaeological sites that contained the word *politarch*. Nineteen of the thirty-two were found at Thessalonica. At least three of them dated to the first century AD— the exact time when Paul and Luke spent time there on their second missionary journey.

> **What would you like your job title to be when you become an adult?**
>
> **How might you feel about someone getting your title wrong?**

Jesus, you are the Messiah, the Son of God, and your titles are all amazing. Help me live so my title as Christian is obvious to everyone.

157

Luke's Accuracy: Titles, Countries & More

After his suffering, he presented himself to them and gave many convincing proofs that he was alive. He appeared to them over a period of forty days and spoke about the kingdom of God.

ACTS 1:3

During other travels that Luke writes about in Acts, he correctly identifies the rulers in Philippi as *praetors* (translated as "magistrates" in Acts 16:20), members of the court in Athens as members of the *Areopagus* (Acts 17:34), and the city clerk in Ephesus as a *grammateus* (Acts 19:35).

One prominent archaeologist carefully examined Luke's references to thirty-two countries, fifty-four cities, and nine islands. He didn't find a single mistake.

Again and again, archaeology has proven Luke to be an accurate historian. And given the large portion of the New Testament he wrote, that's extremely significant. If Luke's historical reporting was precise, then his account of Jesus's words and actions can also be trusted.

To be honest, it probably didn't matter much that Luke correctly identified Lysanias as tetrarch. It was great that he got that detail correct, but there were far more important matters with eternal consequences that Luke wrote about. One of those events was Jesus rising from the dead. And on the issue of the empty grave, Luke reported that event was firmly established by "many convincing proofs" (Acts 1:3).

Why would Luke's verified details about titles and places make his claims about Jesus more convincing?

What is significant about Jesus's empty grave?

Lord, as trustworthy as Luke's details are, you are more worthy of my trust.

John's Accuracy: The Pool of Bethesda

Now there is in Jerusalem near the Sheep Gate a pool, which in Aramaic is called Bethesda and which is surrounded by five covered colonnades.

JOHN 5:2

What do scientists have to say about the apostle John?

John's gospel tells different stories and covers different parts of Jesus's life than Matthew, Mark, and Luke. Some scholars have argued John wrote about locations which couldn't be verified, such as a mysterious healing at the Pool of Bethesda. We actually looked at this miracle earlier in this book (Day 60). Since basic details of this event didn't appear to be accurate, these skeptics said, John must have made other "mistakes" too.

Professor John McRay knew all about the controversy about the Pool of Bethesda. For nearly 1,900 years critics said John's record of Jesus healing a person who couldn't walk was false. No pool near the Sheep Gate in Jerusalem had been found, especially one that had five porticoes.

"But more recently the Pool of Bethesda has been located and excavated," Professor McRay explained. "It lies maybe forty feet below ground, and there are five porticoes exactly as John had described."

Although the pool was buried, it was still there. When the circumstances of life try to bury our faith, it is still there. We just need God's help to excavate it from time to time.

> **What was the miracle that happened at the Pool of Bethesda?**
>
> **Do you remember why John's gospel is so different from Matthew's, Mark's, and Luke's?**

Lord, don't let my faith get buried by doubts.

159

John's Accuracy: The Pool of Siloam

*"Go," he told him, "wash in the Pool of Siloam"
(this word means "Sent"). So the man went
and washed, and came home seeing.*

JOHN 9:7

The water of the Pool of Siloam was thought to be sacred. According to tradition, priests would draw water from this pool and carry it to the temple as part of the Festival of Booths. It was during this festival when Jesus said, "Whoever believes in me, as Scripture has said, rivers of living water will flow from within them." (John 7:38)

John 9 tells a story about Jesus healing a man who was blind from birth. Jesus explained to his disciples the man's condition wasn't because of his sin or the sin of his parents, but so God could show his power through Jesus's healing. He then spit on the ground, made some mud, then rubbed it on the blind man's eyes and told him to wash it all off in the Pool of Siloam.

Archaeologists discovered this pool in 2004, and they found it was actually two pools fed by the same spring: one inside the historical walls of Jerusalem (so the city would have clean drinking water in the event of a battle) and the other outside the walls. It was this outer pool where Jesus sent the blind man, but it wasn't the sacred waters which healed him. It was acting on his faith in the one who places living water within us.

Have you ever wondered if someone's illness was because of their sin?

What does Jesus say about the reason for the blind man's condition?

Lord, you are the healer and the giver of living water. Refresh me today.

160

John's Accuracy: Jacob's Well

So he came to a town in Samaria called Sychar, near the plot of ground Jacob had given to his son Joseph. Jacob's well was there, and Jesus, tired as he was from the journey, sat down by the well. It was about noon.

JOHN 4:5–6

Another passage of John in which Jesus claims to provide living water is told in John 4:4–26. On his way through Samaria, Jesus stopped around noon at Jacob's Well.

The land where Jacob dug his well had been purchased from the sons of Hamor during Old Testament times (Genesis 33:19). For more than 2,300 years, both Samaritans and Jews have identified modern Bir Ya'kub as the biblical Jacob's Well.

When Jesus sat down by the well for a drink, he asked a nearby Samaritan woman to help him. Normally, people drew water for themselves at the end of the day in order to avoid the heat of noon. Whether this woman was trying to avoid other people or it was just when she liked to draw water, she wasn't expecting Jesus or his request.

Jews typically avoided interactions with Samaritans. But Jesus wanted more than a cup of water. He wanted her to know he was the Messiah, and that salvation was not only for the Jews, but for all people would put their faith in him.

John's location for Jacob's Well checks out with archaeology, and John's message about salvation checks out too!

> **What in the passage showed the woman Jesus was more than a thirsty traveler?**
>
> **Have you ever tried to avoid other people and found Jesus waiting for you?**

Jesus, you know me inside and out. Thank you for loving me anyway.

Mark's Accuracy: Traveling to the Decapolis

> *Then Jesus left the vicinity of Tyre and went through Sidon, down to the Sea of Galilee and into the region of the Decapolis.*
>
> **MARK 7:31**

Some critics have attacked the gospel of Mark as being ignorant of geography. Atheist Michael Martin says Mark couldn't have lived in the region at the time of Jesus, citing Mark 7:31, which says, "Then Jesus left the vicinity of Tyre and went through Sidon, down to the Sea of Galilee and into the region of the Decapolis."

"It has been pointed out," says Martin, "that given these directions Jesus would have been traveling directly away from the Sea of Galilee."

After looking through Mark and pulling some maps of ancient Palestine off the shelf, archaeologist John McRay disagrees. "What these critics seem to be assuming is that Jesus is getting in his car and zipping around on an interstate," says McRay, "but he obviously wasn't."

Reading the text in the original language, taking into account the terrain and roads of the region, and considering the loose way "Decapolis" was used to refer to a list of ten cities which varied from time to time, McRay traces a logical route on the map that corresponds precisely with Mark's description.

How do you think Jesus traveled if not by car?

What is your favorite traveling activity?

"When everything is put into the appropriate context," he concludes, "there's no problem with Mark's account."

> *Jesus, no matter how you got from Tyre to the region of the Decapolis, your way is always best.*

162

Archaeological Puzzle #1: The Census

*In those days Caesar Augustus issued a
decree that a census should be taken of
the entire Roman world. And everyone
went to their own town to register.*

LUKE 2:1–3

The second chapter of Luke is often read aloud at Christmastime.
Although it is familiar, is it likely the government at the time really
made its citizens return to their birthplace? Is there any archaeological
evidence this kind of census ever took place?

John McRay thinks so. "Actually, the discovery of ancient census
forms has shed quite a bit of light on this practice," he says, pulling out
an official government order dated AD 104.

> Gaius Vibius Maximus, Prefect of Egypt [says]: Seeing that the time
> has come for the house to house census, it is necessary to compel
> all those who for any cause whatsoever are residing out of their
> provinces to *return to their own homes,* . . .

"As you can see," says McRay, "that practice
is confirmed by this document, even though
this particular manner of counting people
might seem odd to you. And another papyrus,
this one from AD 48, indicates that the entire
family was involved in the census."

> **Why do you think
> a government would
> want to know how many
> people live in the land?**
>
> **How would you try to
> count everyone?**

*Lord, thank you for counting me as part
of your family in the census of heaven.*

163

Archaeological Puzzle #2: Nowhere Nazareth

> *He went to Nazareth, where he had been brought up, and on the Sabbath day he went into the synagogue, as was his custom.*
>
> **LUKE 4:16**

In the mid-1990s, atheist Frank Zindler wrote an article called "Where Jesus Never Walked." In the article, he argued the city of Nazareth didn't exist when Jesus was a baby. Therefore, Jesus couldn't have grown up there, and everything about him is a myth.

In 2006, the Nazareth Archaeological Project began digging beneath the Sisters of Nazareth Convent. Ken Dark, the project director, described the remains of a first-century home that was found. "Taken together, the walls conformed to the plan of a so-called courtyard house, one of the typical architectural forms of Early Roman-period settlements in the Galilee," Dark said.

Evidence continues to support that the biblical location of Nazareth is consistent with what archaeologists would call a "small town."

Did Dark's team find the very home where Jesus grew up? Dark doesn't discount this idea, but says, "it is impossible to say on archaeological grounds. On the other hand, there is no good archaeological reason why such an identification should be discounted."

If future archaeologists dug up your home, what would they find out about you?

Why do you think Jesus made Nazareth his hometown instead of a larger city?

Regardless if archaeologists have found Jesus' boyhood home or not, the case for the existence of Nazareth in the first century has gotten stronger over the years.

> *Lord, you choose the humble to do your work. Help me to be humble.*

Archaeological Puzzle #3: The Babies of Bethlehem

When Herod realized that he had been outwitted by the Magi, he was furious, and he gave orders to kill all the boys in Bethlehem and its vicinity who were two years old and under, . . .

MATTHEW 2:16

The gospel of Matthew paints a shocking scene: Herod the Great, king of Judea, feeling threatened by a baby who might one day take his throne, orders his troops to kill all the boys in Bethlehem under the age of two. Warned by an angel, Jesus's family escapes to Egypt.

The problem: There's no independent confirmation this order ever happened. Isn't it logical to say it never happened?

"I can see why you'd say that," replies archaeologist John McRay, "since today an event like that would probably be splashed all over the news media. But you have to put yourself back in the first century and keep a few things in mind."

McRay points out how Bethlehem wasn't a large town, so Herod wasn't ordering the death of thousands of children. Second, Herod was known for being a violent king, so the order fits with his other recorded actions. Third, there was no news media which would have written about it. Sadly, Herod's order to kill the babies in Bethlehem wouldn't have been much of a story for ancient historians to record.

Has fear ever made you act out in bad ways?

What makes God a better king than Herod?

Praise God our king is loving, compassionate, and not threatened by others, and he encourages us to be like him.

Lord, help me be loving, compassionate, and confident.

The Riddle of the Dead Sea Scrolls

Jesus replied, "Go back and report to John what you hear and see . . ."

MATTHEW 11:4–5

No inquiry into the archaeology of the first century would be complete without asking about the Dead Sea Scrolls (which we learned about on Day 102). But do these scrolls tell us anything directly about Jesus?

"Well, no, Jesus isn't specifically mentioned in any of the scrolls," says John McRay. "Although, there is a very interesting development involving a manuscript called 4Q521 that could tell us something about who Jesus was claiming to be."

Matthew's gospel describes how John the Baptist, imprisoned and wrestling with doubts about Jesus's identity, sent his followers to ask Jesus: "Are you the one who is to come, or should we expect someone else?" (Matthew 11:3).

As an answer, Jesus quotes a messianic passage from Isaiah 35. But for some reason Jesus included the phrase "the dead are raised," which isn't in the Old Testament text. This is where 4Q521 comes in. This scroll from the Dead Sea collection contains a version of Isaiah that includes the missing phrase.

> **Which piece of archaeological evidence do you find most convincing?**
>
> **Which of Jesus's miracles do you think are most impressive?**

When Jesus gave his response to John, he wasn't being ambiguous or cryptic. He was telling John, "Yes, look at the signs. I am the Messiah that Isaiah foretold."

Lord, when I have doubts about you, reassure me with your word like you did with John the Baptist.

Not the Tooth Fairy

"He himself bore our sins" in his body on the cross, so that we might die to sins and live for righteousness; "by his wounds you have been healed."

1 PETER 2:24

The idea of the tooth fairy is pretty strange. She sneaks into our room, digs around under our pillow, and steals a tooth. Sure, we receive something in return, but it's still a little creepy.

Christmas can also get a little crazy with its traditions. Forget about Santa Claus. In Denmark, Sinterklaas arrives by boat in early December. Instead of putting out cookies for him, children fill a wooden shoe with hay and carrots.

Many traditions began with a small piece of history. Then things get exaggerated and mixed up. Some people say Jesus is like that. They think, *He's just a myth. No person could do everything Jesus did.* But when we look at the historical evidence, dig into his claims of being God, and explore the effect he's had on the world and in individual lives then we'll come to one conclusion: Jesus is no myth. He's 100 percent real.

Jesus is the Son of the living God who saved us from our sins. First Peter 2:24 says, "'He himself bore our sins' in his body on the cross, so that we might die to sins and live for righteousness; 'by his wounds you have been healed.'"

Who's your favorite mythical person?

How does Jesus differ from that person?

Lord, thank you for bringing me life and being real!

Rebuttal Evidence

"Isn't this the carpenter? Isn't this Mary's son and the brother of James, Joseph, Judas and Simon? Aren't his sisters here with us?" And they took offense at him. He was amazed at their lack of faith.

MARK 6:3,6

In a courtroom, after the prosecution makes its case, the defense team has to explain why their client is not guilty. To do this, they have to present their own evidence to support their case. This is called rebuttal evidence.

In the case for Christ, we've seen some compelling evidence from science, documents, eyewitnesses, and even from fingerprints. But is there any evidence to rebut what we've seen so far? Do any credible sources say Jesus was a historical figure, but that he was just a normal person misunderstood by history?

Actually, there's a group called "The Jesus Seminar" who claims exactly that. So what version of Jesus did they find?

According to theology professor Dr. Gregory Boyd, "Basically, they've discovered what they set out to find. Some think he was a political revolutionary, some a religious fanatic, some a wonder worker. But they all agree that Jesus was not supernatural."

As we look into the claims of the Jesus Seminar, we must be careful not to make Jesus into someone we expect to find. When Jesus looks exactly like us, he stops being God.

Who do you think Jesus is?

Why do some people want to make Jesus look like them?

*Jesus, you love me for who I am.
May I love you for who you are.*

What is Naturalism?

> Jesus replied, "What is impossible
> with man is possible with God."
>
> **LUKE 18:27**

Remember when we learned what a *bias* is? (Day 90, if you forgot). The participants of the Jesus Seminar—who deny Jesus was anything more than a regular man—say they are on an unbiased quest for truth.

"Ah, but that's not what's really going on," says Dr. Gregory Boyd. "Their major assumption—which, incidentally, is not the product of unbiased scholarly research—is that the gospels are not even generally reliable. They conclude this at the outset because the gospels include things that seem historically unlikely, like miracles. These things, they say, just don't happen. That's naturalism, which says that for every effect in the natural or physical world, there is a natural cause."

But that's how the world works, right?

"I would grant that you shouldn't appeal to the supernatural until you have to," says Boyd. "But what I can't grant is the tremendous presumption that we know enough about the universe to say that God can never break into our world in a supernatural way."

By denying the possibility of miracles, the Jesus Seminar refuses to look at evidence showing Jesus *did* work in supernatural ways. If there's no other way to account for the evidence, we need to investigate the possibility. That's the only way to give the evidence a fair hearing.

How would a naturalist explain a tree spontaneously falling over?

What is a supernatural way to explain a tree spontaneously falling over?

> Lord, don't let me presume to tell you
> what you are allowed to do.

Jesus the Wonder Worker?

> *But if I drive out demons by the finger of God,*
> *then the kingdom of God has come upon you.*
>
> **LUKE 11:20**

One approach taken by naturalistic scholars has been to look for parallels between Jesus and others from ancient history as a way of showing his claims and deeds weren't completely unique. For example, there were ancient rabbis called wonder workers who did exorcisms or prayed for rain and it came. So some scholars have said Jesus was just another Jewish wonder worker.

"Actually," says Dr. Gregory Boyd, "the parallels break down quickly when you look more closely. The radical nature of his miracles distinguishes him. It didn't just rain when he prayed for it; we're talking about blindness, deafness, leprosy, and scoliosis being healed, storms being stopped, bread and fish being multiplied, sons and daughters being raised from the dead. This is beyond parallels."

The other major difference is how Jesus claimed to do miracles using his own authority. Wonder workers always worked by asking God to do something rather than trying to do it on their own. So when Jesus said in Luke 11:20, "But if I drive out demons by the finger of God, then the kingdom of God has come upon you," he's referring to himself. Jesus didn't ask God the Father to do something. He did things with the power of God the Father.

And he did those things so we would believe in him and accept him as our Savior.

How would you react if you saw Jesus doing a miracle in front of you?

What would you say to someone who believed Jesus was just a wonder worker?

> *Lord, you have the authority of God, help*
> *me live a blameless life in your power.*

Jesus vs. Apollonius of Tyana

> *Very truly I tell you, whoever believes in me will do the works I have been doing, and they will do even greater things than these, because I am going to the Father.*
>
> **JOHN 14:12**

Jesus may not have much in common with Jewish wonder workers, but what about with Apollonius of Tyana? He was someone from the first century who was said to have healed people and to have exorcised demons; who may have raised a young girl from the dead; and who appeared to some of his followers after he died. People point to these exploits and say, "Aha! If you're going to admit that the Apollonius story is legendary, why not say the same thing about the Jesus story?"

"I'll admit that initially this sounds impressive," says Dr. Gregory Boyd. "But if you do the historical work calmly and objectively, you find the alleged parallels just don't stand up."

He points out, Apollonius' biographer, Philostratus, was writing a century and a half after Apollonius lived, whereas the gospels were written within a generation of Jesus.

Also, Philostratus was paid by an admirer of Apollonius to write his biography, so he had a financial motive for making him look good. The gospel writers were rewarded for their works by being martyred (or nearly so in the case of John).

While some people may not want to believe it, Jesus stands alone as the verifiable Son of God.

> Since it was written later in an area where Christianity was present, do you think Philostratus borrowed some details about Jesus to write his biography of Apollonius?

> *Jesus, you are unique. Keep me away from anyone who would take your place.*

171

Jesus vs. the Mystery Religions

He appeared in the flesh, was vindicated by the Spirit, was seen by angels, . . . was believed on in the world, was taken up in glory.

1 TIMOTHY 3:16

Some critics point to the mystery religions of the Roman Empire and say Christianity borrowed its stories from them.

The mystery religions were secret gatherings, or cults, who weren't part of the officially recognized group. Some of these mystery religions included mythical tales of gods dying and rising again. Was worshiping Jesus just another unofficial Roman cult?

"The mystery religions were do-your-own-thing religions that freely borrowed ideas from various places," says Dr. Gregory Boyd. "While it's true that some had stories of gods dying and rising, these stories always revolved around the natural life cycle of death and rebirth.

"Crops die in the fall and come to life in the spring," he continues. "People express the wonder of this ongoing phenomenon through mythological stories of gods dying and rising."

"And Christianity has nothing to do with life cycles or the harvest," says Boyd. "It has to do with a very Jewish belief—which is absent from the mystery religions—about the resurrection of the dead and about life eternal and reconciliation with God."

Would you describe Christianity as a do-your-own-thing religion?

How would you describe Christianity?

Lord, your ways are mysterious, but your love is obvious.

Jesus vs. Secret Mark

"Do not let your hearts be troubled. You believe in God; believe also in me."

JOHN 14:1

John Dominic Crossan, perhaps the most influential scholar from the Jesus Seminar—the group who says Jesus was just a normal man—has made some strong claims about a gospel called Secret Mark. He says that Secret Mark may be the real version of Mark's gospel. What is his proof?

Dr. Gregory Boyd, biblical professor, says there is no proof. "You see, we don't have Secret Mark," he says. "What we have is one scholar who found a quote from Clement of Alexandria, from late in the second century, that supposedly comes from this gospel. And now, mysteriously, even that is gone, disappeared."

So what does Secret Mark mean for our understanding of Jesus?

"We don't have it," says Boyd, "we don't have a quote from it, and even if we did have a quote from it, we don't have any reason to think that it has given us any valid information about the historical Jesus or what early Christians thought about him."

Boyd says the vast majority of scholars don't give Secret Mark any credibility. There's only a rumor it existed and no one knows what it would have said. Fortunately, we do have lots of documentary evidence for the real gospels, and we know they tell us Jesus died for our sins and rose again to give us life.

> **How convincing is a secret document that's gone missing?**
>
> **Do you think Jesus was just a normal man or was he something more?**

Lord, help me see your opponents' evidence as it really is: Non-existent.

Jesus vs. the Cross Gospel

> *For the message of the cross is foolishness to those who are perishing, but to us who are being saved it is the power of God.*
>
> **1 CORINTHIANS 1:18**

There is another gospel, rejected by the majority of scholars, but embraced by the Jesus Seminar called the Cross Gospel. Does it fare any better than the nonexistent book of Secret Mark?

"No," says Dr. Gregory Boyd, "most scholars don't give it credibility, because it includes such outlandishly legendary material. For instance, Jesus comes out of his tomb and he's huge—he goes up beyond the sky—and the cross comes out of the tomb and actually talks!"

The Bible says in 1 Corinthians 1:18, "For the message of the cross is foolishness to those who are perishing, but to us who are being saved it is the power of God." This verse is saying that to people who don't believe in Jesus, it seems silly to believe eternal life is available because of what Jesus did on the cross. How could an embarrassing and horrible form of punishment be something worth celebrating?

But the Cross Gospel's version of the resurrection *is* foolishness. Our faith is not in a gigantic Jesus or a talking cross. It is in the God who sent Jesus, according to the promises made in the Old Testament, to be the perfect sacrifice for our sins. Why? Because it was the only way we could be with him in his holiness. Praise God for a Jesus we can actually believe in!

Why is the cross worth celebrating?

How does the cross represent the power of God?

> *Jesus, your power is not in your physical size, but the amount of your love. Help me love big like you.*

Circular Reasoning with Thomas

So Jesus said, "When you have lifted up the Son of Man, then you will know that I am he and that I do nothing on my own but speak just what the Father has taught me.

JOHN 8:28

Here is an example of circular reasoning: "If A is true, then B is true. And if B is true, then A is true."

Critics of Christianity think the Bible uses circular reasoning because it claims to be true, but we know it *is* true because it has been backed up by science, history, archaeology, and personal experience.

People from the Jesus Seminar believe the Gospel of Thomas should be part of the Bible. They believe it represents an earlier version of Jesus because there are passages where he doesn't do supernatural things.

Dr. Gregory Boyd says, "The only reason for thinking these passages in Thomas are early in the first place is because they contain a view of Jesus that these scholars already believed was the original Jesus. In truth, there is no good reason for preferring the second-century Gospel of Thomas over the first-century gospels of the New Testament."

When talking to others about Jesus, we don't need to use circular reasoning to prove he's truly God. Even though the Bible says he's real, we have many other non-biblical reasons to know he's real too.

How do you know the Bible is true?

Why do you believe Jesus is real?

Lord, help me avoid circular reasoning to justify my beliefs.

175

History vs. Faith

*And if Christ has not been raised, your
faith is futile; you are still in your sins.*

1 CORINTHIANS 15:17

People who say Jesus was just a normal guy think he was made into
some kind of religious symbol by Christians. They say the historical
Jesus is probably nothing like the Jesus of the Christian faith, because
it is too unlikely his miracles ever happened. Still, they say Jesus's
teachings could be inspirational to people without the miracles.

"But listen," says Dr. Gregory Boyd. "Jesus is not a symbol of anything unless he's rooted in history. The theological truth is based on
historical truth. That's the way the New Testament talks. Look at the
sermon of Peter in the second chapter of Acts. He stands up and says,
'You guys are a witness of these things; they weren't done in secret.
David's tomb is still with us, but God has raised Jesus from the dead.
Therefore we proclaim him to be the Son of God.'

"Take away miracles and you take away the resurrection, and then
you've got nothing to proclaim. Paul said that if
Jesus wasn't raised from the dead, our faith is
futile, it's useless, it's empty."

**Why would our
faith be useless
if Jesus wasn't raised
from the dead?**

**What does Jesus's
resurrection mean for
your own life?**

We crave for reality, and Christianity has
always been rooted in reality. Jesus was really
both God and man. He taught wisdom and
he performed miracles. He died and he rose
again. The power of Jesus is only real to those
who put their faith in his historical reality.

*Lord, you've raised me from
death to new life in you.*

176

Combining History & Faith

*So then, just as you received Christ Jesus as Lord,
continue to live your lives in him, rooted and
built up in him, strengthened in the faith as you
were taught, and overflowing with thankfulness.*

COLOSSIANS 2:6–7

As Christians, we worship the real Jesus. The Jesus preached about in church, the one we sing worship songs to, is the same Jesus who walked on the earth, hung on a cross for our sins, and rose again on the third day.

Dr. Gregory Boyd describes it like this: "If you love a person, your love goes beyond the facts of that person, but it's rooted in the facts about that person."

For example, you love your mom because she's nice, she takes care of your needs, she gives good hugs. All these things are facts about your mom; therefore you love her.

"But your love goes beyond that," says Boyd. "You can know all these things and not love her, but you do. So the decision goes beyond the evidence, yet it is there also on the basis of the evidence."

That's what it's like with Jesus. To have a relationship with him goes beyond just knowing the historical facts about him, yet it's rooted in those facts. We believe in Jesus on the basis of the historical evidence, but our relationship goes beyond the evidence.

How are knowing facts and being in love different?

How well could you love someone if you don't know any facts about them?

Lord, strengthen my faith with knowledge about you.

179

On Target

> *Let us keep looking to Jesus. He is the one*
> *who started this journey of faith. And he is the*
> *one who completes the journey of faith....*
>
> **HEBREWS 12:2 (NIRV)**

Matt Emmons focused on the target more than fifty yards away. After shooting 129 shots in the three-position rifle final at the 2004 Summer Olympics, Matt needed just one more decent shot to win gold. He locked in on the bull's-eye, pulled the trigger, and saw the shot strike. The gold medal was his!

The twenty-three-year-old looked at the scoreboard. Something was wrong. After a brief huddle, one of the officials walked over and said he'd hit the wrong target. Matt was competing in lane two, but the shot hit the target in lane three. Matt received zero points and dropped from first to eighth place.

On the most important shot in the Olympics, his aim was perfect but on the wrong target.

How could somebody so skilled hit the wrong target? Impossible, right? Sadly, a lot of smart people live their lives aimed at the wrong target. Instead of focusing on God and hitting the target, they aim at a different target.

What target are you aimed at?

How does your aim affect your decisions?

The Bible says to look to Jesus for guidance. Being sincere about your search for spiritual truth is important. We need to make sure we're aimed at the right target—Jesus Christ—as we make decisions about our life.

> *Lord, keep me aimed at your bull's-eye.*

Identity Evidence

> *Jesus, knowing all that was going to happen to him,*
> *went out and asked them, "Who is it you want?"*
> *"Jesus of Nazareth," they replied.*
> *"I am he," Jesus said.*
>
> **JOHN 18:4–5**

By the time Jesus was born, more than four hundred years had passed since the ministry of the prophet Malachi. The Jewish people had expected and looked for a Messiah during that long stretch of time. Earlier, we looked at how many Jewish Scriptures included prophecies about a coming Savior. If Jesus knew he was the Messiah, some people think he should have walked into the temple and said, "Hey, it's me! I'm God."

Critics of the Bible argue Jesus didn't walk around boldly proclaiming himself to be the Messiah or the Son of God because he didn't believe it was true. They say Jesus just considered himself to be a good teacher or prophet and all the "God stuff" was added later by Jesus's misguided followers.

But could there be other reasons why Jesus didn't stroll out of Nazareth in a big caravan of camels and say, "Hi, everyone. I'm God"? The question of what Jesus thought about himself is a critical issue in the case for Christ. To truly figure out who Jesus thought he was, evidence must be gathered about what he did, what he said, and how he related to others.

What would have happened if Jesus walked into the temple and said, "I'm God"?

What things do you remember Jesus saying about himself?

> *Jesus, you didn't come as people expected,*
> *but you still showed us that you are God.*

179

Jesus's Reputation

A good name is more desirable than great riches;
to be esteemed is better than silver or gold.

PROVERBS 22:1

Picture someone with a lightly inked stamp and a fresh piece of paper. If the stamp is lightly pressed to the paper, it leaves an impression. The more times the stamp is re-inked and pressed to the same place on the paper, the greater the impression it will leave. Reputations are the same way.

Good reputations require a lifetime of repeatedly doing good things: being trustworthy, making wise decisions, being kind. But just like one sloppily lined up stamp can ruin all the previous stampings bad choices can ruin a good reputation.

Jesus didn't have to worry about having a bad reputation because of his actions. He was perfectly trustworthy, perfectly wise, and perfectly kind. Jesus's reputation problem was that for hundreds of years, the people of Israel had been stamping out an image of someone to suit their own desires. Jesus didn't fit their idea of an earthly Messiah; he fit God's idea of the perfect Messiah.

Just like it takes time to restore a good reputation after a bad choice, Jesus knew it was going to take time to correct Israel's false reputation of the Messiah. Instead of instantly announcing himself to be God, Jesus took time to show people with his loving actions what kind of God he was.

What is your reputation like?

How could you improve your reputation?

Lord, fix the areas in my life that don't fit
your stamp of what a Christian should be.

Humble Hero

Do nothing out of selfish ambition or vain conceit. Rather, in humility value others above yourselves, not looking to your own interests but each of you to the interests of the others.

PHILIPPIANS 2:3–4

New York Yankees pitcher Mariano Rivera set more than twenty-five pitching records, including becoming the all-time saves leader.

At his retirement from baseball, Rivera notched a record 652 saves. When asked during an ESPN radio interview if being called the greatest closer embarrassed him, Mariano answered: "Yes, it does. It does make me uncomfortable because I don't like to talk about myself. I just want to be able to contribute as much as I can for the team. And the rest is just blessings from the Lord."

Mariano Rivera played baseball like he lived his life, according to Philippians 2:3–4.

Jesus lived out those words to the greatest degree. Nobody had more to brag about than Jesus Christ. But he never said, "Hey, check me out. I'm God's Son. I can walk on water." Instead of demanding to be served on earth, he made himself a servant and humbled himself on the cross to die for our sins.

When we're tempted to brag about acing a test, nailing a game-winning shot, or getting the lead in a play, we must remember Jesus's example and act humbly.

Do you find it hard to be humble?

How can you show others you are interested in their accomplishments more than your own?

Lord, turn my attention to helping others more than myself.

181

Jesus & the Twelve

We know Jesus was concerned about what would happen if he loudly announced he was the Messiah. We know he was humble and never bragged about his abilities. Critics have pointed to these facts as reasons why Jesus didn't claim to be more than just a good teacher. So what are some details about his life that say otherwise? How did Jesus show the world he was the promised Messiah?

"Look at his relationship with his disciples," advises Ben Witherington, theologian, author, and Bible professor. "Jesus has twelve disciples, yet notice that he's not one of the Twelve." Why is this significant?

"If the Twelve represent a renewed Israel, where does Jesus fit in?" says Witherington. "He's not just part of Israel, not merely part of the redeemed group, he's forming the group—just as God in the Old Testament formed his people and set up the twelve tribes of Israel. That's a clue about what Jesus thought of himself."

Jesus had thousands of followers, but only twelve he called to be his disciples. Twelve is a significant number for Judaism and Jesus used it to signal to the Jews how God was about to engage in some hands-on activity not seen since the tribes of Israel were first established.

What position did God have with the twelve tribes of Israel?

What position did Jesus have with the twelve disciples?

Jesus, you called twelve disciples during your earthly ministry, but you've called all of us to find salvation in you. May I serve you as a devoted disciple today.

182

Who Do People Say the Son of Man Is?

When Jesus came to the region of Caesarea Philippi, he asked his disciples, "Who do people say the Son of Man is?" They replied, "Some say John the Baptist; others say Elijah; and still others, Jeremiah or one of the prophets."

MATTHEW 16:13–14

Some critics of Christianity have suggested Jesus had an identity crisis, which is why he asked his disciples who the people thought he was in Matthew 16:13. But Jesus knew exactly who he was.

Jesus was well into his ministry when he asked his disciples the question. Matthew 15:30–31 says, "Great crowds came to him, bringing the lame, the blind, the crippled, the mute, and many others, and laid them at his feet; and he healed them. The people were amazed when they saw the mute speaking, the crippled made well, the lame walking and the blind seeing. And they praised the God of Israel."

Afterward, Jesus fed four thousand people with seven loaves of bread and a few small fish. Matthew 15:36–37 records this event.

Jesus showed power through his miracles. He showed love by meeting people's needs. His question of "Who do people say the Son of Man is?" was a test to see if by his actions, people knew what he already knew: Jesus was God.

How can you meet the needs around you like Jesus did?

How would you answer Jesus's question?

Lord, you fed the hungry and helped the hurting. Open my eyes to the needs I can meet.

Who Was John the Baptist?

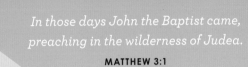

In those days John the Baptist came,
preaching in the wilderness of Judea.

MATTHEW 3:1

When Jesus asked his disciples, "Who do people say the Son of Man is?" in Matthew 16:13, they responded with a list of famous prophets. First on the list was John the Baptist.

His birth was announced by angels. His mom shouldn't have been able to be pregnant. He spent time in the wilderness, called people to repentance, and said the kingdom of heaven was at hand. He had loyal disciples. He was killed unjustly at Roman hands, and is attested outside of the Bible by the historian Josephus.

On top of these similarities, it's possible Jesus and John the Baptist looked alike. They were the same age and their moms were cousins.

But why would people confuse Jesus with John?

John the Baptist's ministry began first. As he called the nation of Israel to repent and be baptized, he gathered a sizable following. Threatened by his rising popularity, as well as his willingness to call out his sin, Herod Antipas had him killed.

By this time, Jesus's ministry had begun, and people wondered if John had returned from the grave. Of course, Jesus was the only one who would rise again, but given all the similarities, it made sense why people were confused.

Can you think of any other similarities between Jesus and John the Baptist?

What made them different?

Lord, you are more than a prophet.
You are my Savior.

Who was Elijah?

> *Elijah picked up the child and carried him down from the room into the house. He gave him to his mother and said, "Look, your son is alive!"*
>
> **1 KINGS 17:23**

Elijah was the second person mentioned by his disciples in answer to Jesus's question in Matthew 16:13. Why did people think Jesus might be Elijah?

Elijah is one of the most popular Old Testament prophets. He performed miracles, fought against corruption in religious circles, and he avoided death by heading straight into heaven in a whirlwind (seriously, read the second chapter of 2 Kings). Plus, Malachi 4:5–6 says Elijah would come again, "See, I will send the prophet Elijah to you before that great and dreadful day of the Lord comes. He will turn the hearts of the parents to their children, and the hearts of the children to their parents."

One of Elijah's miracles involved bringing a child back to life. First Kings 17:21–22 says, "Then he stretched himself out on the boy three times and cried out to the LORD, 'LORD my God, let this boy's life return to him!' The LORD heard Elijah's cry, and the boy's life returned to him, and he lived."

In addition to raising a widow's son from the dead (check out the devotional from Day 51), Jesus also raised a young girl and his friend Lazarus. It seemed like Elijah had indeed come back, but for some reason, he was calling himself Jesus.

Elijah prayed for miracles to happen. How did Jesus perform miracles?

What are some other differences between Elijah and Jesus?

Lord, not only can you bring the dead to life, you can give eternal life. Thank you for my salvation!

Who was Jeremiah?

> *"The days are coming," declares the LORD,*
> *"when I will make a new covenant with the*
> *people of Israel and with the people of Judah."*
>
> **JEREMIAH 31:31**

The third person Jesus was compared to was Jeremiah.

Jeremiah told the people of Jerusalem if they did not repent, God would allow them to be conquered. His message didn't make him popular. In the end, Jeremiah was proven right. Jerusalem fell to Babylonian forces, and the nation of Israel was scattered.

Like Jeremiah, Jesus's harsh message for the religious elite of Jerusalem was rejected. His call to repentance was met with violence. Interestingly, it was Jeremiah who prophesied that Jesus would set up a new covenant with the people of Israel in Jeremiah 31.

Jeremiah 31:33–34 says, "'This is the covenant I will make with the people of Israel after that time,' declares the LORD. 'I will put my law in their minds and write it on their hearts. I will be their God, and they will be my people. No longer will they teach their neighbor, or say to one another, "Know the LORD," because they will all know me, from the least of them to the greatest,' declares the LORD. 'For I will forgive their wickedness and will remember their sins no more.'"

When we recognize our need for a Savior, repent, and trust Jesus, we are forgiven and the Holy Spirit lives within us.

What does it mean that God puts his law in your mind and writes it on your heart?

Have you ever had to deliver bad news like Jeremiah did?

> *Lord, give me the truth, whether*
> *I want to hear it or not.*

Jesus the Prophet

Then I heard the voice of the LORD saying,
"Whom shall I send? And who will go for us?"
And I said, "Here am I. Send me!"

ISAIAH 6:8

Jesus was also compared to "one of the prophets" in Matthew 16:14.

A prophet is a messenger of God. A good portion of the Old Testament is a record of the prophets. The messages given by the prophets could be for cities, like Jonah gave to Nineveh, or countries, like Amos gave to Israel, or for individuals, like Nathan gave to King David. A prophet's job wasn't easy, because the truth is often difficult to hear, and true prophets only spoke the truth.

When Jesus asked who the people thought he was, his disciples answered maybe he was one of the prophets. Jesus told the truth. Even more than that, Jesus is the truth.

In John 14:6, Jesus says, "I am the way and the truth and the life." Jesus didn't just have a message from God, he had an invitation to eternal life. When we accept it, we are also given a mission. "Go into all the world and preach the gospel to all creation" (Mark 16:15).

We are prophets entrusted with a message from God. Our message from God is found in John 3:16, "For God so loved the world that he gave his one and only Son, that whoever believes in him shall not perish but have eternal life."

What qualifies you to be a prophet?

To whom can you give your message from God?

God, help me deliver your truth in love.

Jesus's Identity in the Trinity

Therefore go and make disciples of all nations,
baptizing them in the name of the Father
and of the Son and of the Holy Spirit.

MATTHEW 28:19

Judaism and Christianity are monotheistic religions; that means we both recognize and worship only one God. At the same time, Christianity seems complicated because we recognize the Trinity.

When Jesus came to earth, the Jews had no concept of the Trinity. There was only Yahweh, who we would call the Father. In fact, Jews called him the Father too. Isaiah 63:16 says, "But you are our Father, though Abraham does not know us or Israel acknowledge us; you, LORD, are our Father, our Redeemer from of old is your name."

Then Jesus came as the Son of God. Jewish priests and rabbis weren't expecting a Son. And yet, Isaiah 9:6 says (emphasis added), "For to us a child is born, to us **a son is given**, and the government will be on his shoulders. And he will be called Wonderful Counselor, **Mighty God**, Everlasting Father, Prince of Peace."

The Holy Spirit was present at different times in the Old Testament too. Genesis 1:2 says, "Now the earth was formless and empty, darkness was over the surface of the deep, and the Spirit of God was hovering over the waters."

Jesus identified as a member of the Trinity. The Jews rejected him as a liar, but we know he was telling the truth.

> **If you only knew the Father, how would you treat someone claiming to be God's Son?**
>
> **What does Jesus say about the Holy Spirit in John 16:7–11?**

Jesus, you are the Son. Thank you for sending the Spirit and for representing me to the Father.

188

The Voice from Heaven

And a voice from heaven said, "This is my Son, whom I love; with him I am well pleased."

MATTHEW 3:17

Although God exists in a Trinity—as one God with three distinct identities—we don't often get to see each identity in the same place at the same time. But it did happen at least once.

At Jesus's baptism, the Trinity is seen all together. Matthew 3:16–17 says, "As soon as Jesus was baptized, he went up out of the water. At that moment heaven was opened, and he saw the Spirit of God descending like a dove and alighting on him. And a voice from heaven said, 'This is my Son, whom I love; with him I am well pleased.'"

In the middle of his ministry the voice from heaven showed up again at the transfiguration. Matthew 17:5 says, "While he was still speaking, a bright cloud covered them, and a voice from the cloud said, 'This is my Son, whom I love; with him I am well pleased. Listen to him!'"

But at his crucifixion, there was no voice from heaven. The Father was silent. Jesus felt abandoned (Matthew 27:46). After he died, it was a Roman soldier who repeated what the voice of heaven had been saying all along. Matthew 27:54 says, "'Surely he was the Son of God!'"

Heaven has testified Jesus was God. Now it's our turn to tell others about Jesus.

Did Jesus deny he was God in any of these passages?

If you heard a voice from heaven, would you believe it?

Lord, help me listen to your words in the Bible as loudly as if they were shouted from heaven.

189

John the Baptist's Testimony

But John tried to deter him, saying, "I need to be baptized by you, and do you come to me?"

MATTHEW 3:14

Along with the voice from heaven, Jesus had a number of other identity confirmations. One of them was John the Baptist, who we've already seen a couple of times.

Jesus had some great things to say about him. "Truly I tell you, among those born of women there has not risen anyone greater than John the Baptist" (Matthew 11:11). But Jesus knew John wasn't the Messiah.

John knew it too. Luke 3:15-16 says, "The people were waiting expectantly and were all wondering in their hearts if John might possibly be the Messiah. John answered them all, 'I baptize you with water. But one who is more powerful than I will come, the straps of whose sandals I am not worthy to untie. He will baptize you with the Holy Spirit and fire.'"

John the Baptist wasn't the Messiah, but he recognized Jesus was. Matthew 3:13-14 says, "Then Jesus came from Galilee to the Jordan to be baptized by John. But John tried to deter him, saying, 'I need to be baptized by you, and do you come to me?'"

Why would he say that? Because John's baptism was for the repentance of sins, and John knew Jesus was perfectly sinless. Like John, we also know Jesus is the sinless Son of God.

> In Matthew 3, what reason does Jesus give John for wanting to be baptized?
>
> Why is it important for Jesus to be sinless?

Lord, because you were sinless, you were able to pay for my sins. Thank you for salvation!

The Demons' Testimony

> *"What do you want with us, Jesus of Nazareth? Have you come to destroy us? I know who you are—the Holy One of God!"*
>
> **MARK 1:24**

The next category of witnesses aren't nearly as trustworthy as John the Baptist, but they do reinforce what John said. We're talking about demons.

Matthew 8:29 records the response of the demon-possessed man known as Legion: "What do you want with us, Son of God?" they shouted. "Have you come here to torture us before the appointed time?"

In Mark 1:24, another demon says, "What do you want with us, Jesus of Nazareth? Have you come to destroy us? I know who you are—the Holy One of God!"

Why would these demons so freely identify Jesus as the Holy Son of God? For one thing, demons aren't necessarily liars. They may be evil, but they don't need to lie.

Second, by revealing the truth of who Jesus was, they were working against Jesus's plan. Jesus didn't want to reveal himself as the Messiah with his words because he knew people would misunderstand his intentions. He wanted to reveal himself through his actions, so people would see he was God, but a more loving kind of God than they were expecting.

How is it possible to tell the truth in a hurtful way?

How could you tell the truth in a kind way?

Fortunately, we don't need to take the demons' word for Jesus's deity because we have other testimonies as well.

Lord, make me both truthful and kind.

The Disciples' Testimony

Simon Peter answered, "You are the Messiah, the Son of the living God."

MATTHEW 16:16

When Jesus asked the disciples who the people said he was, he followed it up by asking the disciples who *they* said he was.

Matthew 16:16–17 says, "Jesus replied, 'Blessed are you, Simon son of Jonah, for this was not revealed to you by flesh and blood, but by my Father in heaven.'"

No one knew Jesus was God better than the disciples. They watched him do countless miracles. They heard him share wisdom with the masses. They saw him control the wind and waves.

Seeing should have meant believing, but even the disciples sometimes forgot who Jesus was. It is easy to believe Jesus is God when things are going well, but doubts creep in when life gets hard. We start to question whether Jesus really loves us or why he would allow us to experience hard times.

Jesus told his disciples to expect the hard times. John 16:33 says, "I have told you these things, so that in me you may have peace. In this world you will have trouble. But take heart! I have overcome the world."

We can believe in him like the disciples did, and even better than they did. We aren't waiting to see if Jesus really is the Messiah. He is, and he rose from the grave to prove it.

> **Why is it easy to believe in Jesus in the good times?**
>
> **Why is it important to believe in him in the hard times?**

> *Jesus, help me overcome my doubts like you have overcome the world.*

Fighting with the Pharisees

"Nothing outside a person can defile them by going into them. Rather, it is what comes out of a person that defiles them."

MARK 7:15

Jesus said and did a lot to show what he thought about himself.

Ben Witherington, professor and Bible expert says: "Jesus makes the truly radical statement that it's not what enters a person that defiles him but what comes out of his heart. Frankly, this sets aside huge portions of the Old Testament book of Leviticus, with its meticulous rules concerning purity.

"Now, the Pharisees didn't like this message. They wanted to keep things as they were, but Jesus said, 'No, God has further plans. He's doing a new thing.' We have to ask, what kind of person thinks he has the authority to set aside the divinely inspired Jewish Scriptures and supplant them with his own teaching?"

The answer? A book's author wants to make sure the reader understands the message clearly. God relayed detailed purity rules to the Israelites because he wanted them to know he was pure. But Jesus saw those rules as getting in the way of what God really wanted— their hearts.

God does want us to live pure lives, but purity doesn't come from keeping our bodies clean. It comes from loving him first and loving others as ourselves.

If you love God, would you live an impure life?

What does Jesus's response to the pharisees mean about how he sees himself?

God, you gave us rules to help us live, but you gave us love to give us a reason to follow the rules.

By the Finger of God

Jesus knew their thoughts and said to them: "Any kingdom divided against itself will be ruined, and a house divided against itself will fall."

LUKE 11:17

While Jesus's relationships provide one window into his self-understanding, Jesus's deeds—especially his miracles—offer additional insights. But it wasn't *that* he did miracles. His disciples did miracles too.

Acts 3:2,6–7 says, "Now a man who was lame from birth was being carried to the temple gate called Beautiful, where he was put every day to beg from those going into the temple courts. Then Peter said, 'Silver or gold I do not have, but what I do have I give you. In the name of Jesus Christ of Nazareth, walk.' Taking him by the right hand, he helped him up, and instantly the man's feet and ankles became strong."

Professor Ben Witherington says the difference between the disciples' miracles and Jesus's is found in how Jesus interpreted his miracles.

Luke 11:14–28 tells the story of Jesus casting out a demon. Some people who witnessed this thought that meant Jesus got his power from the prince of demons. Jesus explained that a house divided will fall. Satan can't cast out evil demons. Then he added, "If I drive out demons by the finger of God, then the kingdom of God has come upon you."

To Jesus, his miracles were a sign of the coming of the kingdom of God. Life wasn't going to continue like normal.

> **By what power is Jesus claiming to cast out demons?**
>
> **Whose power did Peter use to heal the lame man?**

Lord, help me rely on your power, not my own.

194

Jesus & His Abba

> *"Why were you searching for me?"*
> *he asked. "Didn't you know I had*
> *to be in my Father's house?"*
>
> **LUKE 2:49**

Jesus's miracles provided one window into who he understood himself to be. His teaching provided another.

Jesus taught in a radical new way. It started when Jesus was twelve years old in the temple (see Luke 2:41–50). He sat among the teachers and amazed everyone with his understanding of the Scriptures. When Mary and Joseph showed up to take him home, Jesus said, "Didn't you know I had to be in my Father's house?"

In fact, Jesus often used the term *Abba* when he was referring to God.

"'Abba' connotes intimacy in a relationship between a child and his father," Ben Witherington explains. "Jesus used it of God—and as far as I can tell, he and his followers were the only ones praying to God that way."

Normally, when the Jews spoke about God or prayed to him, they would call him something like "The Holy One." *Abba* is an incredibly personal term, like something a child would say to a parent.

"The question is," Ben says, "what kind of person can relate to God that way and change the way that others relate to God as a father?" The answer again is clear: Someone who knows he's the Son of God.

How do you address God in prayer?

Do you ever talk to God like you would one of your earthly parents?

Father, thank you for treating me like a beloved child.

195

John's Portrait of Jesus

The Word became flesh and made his dwelling among us. We have seen his glory, the glory of the one and only Son, who came from the Father, full of grace and truth.

JOHN 1:14

The Gospel of John is rich with Jesus's self-identification as God. In its opening scene, John uses majestic and bold language to assert the deity of Jesus, calling him "the Word."

> In the beginning was the Word, and the Word was with God, and the Word was God. He was with God in the beginning. Through him all things were made; without him nothing was made that has been made...

JOHN 1:1-3, 14

"When you're dealing with the Gospel of John, you're dealing with a somewhat interpreted picture of Jesus," explains Ben Witherington. John didn't follow the same stories as the other three "synoptic" Gospels. He wrote to show that Jesus was God. "But," Ben added, "I also believe it's a logical drawing out of who was the historical Jesus."

How would Jesus have reacted to John's version of him? Scholar Raymond Brown once said, "I have no difficulty with the thesis that if Jesus ... could have read John he would have found that gospel a suitable expression of his identity."

> **John compares Jesus to the Word. What would you compare him to?**
>
> **What do you think it means to be "full of grace and truth"?**

Lord, fill me with grace and truth.

John's Jesus Wasn't Shy

"You call me 'Teacher' and 'Lord,' and you are right, because that's what I am."

JOHN 13:13

In John's Gospel, Jesus isn't shy about saying who he is:

- In John 8:58, Jesus said, "Very truly I tell you, before Abraham was born, I am!"
- In John 13:13, after Jesus washed the disciples' feet, he said, "You call me 'Teacher' and 'Lord,' and rightly so, for that is what I am."
- In John 10, Jesus says, "I and the Father are one" (John 10:30).

Specifically referencing John 10, Professor Ben Witherington notes Jesus was plainly stating, "I have the authority to speak for the Father; I have the power to act for the Father; if you reject me, you've rejected the Father."

As Christians, we should boldly proclaim our identity too, not because we go around saying, "Look at me! I love Jesus!" but because our lives should look different from the lives of nonbelievers.

When we love with Jesus's unconditional love, when we forgive like God has forgiven us, the world will notice Jesus in us. Once people know we care, they will care what we know.

> **What is one difference you notice between Christians and the rest of the world?**
>
> **How can you share Jesus's love boldly with others?**

Lord, help me not be shy when it comes to living (and loving) like you.

Jesus On a Mission

"Very truly I tell you, whoever hears my word and believes him who sent me has eternal life and will not be judged but has crossed over from death to life."

JOHN 5:24

In most spy stories, the action starts when the main character gets a mission from spy headquarters. This character is equipped with the cool spy gear and the authority to do the job on behalf of their agency. Things may go sideways, but the main character is usually able to complete the mission and bring glory to their agency.

"Jesus believed he was on a divine mission, and the mission was to redeem the people of God," says Ben Witherington. "The people of God were lost and God had to do something—as he had always done—to intervene and set them back on the right track."

But here's where Jesus's mission goes sideways. The way God was going to save the world was by his Son dying. This statement is at the same time horrific and one of the most glorious statements of God's love. Jesus was willing to die in our place so we may have life.

Jesus isn't the main character in a spy story. He's the main character in the story of the universe, and he has already completed the mission and brought glory to the one who sent him.

What do you feel like God's mission is for you?

What gear do you need to do that mission?

Lord, may I bring glory to you in how I complete my mission.

A Ransom for Many

*"For even the Son of Man did not come
to be served, but to serve, and to give
his life as a ransom for many."*

MARK 10:45

In the gospel of John, we get to see Jesus as he understood himself.

- Did Jesus believe he was the Son of God, the anointed one? Yes.
- Did he see himself as the Messiah? Yes.
- Did he believe that anybody less than God could save the world? No.

That's a problem. God, in his divine nature, can't die.

"So how was God going to get this done? How could God be the Savior of the human race?" asks Ben Witherington. "He had to come to earth as a human being to accomplish that task. And Jesus believed he was the one to do it."

John's Gospel isn't the only one where Jesus made bold claims about himself. Jesus said in Mark 10:45: "I did not come to be served, but to serve, and give my life as a ransom in place of the many."

God sent Jesus to earth to be the ransom for our sins, which stole us away from him. God wants us back, and he was willing to take on flesh and blood to get us.

Why would God accept Jesus's life as a ransom for many?

Is there anyone you'd be willing to die for so they could live?

Lord, you made the ultimate sacrifice to save me. Help me live for you.

199

King of the Jews

> *The chief priests of the Jews protested to Pilate,*
> *"Do not write 'The King of the Jews,' but that*
> *this man claimed to be king of the Jews."*
>
> **JOHN 19:21**

Another identity clue for Jesus is the relationship he had with the Roman authorities. We have to ask why they crucified him.

"If he had merely been an innocuous sage telling nice little parables, how did he end up on a cross, especially at a Passover season, when no Jew wants any Jew to be executed?" asks Professor Ben Witherington. "There had to be a reason why the sign above his head said, 'This is the King of the Jews.'"

This title for Jesus is found in all four gospels. Matthew included it at Jesus's birth (Matthew 2:2) as well as at the crucifixion (Matthew 27:11). Mark and Luke echo the same thing (Mark 15:2 and Luke 23:3). And John 19:19–20 says, "Pilate had a notice prepared and fastened to the cross. It read: JESUS OF NAZARETH, THE KING OF THE JEWS. Many of the Jews read this sign, for the place where Jesus was crucified was near the city, and the sign was written in Aramaic, Latin, and Greek."

"Either Jesus had made that verbal claim," says Ben, "or someone clearly thought he did."

Did Jesus identify as a king? Yes, but not only King of the Jews; he is the King of Kings and Lord of Lords.

Is Jesus king of your heart?

What can you do when you feel like sitting on his throne?

> *Lord, be the king of my life.*

Evidence from the Early Church

If anyone does not love the Lord, let that person be cursed! Come, Lord!

1 CORINTHIANS 16:22

In addition to Jesus's identity claims in the gospels, church tradition gives us a glimpse of who the earliest believers understood Jesus to be.

Church historian Jaroslav Pelikan has pointed out that the oldest Christian sermon, the oldest account of a Christian martyr, the oldest non-Christian report of the church, and the oldest liturgical prayer (1 Corinthians 16:22) all refer to Jesus as Lord and God. Pelikan says, "Clearly, it was the message of what the church believed and taught that 'God' was an appropriate name for Jesus Christ."

Is there any possible way the early church would think of Jesus as God if he had never said he was the Messiah?

Ben Witherington says, "Not unless you're willing to argue that the disciples completely forgot what the historical Jesus was like and that they had nothing to do with the traditions that start showing up twenty years after his death."

Today, we still claim Jesus is God, and our faith is built not on wishful thinking, but on evidence. Jesus was both a verifiably historical figure and a unique member of the Trinity. In his humanity, he died for our sins. In his deity, he rose from the grave. And in his love, we have become members of his family.

Who do you tell others Jesus is?

When was the last time you talked to someone else about Jesus?

Lord, the early church knew you were God. In all the years since then, that hasn't changed.

Why the Disciples Came Back

> *Immediately Jesus reached out his hand and caught him. "You of little faith," he said, "why did you doubt?"*
>
> **MATTHEW 14:31**

Jesus's disciples heard his claims. They heard his teaching and saw his miracles. But when Jesus was betrayed by Judas and taken from the Garden of Gethsemane by soldiers, the disciples ran.

Peter went from confidently saying Jesus was the Messiah (Matthew 16:16) and assuring him that he'd stand by his side (Matthew 26:33) to pretending not even to know Jesus three times on the night he was arrested (Matthew 26:69–75).

There will be times in life where the things we've learned about Jesus and the prayers he's answered for us won't seem as real as the problem right in front of us. We may deny him like Peter did. Our actions may not tell others that Jesus is our Lord.

The thing about the disciples is, they came back. Something happened after Jesus's death on the cross to change their direction. They stopped running away from Jesus and started running toward him.

What changed? They encountered the resurrected Jesus. When things went bad, doubts crept in, but then they came back to Jesus because Jesus came back for them. When we have doubts, he'll come back for us too.

Have you ever doubted God because something bad happened?

How has Jesus come back for you?

> *Jesus, keep me from turning away when things get rough.*

Psychological Evidence

Many of them said, "He is demon-possessed and raving mad. Why listen to him?"
JOHN 10:20

Critics of Jesus often accused him of being demon-possessed or crazy. Even his own family questioned his sanity. Mark 3:20–21 says, "Then Jesus entered a house, and again a crowd gathered, so that he and his disciples were not even able to eat. When his family heard about this, they went to take charge of him, for they said, 'He is out of his mind.'"

With such charges recorded in the New Testament, is it any wonder that people today would question Jesus's sanity?

Merriam-Webster defines *megalomania* as: "a delusional mental illness that is marked by feelings of personal omnipotence and grandeur."

Or maybe Jesus suffered from a *god complex*, (also known as Narcissistic Personality Disorder), which is defined by an exaggerated sense of self-importance and a persistent need for admiration.

Do either of these diagnoses fit Jesus? "If you want the short answer," says psychology expert Gary R. Collins, "it's no."

Still, this is a legitimate topic that's worthy of further analysis. Experts say people suffering from delusional psychosis may appear rational most of the time. Some can even attract followers who believe they're geniuses. In the end, we'll come to the same conclusion as Gary.

Jesus wasn't crazy and it would be crazy to say he was.

> **Do you think Jesus was crazy?**
>
> **Does belief in Jesus make you crazy?**

Lord, I would be out of my mind NOT to put my trust in you.

Jesus's Mental State

"Who can ever know what is in the Lord's mind? Can anyone ever teach him?" (Isaiah 40:13) But we have the mind of Christ.

1 CORINTHIANS 2:16 (NIRV)

To figure out whether Jesus's claim to be God is a crazy idea, let's get an overview of his mental state as described in the Bible.

According to psychology professional Gary R. Collins: "He never demonstrated inappropriate emotions. For instance, he cried at the death of his friend Lazarus—that's natural for an emotionally healthy individual."

"Deluded people will have misperceptions," says Collins. "They think people are watching them or are trying to get them when they're not. They're out of contact with reality. They misperceive the actions of other people and accuse them of doing things they have no intention of ever doing. Again, we don't see this in Jesus. He was obviously in contact with reality. He wasn't paranoid, although he rightfully understood that there were some very real dangers around him."

Those dangers were real enough to result in his death on a cross. Jesus wasn't delusional. He was loving. He didn't have a bloated ego, even though he was surrounded by adoring crowds. He maintained balance despite a demanding schedule. He cared about all people.

"All in all," says Collins, "I just don't see signs that Jesus was suffering from any known mental illness."

> Do you ever feel like showing emotions means you're crazy?
>
> What does it mean that Jesus showed emotions like sadness and anger?

Lord, give me a mind and emotions like Jesus had.

Identity Claims

> *Yet to all who did receive him, to those*
> *who believed in his name, he gave the*
> *right to become children of God.*
>
> **JOHN 1:12**

If we visited a mental health facility, we'd probably be able to find a few people who believed they were God. How is Jesus's claim to deity any different? Because Jesus wasn't just making outrageous claims about himself. He was backing them up with miracles, like healing the blind.

"You see," says Gary R. Collins, "if I claimed to be the president of the United States, that would be crazy. I wouldn't look like the president. People wouldn't accept my authority as president. No Secret Service agents would be guarding me. But if the real president claimed to be president, that wouldn't be crazy, because he *is* president and there would be plenty of confirming evidence of that."

Jesus didn't just claim to be God—he backed it up with amazing miracles of healing, with divine insights into people, and ultimately with his own resurrection from the dead, which absolutely nobody else has been able to duplicate.

"So when Jesus claimed to be God," says Collins, "it wasn't crazy. It was the truth."

What evidence do you have to support your identity in Christ?

Who do you tell other people you are?

Pretending to be something we're not is a dangerous game. If we profess to be a Christian, but act just like the rest of the world, it reflects badly on the God we serve. We need to live into our true identities as God's adopted children through Christ.

> *Jesus, you weren't crazy in claiming*
> *to be God. Help my claim to be your*
> *follower be just as strong.*

205

Jesus and the Placebo Effect

*And he did not do many miracles there
because of their lack of faith.*

MATTHEW 13:58

A *placebo* is a fake drug or pill, and the *placebo effect* is when that fake drug or pill makes real change to a patient's condition simply because the patient *believes* it will work.

Skeptic Charles Templeton says, "Many illnesses, then as now, were psychosomatic, and could be "cured" when the sufferer's perception changed. Just as today a placebo prescribed by a physician in whom the patient has faith can effect an apparent cure, so, in an early time, faith in the healer could banish adverse symptoms."

Does this explain away Jesus's miracles supporting his claim to being the Son of God?

Psychology expert Gary Collins answers, "Might Jesus have sometimes healed by suggestion? I have no problem with that. Regardless of how he did it, Jesus did heal them.

"Of course," Collins continues, "that doesn't explain all of Jesus's healings. Often a psychosomatic healing takes time; Jesus's healings were spontaneous. And Jesus healed conditions like lifelong blindness and leprosy, for which a psychosomatic explanation isn't likely."

Jesus also brought people back from the dead—and death isn't a psychologically induced state! Jesus's miracles still stand up to criticism because Jesus really is the Son of God.

Have you ever experienced the placebo effect?

How effective would a placebo be on calming a storm or walking on water?

*Lord, no matter how you heal
people, you are still God.*

Jesus the Hypnotist?

> *What Jesus did here in Cana of Galilee was the first of the signs through which he revealed his glory; and his disciples believed in him.*
>
> **JOHN 2:11**

While at a wedding feast, Jesus heard there was not enough wine for the celebration. So Jesus performed a miracle.

John 2:7–10 says, "Jesus said to the servants, 'Fill the jars with water'; so they filled them to the brim. Then he told them, 'Now draw some out and take it to the master of the banquet.'

"They did so, and the master of the banquet tasted the water that had been turned into wine. He did not realize where it had come from, though the servants who had drawn the water knew. Then he called the bridegroom aside and said, 'Everyone brings out the choice wine first and then the cheaper wine after the guests have had too much to drink; but you have saved the best until now.'"

British author Ian Wilson has suggested Jesus may have been a master hypnotist. Could hypnotism account for this miracle?

No. Hypnotists typically look for people who are susceptible to suggestion. They don't often try to hypnotize a whole audience or wedding party.

What miracles wouldn't hypnotism explain?

Do you trust in Jesus's power?

Hypnotism would be a clever explanation, but ultimately it would require us to have more faith in the power of hypnotism than trusting in the power of Jesus.

Lord, help me believe what is true about you.

207

Dig Deeper—Hypnotic Healing

British author and religious skeptic Ian Wilson thinks Jesus's miracles were nothing more than a well-done hypnotism performance. As evidence, Wilson cites the modern example of a sixteen-year-old boy whose serious skin disorder was inexplicably healed through hypnotic suggestion.

Wilson's hypothesis would explain the reference in the gospels to Jesus's inability to perform many miracles in his hometown of Nazareth.

"Jesus failed precisely where as a hypnotist we would most expect him to fail," says Wilson, "among those who knew him best, those who had seen him grow up as an ordinary child."

Does Wilson's theory stand up to scrutiny?

Psychologist Gary Collins doesn't think so, asking about the previously mentioned sixteen-year-old. "The skin healing that Wilson talks about wasn't spontaneous, was it?" he asks.

According to the *British Medical Journal*, the healing took five days after the hypnosis for the reptilian skin, called *ichthyosis*, to fall off the teenager's left arm, and several more days for the skin to appear normal. The hypnotic success rate for dealing with other parts of his body over a period of several weeks was 50 to 90 percent.

"Compare that," says Collins, "with Jesus healing ten lepers in Luke 17. They were instantaneously healed—and 100 percent. That's not explainable merely by hypnosis. Even if people were in a trance and merely thought his hand had been healed, eventually they would have found out the truth. Hypnosis doesn't last a real long time."

Jesus didn't use hypnotist tricks to control the minds of his followers. He really healed and people really believed. In fact, belief in the real Jesus is the first step toward seeing the world as it truly is. And ironically, once we believe in Jesus, we will *want* him to control our minds (see 2 Corinthians 10:5).

Liar, Lunatic, or the Lord

> *If you declare with your mouth, "Jesus is Lord," and believe in your heart that God raised him from the dead, you will be saved.*
>
> **ROMANS 10:9**

C. S. Lewis, author of the Chronicles of Narnia series, was once skeptical about Jesus. After Lewis came to faith, he wrote about the evidence which convinced him in his thought-provoking book *Mere Christianity*.

> I am trying here to prevent anyone saying the really foolish thing that people often say about Him: "I'm ready to accept Jesus as a great moral teacher, but I don't accept His claim to be God." That is the one thing we must not say. A man who was merely a man and said the sort of things Jesus said would not be a great moral teacher. He would either be a lunatic … or else he would be the Devil of Hell. You must make your choice. Either this man was, and is, the Son of God: or else a madman or something worse. You can shut Him up for a fool, you can spit at Him and kill Him as a demon; or you can fall at His feet and call Him Lord and God. But let us not come with any patronizing nonsense about His being a great human teacher. He has not left that open to us. He did not intend to.

What would you say to someone who believed Jesus was just a great teacher?

How do you know he is Lord?

We know Jesus wasn't a liar. Gary R. Collins says Jesus wasn't a lunatic. That must mean he really is the Lord.

> *Lord, prepare me to defend you with my words and actions.*

DAY 200

Profile Evidence

> *"Who has done this and carried it through,*
> *calling forth the generations from the*
> *beginning? I, the LORD—with the first of*
> *them and with the last—I am he."*
>
> **ISAIAH 41:4**

In criminal investigations, police look for clues to help them solve crimes and bring justice to victims. When a crime isn't caught on camera, eyewitnesses can describe a suspect's appearance to a police sketch artist. The artist creates a picture which is released to the public who can then keep an eye out for people matching the suspect's profile.

According to the *Guinness World Records*, Lois Gibson of the Houston Police Department has helped to positively identify 751 criminals and secure over 1,000 convictions with her work as an artist. But can we use profile evidence to help us in the case for Christ?

The Old Testament provides numerous details about God that sketch out in great detail what he's like. For instance, God is described as omnipresent, or existing everywhere; as omniscient, or knowing everything; as omnipotent, or all-powerful; as eternal or being both beyond time and the source of all time; as immutable, or unchanging in his attributes. He's loving, he's holy, he's righteous, he's wise, he's just.

Now Jesus claims to be God. But does he fulfill these characteristics of God?

Let's see what we can find.

> **Which of God's attributes do you think will be easiest for Jesus to fit?**
>
> **Which attribute do you think Jesus will struggle to fit?**

> *God, help me follow the clues where they lead*
> *and see Jesus in all of your attributes.*

210

God and the Forgiveness of Sin

If you, LORD, kept a record of sins, LORD, who could stand? But with you there is forgiveness, so that we can, with reverence, serve you.

PSALM 130:3–4

Professor D. A. Carson identified God's authority and ability to forgive as one of the most striking identity traits we'll test against Jesus's profile. To test this accurately, we first need to understand a bit about God's forgiveness.

"If you do something against me," says Carson, "I have the right to forgive you. However, if you do something against me and somebody else comes along and says, 'I forgive you,' what kind of cheek is that? The only person who can say that sort of thing meaningfully is God himself, because sin, even if it is against other people, is first and foremost a defiance of God and his laws."

When David sinned with Bathsheba and arranged the death of her husband to cover his tracks, he eventually repented and said to God in Psalm 51:4, "Against you, only you, have I sinned and done what is evil in your sight."

"He recognized," says Carson, "that although he had wronged people, in the end he had sinned against the God who made him in his image, and God needed to forgive him."

God's forgiveness is always available and is only a prayer away.

How would you define sin?

Why is it important to confess our sins and ask for forgiveness?

Lord, forgive me when I sin against you and help me seek restoration when I sin against others.

Jesus and the Forgiveness of Sin

"Which is easier: to say to this paralyzed man, 'Your sins are forgiven,' or to say, 'Get up, take your mat and walk'? But I want you to know that the Son of Man has authority on earth to forgive sins."

MARK 2:9–10

Because sin is a violation of God's law, all sins—even sins against other people—are God's to forgive. No one else has the right to forgive sins.

"So along comes Jesus," says Professor D. A. Carson, "and says to sinners, 'I forgive you.' The Jews react by saying, 'Who can forgive sins but God alone?' To my mind, that is one of the most striking things Jesus did."

Jesus also asserted he was without sin. And certainly sinlessness is an attribute of God.

"Yes," agrees Carson. "Historically, people considered most holy have also been the most conscious of their failures and sins. But along comes Jesus, who can say with a straight face, 'Which of you can convict me of sin' If I said that my wife and children and all who know me would be glad to stand up and testify, whereas no one could with respect to Christ."

Jesus's sinlessness was part of what made him the perfect sacrifice for our own sins. His was the only death which could make eternal life possible. And because of Jesus's sacrifice, we are able to be perfectly forgiven for sins we've already committed and the sins we'll commit moving forward.

How close to sinless are you?

If you have been forgiven, what does God see when he looks at your sin?

Jesus, thank you for taking the penalty for my sin and making me clean before God.

212

God the Omnipresent

If I go up to the heavens, you are there; if I make my bed in the depths, you are there. If I rise on the wings of the dawn, if I settle on the far side of the sea, even there your hand will guide me, your right hand will hold me fast.

PSALM 139:8–10

What's the largest living thing on earth? Well, the blue whale grows up to 100 feet long and can weigh 200 tons. But blue whales are far from the largest things on earth.

Scientists found a mushroom colony in Oregon that spans about six square miles. Experts estimate this honey fungus weighs as much as 605 tons. But that's not it either.

Aspen trees spread through an intricate root system. One tree shoots out its roots and other trees pop up that are identical to the first. Several years ago a scientist found an aspen grove in Utah, where one tree spread over 106 acres. Its estimated weight: 6,000 tons. The scientist named the aspen "Pando," which is a Latin word meaning "to spread."

Pando is big ... but nowhere close to God's bigness. God is omnipresent. He's everywhere, all of the time. In Psalm 139, David writes, "Where can I flee from your presence? If I go up to the heavens, you are there; if I make my bed in the depths, you are there." David goes on to say that no matter where he goes, God is there to guide him. God is living large, because he's alive everywhere.

How is the church like an aspen tree?

How does God's omnipresence affect your behavior?

Lord, there's nowhere I can go where you aren't there to meet me.

213

Jesus the Omnipresent

*And surely I am with you always,
to the very end of the age.*

MATTHEW 28:20B

We may be able to accept Jesus's authority to forgive sins as God forgives, but is Jesus really omnipresent in the same way God is?

The questions around Jesus's incarnation—the act of God putting on flesh—have kept theologians busy for centuries.

"Historically, there have been two or three approaches to this," says Professor D. A. Carson. One approach involves categorizing the things Jesus did according to either his humanity or his deity, but that approach has some significant flaws.

"The other kind of solution," says Carson, "is some form of *kenosis*, which means 'emptying.' This spins out of Philippians 2. He emptied himself; he became a nobody. Some kind of emptying is at issue, but let's be frank—you're talking about the incarnation, one of the central mysteries of the Christian faith."

No matter how we understand Jesus's limitations while in human form, the fact remains that the New Testament gives specific examples of Jesus's omnipresence (see Matthew 18:20 & Matthew 28:20).

When we've accepted him as our Savior, we can trust Jesus is always with us. He knows our needs and never leaves us to deal with hard things on our own.

What does Philippians 2 say about Jesus's humility?

Do you need to fully understand something in order to believe it?

Lord, you are everywhere and you'll never leave me.

God the Omniscient

If our hearts judge us, we know that God is greater than our hearts. And he knows everything.

1 JOHN 3:20 (NIRV)

In addition to his authority to forgive sins and his omnipresence, God is omniscient, or all-knowing. We may act like we know it all from time to time, but God actually does.

- "Can anyone teach knowledge to God, since he judges even the highest?" (Job 21:22)
- "You have searched me, LORD, and you know me. You know when I sit and when I rise; you perceive my thoughts from afar. You discern my going out and my lying down; you are familiar with all my ways. Before a word is on my tongue you, LORD, know it completely." (Psalm 139:1–4)
- "He determines the number of the stars and calls them each by name. Great is our LORD and mighty in power; his understanding has no limit." (Psalm 147:4–5)
- "Who can fathom the Spirit of the LORD, or instruct the LORD as his counselor? Whom did the LORD consult to enlighten him, and who taught him the right way? (Isaiah 40:13–14)

In what situation do you need God's wisdom?

How successfully could you hide something from God?

God is the source of all knowledge. James 1:5 says, "If any of you lacks wisdom, you should ask God, who gives generously to all without finding fault, and it will be given to you."

Lord, help me ask for your wisdom freely.

Jesus the Omniscient

"Now we can see that you know all things and that you do not even need to have anyone ask you questions. This makes us believe that you came from God."

JOHN 16:30

Jesus's omniscience is probably one of the easiest of God's attributes to see in action in the gospels. It seems like he loved surprising people with knowledge no one else could know.

- He knew the thoughts of the teachers accusing him of blasphemy (Mark 2:8)
- He knew the background of the woman at the well (John 4:18)
- He knew what would happen following his death (John 16:16–30)
- He knew Peter would deny him three times (Luke 22:34)
- He knew Judas would betray him (John 6:64)

Jesus knew more than any human could possibly know. And yet, he grew in wisdom (Luke 2:52), which suggests that he started with less than all wisdom. He also claimed not to know when the end times would be (Matthew 24:36). Does this mean he isn't truly omniscient?

We have to leave his omniscience as one of the mysteries of the incarnation. What we do know is Jesus is no longer bound by his human body and he knows what we need before we ask.

> **If he knew Judas was going to betray him, why did Jesus still chose him as a disciple?**
>
> **What question would you like to ask Jesus?**

Jesus, you know me inside and out. Thanks for loving me anyway.

216

God the Omnipotent

"I know that you can do all things; no purpose of yours can be thwarted."

JOB 42:2

When some critics of Christianity hear God is omnipotent, or all-powerful, they ask, "Could God create a rock too big for him to lift?"

Although God is all-powerful, there are actually several things he *can't* do. He can't cease to exist. God also can't change his nature. He's consistent and solid. He'll always love you and always be there for you.

But what about the rock? As an all-powerful being, God could create an impossibly big rock. So it's logically impossible for God to create a rock he couldn't lift. Got it?

Sometimes questions can be confusing. At times we may ask some tough questions of our own, like "Why does a good God allow bad things to happen?" As humans, we won't always understand why something happens. But we can always trust God has a purpose. And all of his purposes are good.

Do bad things happen in the world? Yes. But God's purposes can be accomplished in the good times and bad. Job experienced that firsthand. He suffered unthinkable losses, yet he never doubted God's power.

We can follow Job's example by always trusting in God's power and goodness.

What questions do you have about God?

Do you trust him in spite of your questions?

God, help me trust in your purposes even when I don't understand them.

Jesus the Omnipotent

Then Jesus came to them and said, "All authority in heaven and on earth has been given to me."

MATTHEW 28:18

To say Jesus had power would be the understatement of all time. Not only did he perform miracles, even Jesus's teaching showed his power. Mark 1:27 says, "The people were all so amazed that they asked each other, 'What is this? A new teaching—and with authority! He even gives orders to impure spirits and they obey him.'"

But miracles and teaching don't equate to the same thing as omnipotence. The prophets of the Old Testament and Jesus's own disciples in the New Testament taught and did miracles. So what sets Jesus apart?

The main difference is one of authority. The Old Testament prophets received messages from God. They prayed for God to do miracles. The New Testament disciples taught what the Holy Spirit told them to say. They did miracles in Jesus's name. Jesus taught and did miracles under his own authority, an authority on the same level as God's.

Which makes sense. Jesus is omnipotent because he's God. Nothing is beyond his ability. So when he died on the cross for our sins, it wasn't because he lacked the power to come down, it was because he chose to die in our place. And because he is God, his sacrifice is powerful enough to give us eternal life.

What are some examples of Jesus's power in the gospels?

What are some examples of Jesus's power in your life?

Jesus, may I live in your power to do good instead of my own.

218

God the Eternal

Before the mountains were born or you brought forth the whole world, from everlasting to everlasting you are God.

PSALM 90:2

One of God's attributes is his eternal nature. Genesis 1:1 opens with God already present at the beginning. In addition to creating the heavens and the earth and separating the light from the darkness, God created time. Genesis 1:5 says, "God called the light 'day,' and the darkness he called 'night.' And there was evening, and there was morning—the first day."

God is not bound by time because he exists outside of it. Humans live sequentially—things happen in order, one thing after another. We use words like yesterday, today, and tomorrow. Time looks different to God. He is always in the present tense. That's why the name he used when talking to the Israelites is "I am."

When he does reference the past and the future, he exists there too. Revelation 1:8 says, "'I am the Alpha and the Omega,' says the Lord God, 'who is, and who was, and who is to come, the Almighty.'"

It is always today to God. Second Peter 3:8 says, "But do not forget this one thing, dear friends: With the Lord a day is like a thousand years, and a thousand years are like a day."

We can take comfort in God's eternal nature because when he says he loves us, he means it forever.

> **Do you think God gets impatient when things don't happen according to his schedule?**
>
> **How could God's eternal nature comfort you?**

God, I can't comprehend your eternal nature, but I know you love me today and that's enough.

219

Jesus the Eternal

For in Christ all the fullness of the
Deity lives in bodily form.

COLOSSIANS 2:9

In testing Jesus's sketch against God's, Jesus has to match the fact that God is an uncreated being who has existed forever. So what do we do about the verses which suggest Jesus was created?

Colossians 1:15 says, "The Son is the image of the invisible God, the firstborn over all creation." For something to be firstborn, doesn't it mean it was created at some point in time?

D. A. Carson explains, "Most commentators recognize that in the Old Testament, because of the laws of succession, the firstborn was the one ultimately with all the rights of the father.

"By the second century before Christ, there are places where the word no longer has any notion of actually being born first but carries the idea of the authority that comes with the position of being the rightful heir. That's the way it applies to Jesus, as virtually all scholars admit. In light of that, the very expression 'firstborn' is slightly misleading."

If we are going to look at Colossians 1:15, we can't ignore Colossians 2:9 which says, "For in Christ all the fullness of the Deity lives in bodily form." The author wouldn't contradict himself.

Jesus was with God before creation and will sit on the throne in heaven when time itself passes away.

What does John 1:1–4, 14 say about Jesus's eternal nature?

Do you believe Jesus is eternal?

Jesus, you didn't just live for 33 years on earth,
you were there when the earth was made.

God the Immutable

"I the LORD do not change. So you, the descendants of Jacob, are not destroyed."

MALACHI 3:6

Immutable is a fancy word that means unchanging, and it is one of the attributes of God. Why is God's immutability important?

As God gave the Ten Commandments to Moses, he told Moses a bit about himself. Exodus 34:6–7a says, "And he passed in front of Moses, proclaiming, 'The LORD, the LORD, the compassionate and gracious God, slow to anger, abounding in love and faithfulness, maintaining love to thousands, and forgiving wickedness, rebellion and sin.'"

If God were to change any of these aspects about himself, we wouldn't like the result. We need God to be compassionate, patient, loving, faithful, and forgiving. If he wasn't, we wouldn't last long because his holiness cannot abide our sin. Malachi 3:6 says, "I the LORD do not change. So you, the descendants of Jacob, are not destroyed."

Second, if God did change, he wouldn't be as worthy of worship. Because God is perfect in all ways, any change would be a change for the worse.

As worshipers of God and people who want to be like him, it is important that we don't change for the worse either. When we resemble God in being compassionate, patient, loving and the rest, it makes it easier for other people to see God through us. If that's not how we are, let's use our mutability and change for the better!

> **Which of God's personality traits you are thankful never changes?**
>
> **How can you change your life to look more like God?**

Lord, thank you for never changing.

Jesus the Immutable

> *Jesus Christ is the same yesterday
> and today and forever.*
>
> **HEBREWS 13:8**

We know God is immutable, or unchanging, but does this description fit Jesus? The author of Hebrews certainly believed so. The book of Hebrews is a letter of encouragement to a church facing persecution. It is a book filled with reasons to keep believing and working for God, even when our faith is challenged.

Hebrews 6:10-11 says, "God is not unjust; he will not forget your work and the love you have shown him as you have helped his people and continue to help them. We want each of you to show this same diligence to the very end, so that what you hope for may be fully realized."

Hebrews 11 is sometimes called the "Faith Hall of Fame" and gives examples of people throughout the Old Testament whose faith led them past hardship to do great things for God.

What does that have to do with Jesus's immutability? Hebrews describes Christ as the perfect high priest who has made everlasting peace between God and sinners. "Unlike the other high priests, he does not need to offer sacrifices day after day, first for his own sins, and then for the sins of the people. He sacrificed for their sins once for all when he offered himself" (Hebrews 7:27).

Our salvation is eternally secure because our sacrifice is unchangeable..

How does Jesus's unchanging nature make his sacrifice eternally perfect?

How can you show perseverance when faith is tough?

> *Jesus, you are unchanging and your
> sacrifice is always enough.*

Jesus the Lesser God?

> *"You heard me say, 'I am going away and I am coming back to you.' If you loved me, you would be glad that I am going to the Father, for the Father is greater than I."*
>
> **JOHN 14:28**

We've seen enough similarities of God's attributes in Jesus to raise another question: If Jesus was God, what kind of God was he? Was he equal to the Father, or some sort of junior God?

Jesus said in John 14:28, "The Father is greater than I." Some read this verse as proof Jesus must have been a lesser God, but what do the experts say?

"It's important to see this passage in its context," says Professor D. A. Carson. "The disciples are moaning because Jesus has said he's going away. Jesus says, 'If you love me, you'd be glad for my sake when I say I'm going away, because the Father is greater than I.' That is to say, Jesus is returning to the glory that is properly his, so if they really know who he is and really love him properly, they'll be glad that he's going back to the realm where he really is greater."

Jesus says in John 17:5, "And now, Father, glorify me in your presence with the glory I had with you before the world began." The comparison only makes sense if they are equal and Jesus has limited his earthly glory according to his incarnation, which is exactly what he did.

Does John 17:5 suggest Jesus was some sort of junior God?

Have you ever wished a visiting relative could stay longer, even if you know they'd be happier in their own home?

Jesus, keep me from treating you like some lesser version of God.

The Question of Hell and Sin

> *And if your right hand causes you to stumble, cut it off and throw it away. It is better for you to lose one part of your body than for your whole body to go into hell.*
>
> **MATTHEW 5:30**

The Bible says God the Father is loving. The New Testament affirms the same about Jesus. But can they really be loving while at the same time sending people to hell?

Critics of Christianity have always tried to use this logic to argue God cannot be truly good, but D. A. Carson paints a different image of what's going on here.

"Picture God in the beginning of creation with a man and woman made in his image. They love him truly. They delight to do what he wants; it's their whole pleasure. They're rightly related to him, and they're rightly related to each other."

Then sin came in and the man and woman start thinking they're the center of the universe.

"Hell is not a place where people go because they didn't believe the right stuff," says Carson. "It's filled with people who, for all eternity, still want to be at the center of the universe."

If God acts like he doesn't care about sin, it's the same as ignoring the people's pain. That's why he made a way to satisfy his justice by becoming the sacrifice needed to restore the right relationship.

Would God be worth serving if he didn't care about justice?

If forgiveness for sin is available, why do people accuse God of being unloving?

> *Lord, in your love, you made a way to restore our relationship. Thank you.*

Jesus and Slavery

There is neither Jew nor Gentile, neither slave nor free, nor is there male and female, for you are all one in Christ Jesus.

GALATIANS 3:28

There's one other issue we should look at. To be God, Jesus must have been ethically perfect. But some critics have said he fell short because he never spoke out about the practice of slavery.

In his book *Race and Culture*, African-American scholar Thomas Sowell points out how every major world culture until the modern period, without exception, has had slavery.

"You have to keep your eye on Jesus's mission," says D. A. Carson. "He didn't come to overturn the Roman economic system, which included slavery. He came to free men and women from their sins."

Jesus's message transforms people so they begin to love God with all their heart, soul, mind, and strength, and to love their neighbors as themselves. Naturally, that has an impact on slavery. Challenging laws won't change people. Only God can change a person—decisively, completely, permanently.

Jesus *did* attack slavery, just like he does every sin, by freeing us to choose a better path than the one offered by this world.

If you love your neighbor, would you seek to enslave them?

How is Jesus transforming you?

Lord, help me live free from sin which seeks to enslave me.

Matching the Sketch

"If you really know me, you will know my Father as well.
From now on, you do know him and have seen him."
Philip said, "Lord, show us the Father
and that will be enough for us."

JOHN 14:7–8

We set out to see if Jesus fit the profile for God by looking at his attributes. We bumped into the mystery of the incarnation and made our way past some tricky questions, but what did we find in the end?

- Omniscience? In John 16:30 the apostle John affirms of Jesus, "Now we can see that you know all things."
- Omnipresence? Jesus said in Matthew 28:20, "Surely I am with you always, to the very end of the age.
- Omnipotence? "All authority in heaven and on earth has been given to me," Jesus said in Matthew 28:18.
- Eternality? John 1:1 declares of Jesus, "In the beginning was the Word, and the Word was with God, and the Word was God."
- Immutability? Hebrews 13:8 says, "Jesus Christ is the same yesterday and today and forever."

Are you convinced by the profile evidence?

Which title for Jesus is your favorite? Why?

Also, the Old Testament calls God Alpha and Omega, Lord, Savior, King, Judge, Light, Rock, Redeemer, Creator, giver of life, and forgiver of sin. The New Testament applies them all to Jesus.

Does the sketch fit?

Lord, you are my God and Savior.
May others see you in me.

Through God's Eyes

> *But now he has reconciled you by Christ's physical body through death to present you holy in his sight, without blemish and free from accusation.*
>
> **COLOSSIANS 1:22**

Pimples, zits, spots, acne. Whatever we call them, blemishes aren't fun. Medical studies show more than 80 percent of young people get acne at some point. As we grow, we might not always be happy with how we look.

Ever wonder how God sees us? Even before we knew him, God loved us and wanted a relationship with us. But our selfish thoughts, lying tongues, and jealous eyes kept us from a one-on-one connection. Once Jesus became our Savior, however, God's view of us changed. Instead of our sins, he sees us under the perfect covering of Jesus's forgiveness.

As followers of Jesus, we're seen as blameless before a perfectly holy God! Colossians 1:22 says, "But now he has reconciled you by Christ's physical body through death to present you holy in his sight, without blemish and free from accusation."

Even if our faces are covered with zits, God sees us as blemish-free and forgiven.

Sadly, many Christians live timid lives filled with guilt from past mistakes. Until we embrace God's view of us, we'll never live the bold lives he has planned. We'll still make mistakes, but becoming more like Christ means learning from our mistakes and trying to act as God would want us to in every situation.

> **Do you like what you see when you look in the mirror?**
>
> **How can you better see yourself like God sees you?**

> *Lord, you don't see my blemishes. Help me see past them too.*

227

What's Our Job?

> *For we are God's handiwork, created in Christ Jesus to do good works, which God prepared in advance for us to do.*
>
> **EPHESIANS 2:10**

As blemish-free and forgiven people, we can look in the mirror and see ourselves as God sees us. But even with an accurate self-image, we may wonder what our purpose is. What are we supposed to do?

Ever since kindergarten, we've been asked what we want to be when we grow up. Back then, we may not have known more options than teacher, parent, or doctor. Since then, we've learned about all kinds of jobs. However, the more options we have, the harder it can be for us to choose.

Fortunately, it doesn't make a difference what we do for a paycheck if we are doing it for God. Colossians 3:23–24 says, "Whatever you do, work at it with all your heart, as working for the Lord, not for human masters, since you know that you will receive an inheritance from the Lord as a reward. It is the Lord Christ you are serving."

If we trust God with our future, he'll help us find whatever job is right for us. Proverbs 16:3 says, "Commit to the LORD whatever you do, and he will establish your plans."

But we don't have to wait until we are grown up to start working for God. According to Ephesians 2:10, he's already prepared things for us to do like obeying our parents and showing kindness to everyone.

What good work could you do today?

Why should you work hard?

Lord, help me work hard for you.

Medical Evidence

> *Pilate was surprised to hear that he was already dead. Summoning the centurion, he asked him if Jesus had already died.*
>
> **MARK 15:44**

In the case for Christ, we've looked at fingerprint evidence, eyewitness evidence, documentary evidence, corroborating evidence, scientific evidence, rebuttal evidence, identity evidence, psychological evidence, and profile evidence. That's a lot of evidence, but if Jesus didn't really die on the cross, it is all worthless.

In spite of all the historical details known about crucifixion, there's a popular idea about what happened to Jesus that's been around for more than a thousand years. It's called the "swoon theory." People suggest Jesus only fainted from exhaustion on the cross. Others say he had been given a drug that made him appear to die and he later revived in the cool, damp air of the tomb. Either way, if he didn't die, then the resurrection was a lie.

Skeptics of the Bible try to use the Bible itself to bolster this idea by pointing out that Pontius Pilate seemed surprised at how quickly Jesus died (Mark 15:44). Consequently, they say, when Jesus walked out of the tomb, it wasn't a miraculous resurrection.

But what does the historical evidence really establish? Is there any possible way Jesus could have survived the crucifixion?

Before looking at the evidence, what do you think about the swoon theory?

What would it mean if Jesus didn't really die on the cross?

Lord, help me see the evidence for what it shows.

Really Human

*Since the children have flesh and blood,
he too shared in their humanity so that
by his death he might break the power of
him who holds the power of death . . .*

HEBREWS 2:14

Before we can look at the medical evidence, we need to know if it was even possible for Jesus to die. Did Jesus have a human body?

It's kind of weird to think about God's Son having normal human bodily responses. But the Bible clearly says Jesus became flesh and dwelt among us (John 1:14). When he got tired, he slept. When he was hungry, his stomach rumbled. When Jesus walked through the countryside teaching about God's kingdom, he probably got sweaty. The fact is Jesus was 100 percent God *and* 100 percent human.

Because Jesus was fully human, he was capable of dying on the cross. He understands everything we go through as humans. He knows what it's like to grow up with siblings and have friends hurt us. But it's also important to remember how Jesus was a real person who lived during a real time in history.

As we put our faith in Jesus, we can be confident about who he really was and still is. He was a real man who lived in a real place during a real time in history. And he's really God's Son who really loves us a lot, right now.

What's the weirdest human thing you can imagine Jesus doing?

How do you feel knowing Jesus was human like you?

Lord, I'm glad you understand me, inside and out.

What Did Jesus Look Like?

> *He grew up before him like a tender shoot,*
> *and like a root out of dry ground. He had no*
> *beauty or majesty to attract us to him, nothing*
> *in his appearance that we should desire him.*
>
> **ISAIAH 53:2**

We live in an image-obsessed culture. About 80 percent of fifteen-to twenty-five-year-olds would like to alter something about their bodies. Many feel being beautiful would make them popular. But instead of a change in appearance, most people just need a change of attitude. The Bible tells us Jesus wasn't attractive, yet thousands of people were drawn to him.

Isaiah 53:2 says the Messiah would have "no beauty or majesty to attract us to him, nothing in his appearance that we should desire him." In other words, Jesus didn't attract followers with his good looks.

Jesus didn't stand out because of his appearance. He was most likely sort of short and common looking. But he was kind, honest, caring, and helpful. As we read about Jesus in the Gospels, we see someone with confidence, not because of the way he looked, but because of how he looked to the needs of others.

As we interact with people, it's important to present ourselves well by being clean and well groomed. But we must be careful not to get caught up in popular culture. Jesus didn't. He stood out in other ways to develop lasting friendships and build popularity. We can do the same.

Do you ever worry about your popularity or how you look?

How can you be confident for reasons which have nothing to do with your looks?

> *Jesus, I don't need to be physically attractive to draw*
> *people to you. Help me not stress about my appearance.*

231

Sweating Blood

*And being in anguish, he prayed more
earnestly, and his sweat was like drops
of blood falling to the ground.*

LUKE 22:44

Since Jesus had a human body, we know he was capable of being put to death, but did he actually die?

Meet Dr. Alexander Metherell. Not only is he a prominent physician, he's also studied the historical, archaeological, and medical data concerning the death of Jesus of Nazareth.

Dr. Metherell says Jesus's torture started after the Last Supper. "Jesus went with his disciples to the Mount of Olives—specifically, to the Garden of Gethsemane. And there, if you remember, he prayed all night. Now, during that process he was anticipating the coming events of the next day. Since he knew the amount of suffering he was going to have to endure, he was quite naturally experiencing a great deal of psychological stress."

The Gospels tell us, he began to sweat blood (Luke 22:44).

"This is a known medical condition called *hematidrosis*," Dr. Metherell said. "It's not very common, but it is associated with a high degree of psychological stress."

He says severe anxiety causes the release of chemicals which break down the capillaries in the sweat glands. As a result, there's a small amount of bleeding into these glands, and the sweat comes out tinged with blood.

How do you deal with stress?

Why would sensitive skin be the first part of Jesus's torture?

*Lord, may I live worthy of your
sacrifice on the cross.*

232

Flogged & Ridiculed

> *Then Pilate took Jesus and had him flogged.*
> *The soldiers twisted together a crown*
> *of thorns and put it on his head ...*
>
> **JOHN 19:1–3**

WARNING Graphic Depiction of Historical Torture

"Roman floggings were known to be terribly brutal," explains Dr. Alexander Metherell. "They usually consisted of thirty-nine lashes, but frequently there were a lot more than that, depending on the mood of the soldier applying the blows."

The soldier would use a braided leather whip with metal balls woven into the cords. When the whip would strike the flesh, these balls would cause deep bruises, which would break open with further blows.

"The back of the victim would be so shredded that part of the spine was sometimes exposed by the deep, deep cuts," Dr. Metherell said. "The whipping would have gone all the way from the shoulders down to the back of the legs. It was just terrible."

The victim would experience tremendous pain and lose a large amount of blood. On top of the flogging, Jesus endured the mocking of soldiers. The King of Kings was crowned with a crown of thorns, but it wasn't the last crown he'll wear.

Do your actions ever mock Jesus?

What's the most physical pain you've endured?

> *Lord, may I always respect you*
> *as the true king of my life.*

How the Body Responds to Blood Loss

> *Later, knowing that everything had now been finished, and so that Scripture would be fulfilled, Jesus said, "I am thirsty."*
>
> **JOHN 19:28**

Beginning with psychological stress enough to cause *hematidrosis*, Jesus endured brutal flogging and ridicule. By the end of the flogging, Jesus would have lost a lot of blood, but what would this do to his body?

"This would do four things," explains Dr. Alexander Metherell, physician and expert on the crucifixion. "First, Jesus's heart would race to try to pump blood that isn't there; second, his blood pressure would drop; third, his kidneys would stop producing urine to maintain what volume is left; and fourth, Jesus would become very thirsty as his body craved fluids to replace the lost blood volume."

Here's how these symptoms were described in the Gospels.

- Jesus staggered up the road to the execution site at Calvary. When Jesus collapsed, Simon was ordered to carry the cross (John 19:16–17 and Luke 23:26).
- As he hung on the cross, Jesus said, "I am thirsty" (John 19:28).

Dr. Metherell concluded, "there's no question that Jesus was already in serious-to-critical condition even before the nails were driven through his hands and feet."

How would you have felt if a Roman soldier ordered you to carry Jesus's cross?

How likely does the swoon theory sound right now?

> *Jesus, your blood was lost for me.*
> *Help me thirst for your truth.*

Nailed Hands & Feet

"They will look on me, the one they have pierced, and they will mourn for him as one mourns for an only child, and grieve bitterly for him as one grieves for a firstborn son."

ZECHARIAH 12:10

When Jesus finally got to Calvary, he was laid down on the horizontal beam. Then spikes were used to nail his hands in an outstretched position.

"The spikes were actually driven through the wrists," Dr. Metherell says, pointing about an inch or so below his left palm. "This was a solid position that would lock the hand. If the nails had been driven through the palms, the weight of the victim would have caused the skin to tear and he would fall off the cross."

Dr. Metherell wasn't done. He pointed out that the nail would crush the median nerve—the largest nerve going out to the hand. Imagine taking pliers and crushing this nerve.

"That effect would be similar to what Jesus experienced," says the doctor. "The pain was literally beyond words. They had to invent a new word—*excruciating*—to describe it. Literally, *excruciating* means 'out of the cross.'"

At this point, the crucifixion was nowhere near done. Jesus was hoisted into the air as the crossbar was attached to the vertical beam. Then nails were driven through Jesus's feet.

> Would you ever voluntarily go through excruciating pain for someone else?
>
> What would you say to Jesus as he hung on the cross?

Jesus, it hurts when I hit my funny bone. I can't imagine the pain you felt. Thank you.

235

Dislocated So We Could Be Healed

> *I am poured out like water, and all my*
> *bones are out of joint. My heart has turned*
> *to wax; it has melted within me.*
>
> **PSALM 22:14**

Beaten and bleeding, Jesus was stretched out on a cross to be crucified. As he hung on the cross, suspended by spikes nailed into his wrists and feet, what stresses were on Jesus's body?

"First of all, his arms would have immediately been stretched, probably about six inches in length," says Dr. Alexander Metherell. "Both shoulders would have become dislocated. You can determine this with simple mathematical equations. And this fulfilled the Old Testament prophecy in Psalm 22:14, 'My bones are out of joint,' which foretold the crucifixion hundreds of years before it happened."

Remember, crucifixion in general didn't exist in King David's day when this psalm was originally written. Still, God knew exactly what lay in store for Jesus, and Jesus was willing to endure this cruel punishment because he knew what came afterward.

First Peter 2:24 says, "'He himself bore our sins' in his body on the cross, so that we might die to sins and live for righteousness; 'by his wounds you have been healed.'"

Because Jesus was willing to suffer, we are able to live in a right relationship with God.

How can you die to sin today?

How can you live for righteousness?

> *Lord, give me your strength as I make*
> *decisions to either sin or live for you today.*

Breath of God

But it is the spirit in a person, the breath of the Almighty, that gives them understanding.

JOB 32:8

Hanging on the cross, Jesus looked down and knew death was only a matter of time. The pain didn't kill. Crucifixion essentially killed people by *asphyxiation*. That means it became difficult to breathe, resulting in a lack of oxygen and, ultimately, suffocation.

"The reason was that the stresses on the muscles and diaphragm put the chest of the victim into the inhaled position," says Dr. Alexander Metherell. "Basically, in order to exhale, the individual had to push up on his feet so the tension on the muscles would be eased for a moment. In doing this, though, the nail would tear through the foot."

After managing to exhale, the person would then be able to relax down and take another breath in. But to exhale, he'd have to push himself up again, scraping his bloodied back against the coarse wood of the cross.

Breath is a very spiritual concept in the Bible. After God formed Adam out of dust, he breathed life into him (Genesis 2:7). Job recognized the link between a man's spirit and God's breath as well (Job 32:8). So for Jesus to suffocate, the pain was not only physical, but profoundly spiritual as well.

With each breath today, let's thank God for his Spirit inside us.

> Why do you think 2 Timothy 3:16 says, "All Scripture is God-breathed"?
>
> How well can you do something when you are short of breath?

> *God, without your breath in my lungs, I can't do anything.*

237

Heart of God

Jesus called out with a loud voice, "Father, into your hands I commit my spirit." When he had said this, he breathed his last.

LUKE 23:46

Hanging upright on the cross, his wrists and feet nailed to the cross, Jesus pushed himself up in order to breathe. But how long would he last?

As Jesus's breathing slowed down, Dr. Alexander Metherell details how he would go into what is called *respiratory acidosis*. Carbon dioxide in the blood would be dissolved, causing the acidity of the blood to increase. This would eventually lead to an irregular heartbeat.

"With his heart beating erratically, Jesus would have known that he was at the moment of death," Dr. Metherell explains, "which is when he was able to say, 'Lord, into your hands I commit my spirit' (Luke 23:46). And then he died of cardiac arrest."

So Jesus died of cardiac arrest?

"Yes," Dr. Metherell says. "But this is important too. Before Jesus died, his sustained rapid heart rate would have resulted in the collection of fluid in the membrane around his heart and lungs."

While his physical heart may have beat erratically and stopped, Jesus's heart continues to beat in us when we accept him as our Savior. Psalm 73:26 says, "My flesh and my heart may fail, but God is the strength of my heart and my portion forever."

Does Jesus have your heart?

What is one way you can show Jesus's love to others today?

Jesus, may your heart for others beat in my chest.

Blood & Water

> *But when they came to Jesus and found that he was already dead, they did not break his legs. Instead, one of the soldiers pierced Jesus' side with a spear, bringing a sudden flow of blood and water.*
>
> **JOHN 19:33–34**

To speed a victim's death on the cross, it was customary to break his legs so he could no longer push himself up to breathe. When Pontius Pilate ordered that the two thieves and Jesus have their legs broken, the soldiers found Jesus already dead. So instead, one of the soldiers took a spear and thrust it into Jesus's side to confirm he was no longer alive.

"The spear was probably stabbed into his right side, between the ribs," says Dr. Metherell. "It apparently went through the right lung and into the heart, so when the spear was pulled out, the fluid around Jesus's heart and lungs came out. This would have the appearance of a clear fluid, like water, followed by a large volume of blood."

Hold up. Water *then* blood? According to John, an eyewitness, it was "blood and water." He put the words in that order in John 19:34.

"I'm not a Greek scholar," says the doctor, "but according to people who are, the order of words in ancient Greek was determined not necessarily by what happened first but by what was most important. This means since there was a lot more blood than water, it would have made sense for John to mention the blood first."

> **According to Ephesians 2:13, why is Jesus's blood important?**
>
> **How can you show others the forgiveness you've been given?**

> *Lord, I can be close to God because of your blood. Help me never put distance between us.*

239

Taking the Prisoner's Place

Greater love has no one than this: to lay down one's life for one's friends.

JOHN 15:13

People who say Jesus didn't die on the cross say the Romans lacked a full understanding of medicine and anatomy. How do we know the Roman soldiers weren't mistaken when they declared Jesus was no longer living?

Dr. Alexander Metherell admits the soldiers didn't go to medical school. "But remember," he says, "they were experts in killing people—that was their job, and they did it very well. They knew without a doubt when a person was dead, and really it's not so terribly difficult to figure out.

"Besides," he continues, "if a prisoner somehow escaped, the responsible soldiers would be put to death themselves, so they had a huge incentive to make absolutely sure that each and every victim was dead when he was removed from the cross."

Dying in someone's place may not have been high on a soldier's list, but it was Jesus's whole mission. It was foretold in Isaiah 53:5: "But he was pierced for our transgressions, he was crushed for our iniquities; the punishment that brought us peace was on him, and by his wounds we are healed."

John 15:13 says, "Greater love has no one than this: to lay down one's life for one's friends." Maybe we won't literally sacrifice our life to save someone else, but we can give up our desires so someone else can have theirs. That's what love is.

How has someone loved you sacrificially before?

How can you love someone else sacrificially today?

Lord, thank you for laying down your life and counting me as your friend.

Death to the Swoon Theory

With a loud cry, Jesus breathed his last.

MARK 15:37

Looking through Dr. Metherell's evidence, it is unimaginable that the Roman soldiers made a mistake about Jesus's condition:

- Jesus was already in shock from the massive blood loss even before the crucifixion started.
- The medical conclusion based on evidence in the Gospels is that Jesus died from cardiac arrest.
- You can't fake the inability to breathe for long.
- The spear thrust into his heart and lung would have settled the issue once and for all.

It would have taken a miracle for Jesus to survive the crucifixion. But if, somehow, he had, he wouldn't have been able to walk or use his arms. And he would have had to heal pretty quickly from the massive wounds on his back from the flogging and the spear wound to his chest.

"Listen," says Dr. Metherell, "a person in that kind of pathetic condition would never have inspired his disciples to go out and proclaim that he's the Lord of life who had triumphed over the grave."

The medical evidence is conclusive. Jesus really died. The swoon theory just doesn't make sense.

After looking at the medical evidence, how convinced are you Jesus died?

Which is easier to believe: Jesus survived the crucifixion or how he rose from the dead?

Jesus, I believe you really died for my sins.

241

But Why?

> *Who gave himself for us to redeem us from all wickedness and to purify for himself a people that are his very own, eager to do what is good.*
>
> **TITUS 2:14**

The medical evidence confirms Jesus died on the cross. The identity evidence confirms Jesus to be God. The historical evidence confirms it all really happened. But why? Why would Jesus have endured the cross if he was powerful enough not to?

- To fulfill the Scriptures (1 Corinthians 15:3)
- To bring us to God (1 Peter 3:18)
- To save us from the wrath of God (Romans 5:9)
- To be a ransom for many (Matthew 20:28)
- To forgive our sins (Ephesians 1:7)
- To sanctify us (Hebrews 13:12)
- To redeem us from lawlessness and to purify us, so we're eager to do good works (Titus 2:14)
- So we might walk in the light and have fellowship with one another (1 John 1:7)
- To give us eternal life (John 3:16)
- Because God loves us (Romans 5:8)

Can you think of any more reasons why Jesus died for you?

How does Jesus's love make you eager to do good works?

Jesus had the power to do what he wanted, but what he wanted most was to make us right with God. He took our punishment so we could live free from sin's curse, eager to do good works, and to love him like he loves us.

Lord, help me walk in the light of your truth today.

Making Sense of Our Suffering

*And the God of all grace, who called you to
his eternal glory in Christ, after you have
suffered a little while, will himself restore you
and make you strong, firm and steadfast.*

1 PETER 5:10

Jesus suffered for us on the cross, but suffering is something we all go through (John 16:33).

The apostle Paul knew a lot about suffering. He was imprisoned, shipwrecked, rejected, beaten, stoned, and left for dead. But each time he got back up and returned to preaching the gospel. In Romans 5:3–4 Paul wrote, "We also glory in our sufferings, because we know that suffering produces perseverance; perseverance, character; and character, hope."

Honestly, we usually don't rejoice about suffering; we complain about it. Nobody likes to suffer, but in the midst of our troubles, we can find peace in knowing our suffering is building something good inside us.

Hard times teach us not to give up. Our persevering attitude builds our character, because we know no matter what happens in our lives, we can overcome it with the Lord's help. And it all leads to hope.

God always loves us, even when we suffer. We can show him love in return by persevering and allowing him to make us "strong, firm and steadfast" (1 Peter 5:10).

> **Can you remember a time in your life when you learned something through suffering?**
>
> **What is one way you can rejoice in your suffering?**

*Lord, when I suffer, help it lead
to hope and not despair.*

Heart of the Matter

*Then Christ will live in your hearts
because you believe in him. And I pray
that your love will have deep roots. I pray
that it will have a strong foundation.*

EPHESIANS 3:17 (NIRV)

Our heart is about the same size as our fist. Protected by our ribs, this amazing organ beats around 100,000 times a day and pumps more than 2,000 gallons of blood every twenty-four hours. Nearly 60,000 miles of blood vessels weave throughout our body, delivering blood packed with life-giving oxygen and nutrients to all our organs and tissues.

God's design of the circulatory system is amazingly complex and powerful. But without a heart, it doesn't work. Likewise, if we remove Jesus from Christianity, our faith is dead. Craig A. Evans, founder of the Dead Sea Scrolls Institute, says the heart of Christianity can be summed up in two words: Jesus Christ.

"So the core message of Christianity . . . is that Jesus is the Messiah," says Evans. "He's God's Son, he fulfills the scriptures, he died on the cross . . . saved humanity, he rose from the dead."

When we put Jesus and our heart together, we get eternal life. Ephesians 3:17 says, "Then Christ will live in your hearts because you believe in him. And I pray that your love will have deep roots. I pray that it will have a strong foundation."

Have you trusted Jesus to live in your heart?

Who is one person you can talk to about your faith in Christ?

*Lord, when I feel my heart beating,
help me remember to trust in you.*

Evidence of the Missing Body

Before long, the world will not see me anymore, but you will see me. Because I live, you also will live.

JOHN 14:19

When the police investigate a murder, the victim's body can give vital clues to the investigation. But what happens when a body disappears?

On February 17, 1977, candy heiress and multimillionaire Helen Vorhees Brach disappeared without a trace. For decades the mystery of what happened to the red-haired, animal-loving philanthropist has baffled police and journalists alike.

While investigators are convinced she was murdered, they haven't been able to determine the specific circumstances, largely because they've never found her body. To this day, no one has been convicted of her murder.

In the case for Christ, investigators also have to deal with a missing body. Christians believe Jesus died on the cross, was buried in a guarded tomb, and rose from the dead. Skeptics claim what happened to Jesus's body is a mystery akin to Helen Brach's disappearance— there's not enough evidence, they say, to reach a firm conclusion.

Unlike Helen Brach—who simply disappeared—we *do* have evidence Jesus died on the cross. There was no way he could have survived. But what can we know about what happened afterward? In the next devotions, we'll see what the evidence of Jesus's missing body will reveal.

What are some differences between the case of Helen Brach and the case for Christ?

Before we dig into the facts, what do you believe happened to Jesus's body?

Lord, help me follow the facts. I believe they will lead me to you.

245

Why Jesus's Missing Body Matters

By his power God raised the Lord from the dead, and he will raise us also.

1 CORINTHIANS 6:14

Let's put ourselves in the shoes of Jesus's followers after his crucifixion. We've seen the torture. We watched him die. His body has been placed in a tomb. We know the prophecies saying how Christ will come back to life. We remember Jesus himself saying he'd rise again.

In the early light of the first day of the week, we hear some of the women wake up, gather a few friends, and walk to the garden tomb. Before we even eat our breakfast, the women return and proclaim that something's not right. The stone is rolled away from the tomb's entrance.

The body of Jesus is gone!

The empty tomb is an enduring symbol of the resurrection. It's the ultimate representation that Jesus's claim of being God is true.

The apostle Paul wrote in 1 Corinthians 15:17 how the resurrection is the foundation of the Christian faith: "If Christ has not been raised, your faith is futile; you are still in your sins." In other words, if Jesus didn't conquer death and rise again, then everything about Christianity is meaningless.

The resurrection is the proof of his triumph over sin and death. It's the foreshadowing of the resurrection of his followers (1 Corinthians 6:14). It's the basis of Christian hope. It's the miracle of all miracles.

Why would we still be in our sins if Jesus didn't rise from the dead?

If Jesus said he would rise again, but didn't, would you believe the other things he said?

Jesus, you triumphed over sin and death. Help me triumph too.

246

Buried in Joseph's Tomb

Joseph took the body, wrapped it in a clean linen cloth, and placed it in his own new tomb that he had cut out of the rock. He rolled a big stone in front of the entrance to the tomb and went away.

MATTHEW 27:59–60

Was there any real evidence to support Matthew 27:57–60?

As evening approached, there came a rich man from Arimathea, named Joseph, who had himself become a disciple of Jesus. Going to Pilate, he asked for Jesus' body, and Pilate ordered that it be given to him. Joseph took the body, wrapped it in a clean linen cloth, and placed it in his own new tomb that he had cut out of the rock. He rolled a big stone in front of the entrance to the tomb and went away.

"For one thing," says William Lane Craig, "the burial is mentioned by Paul in 1 Corinthians 15:3–7, where the apostle passes on a very early creed of the church." Like other experts, Bill (as Craig is called by his friends) agreed this creed could be dated back to within a few years of Jesus's crucifixion. Paul had heard and memorized the creed after his conversion in Damascus or during his subsequent visit to Jerusalem when he met with the apostles James and Peter.

> **Read 1 Corinthians 15:3–7. What does it say about Jesus's resurrection?**
>
> **Why is the creed's mention of the burial significant?**

Bill says, "Essentially, the first line refers to the crucifixion, the second to the burial, the third to the resurrection, and the fourth to Jesus' appearances."

Jesus, you only borrowed Joseph's tomb.

247

Who was Joseph of Arimathea?

Now there was a man named Joseph, a member of the Council, a good and upright man, who had not consented to their decision and action.

LUKE 23:50–51

Since the Sanhedrin, a powerful group of Jewish religious leaders, voted to condemn Jesus, some skeptics argue it's extremely unlikely one of them volunteered to give Jesus an honorable burial.

"Luke may have felt this same discomfort," says Bill Craig, resurrection expert, "which would explain why he added one important detail—Joseph of Arimathea wasn't present when the official vote was taken. But the significant point about Joseph of Arimathea is that he would not be the sort of person who would have been invented by Christian legend or Christian authors."

For one thing, early Christians were still angry at the Jewish leaders who voted for Jesus's execution. It would be unlikely for them to invent one who did the right thing! Besides, when the gospels were written, it would have been easy for people in the region to fact check whether Joseph really existed, so he's undoubtedly a historical figure. And since no competing historical burial stories about Jesus exist, what's in the Bible can be considered trustworthy.

> **How can you use your resources to honor Jesus?**
>
> **Are you ever afraid to stand up for Jesus when your friends may look down on you?**

Lord, give me the bravery of Joseph of Arimathea.

Was Jesus's Resurrection Just a Spiritual Thing?

And if the Spirit of him who raised Jesus from the dead is living in you, he who raised Christ from the dead will also give life to your mortal bodies because of his Spirit who lives in you.

ROMANS 8:11

Jesus's death, burial, and resurrection form the basis for the early church creed found in 1 Corinthians 15:3–7. But the early church creed doesn't specifically say the tomb was empty. What if, even after the resurrection, Jesus's body remained entombed? Was the resurrection just a spiritual thing?

"The creed definitely implies the empty tomb," says Bill Craig, expert on Jesus's resurrection. "You see, the Jews had a physical concept of resurrection. For them, the primary object of the resurrection was the bones of the deceased. After the flesh rotted away, the Jews would gather the bones of their deceased and put them in boxes to be preserved until the resurrection at the end of the world."

Given the Jews understanding of the term "resurrection," it would have been a contradiction for an early Jew to say someone was raised from the dead if their body was still in the tomb.

The new life we have in Christ today is both a spiritual thing *and* a physical thing. One day, God will give us new bodies and we'll live with him in eternity. Until then, we have the Holy Spirit living inside us to help us do God's will.

What is the Spirit living in you asking you to do today?

What do you think our new bodies will be like after this life is over?

Lord, thank you for giving me your Spirit.

Tomb Security: The Stone

And they asked each other, "Who will roll the stone away from the entrance of the tomb?" But when they looked up, they saw that the stone, which was very large, had been rolled away.

MARK 16:3–4

Having heard convincing evidence to say Jesus was in the tomb, it's important to know how secure his grave was from outside influences.

Expert Bill Craig describes the tomb from what archaeologists have found in excavations of first-century sites:

"There was a slanted groove that led down to a low entrance, and a large disk-shaped stone was rolled down this groove and lodged into place across the door," says Bill. "A smaller stone was then used to secure the disk. Although it would be easy to roll this big disk down the groove, it would take several men to roll the stone back up in order to reopen the tomb. In that sense it was quite secure."

The tomb of Joseph of Arimathea was built to be inaccessible. It would have been impossible to open from the inside and it would have required a group of strong people to open it from the outside. So did the disciples steal Jesus's body?

"The idea that the empty tomb is the result of some hoax, conspiracy, or theft is simply dismissed today," says Bill.

And there's another complication to the empty tomb: The guards.

> **What is the heaviest thing you've ever lifted?**
>
> **Why would a secure tomb be important to people?**

Lord, the tomb could not hold you, not even with a heavy stone. Nothing can stop you from keeping your word. Thank you for promising to love me.

Dig Deeper—The Wrong Tomb

As proof for the resurrection, Christians claim Jesus's body went missing from the tomb of Joseph of Arimathea, but is there another explanation? Let's look at John 20:11–15:

> "Now Mary stood outside the tomb crying. As she wept, she bent over to look into the tomb and saw two angels in white, seated where Jesus' body had been, one at the head and the other at the foot.
>
> "They asked her, 'Woman, why are you crying?'
>
> "'They have taken my Lord away,' she said, 'and I don't know where they have put him.' At this, she turned around and saw Jesus standing there, but she did not realize that it was Jesus.
>
> "He asked her, 'Woman, why are you crying? Who is it you are looking for?'
>
> "Thinking he was the gardener, she said, 'Sir, if you have carried him away, tell me where you have put him, and I will get him.'"

In 1907, Kirsopp Lake suggested Mary and the other women merely went to the wrong tomb. He said they got lost and a caretaker at an unoccupied tomb told them, "You're looking for Jesus of Nazareth. He is not here," and they ran away, afraid.

Professor Bill Craig answers, "Lake didn't generate any following with this. The site of Jesus's tomb was known to the Jewish authorities. Even if the women had made this mistake, the authorities would have happily pointed out the tomb and corrected the disciples' error when they began to proclaim Jesus had risen from the dead. I don't know anybody who holds Lake's theory today."

Unlikely though it seems, there is more support for the missing body due to the resurrection than a simple error of visiting the wrong tomb. But God loves to use what is unlikely to prove his power, doesn't he?

Tomb Security: The Guards

> *"You are to say, 'His disciples came during the night and stole him away while we were asleep.'"*
>
> **MATTHEW 28:13**

The gospel of Matthew reports that guards were placed around Jesus's tomb, but he was the only gospel writer to say so. Is there any evidence the guard story is historical?

"Yes, there is," says Bill Craig. "Think about the claims and counterclaims about the resurrection that went back and forth between the Jews and Christians in the first century."

If there had not been any guards, the Jews wouldn't have said the guards fell asleep. They would have said, "What guards? You're crazy! There were no guards!"

"This suggests the guards really were historical and that the Jews knew it," says Bill, "which is why they had to invent the absurd story about the guards having been asleep while the disciples took the body."

Between the heavy stone and the guarded tomb, it would have taken a miracle for Jesus's body to disappear. In fact, it was the miracle of miracles, because that is exactly what happened. Jesus rose in power from the grave, resurrected in his heavenly body.

How does it feel when you are caught in a lie?

What's the best way to avoid getting caught in a lie? (*Hint: Don't lie.*)

Lord, help me be truthful about the amazing things you do in my life.

252

Who Was Guarding the Tomb? And Why?

"Take some guards with you," Pilate answered. "Go. Make the tomb as secure as you can." So they went and made the tomb secure. They put a royal seal on the stone and placed some guards on duty.

MATTHEW 27:65–66

The fact guards were present at Jesus's tomb is indisputable, but why were they there?

If the Jewish authorities were anticipating a resurrection or the disciples faking one, it would mean they had a better understanding of Jesus's predictions than the disciples did! After all, the disciples were surprised by the whole thing. And doesn't it seem unlikely for Roman guards to report to the Jewish authorities?

"If you look carefully," says Bill Craig, "Matthew doesn't say the guards are Romans. When the Jews go to Pilate and ask for a guard, Pilate says, 'You have a guard.' Now, does he mean, 'All right, here's a detachment of Roman soldiers'? Or does he mean, 'You've got your own temple guards; use them'?

Whether the guards were temple guards or Roman soldiers doesn't change the story. John tells us it was a Roman centurion who led Roman soldiers to arrest Jesus under the direction of Jewish leadership. So there is a precedent for either situation.

The point is the tomb was guarded, but Jesus rose anyway.

> **What sins should you let die today?**
>
> **How could you guard yourself against those sins?**

Jesus, help me overcome death and sin with your power.

253

Contradictions at the Tomb

> *There was a violent earthquake, for an angel of the Lord came down from heaven and, going to the tomb, rolled back the stone and sat on it.*
>
> **MATTHEW 28:2–3**

Critics of Christianity have pointed out some differences between the Gospel accounts of the empty tomb. Dr. Michael Martin of Boston University wrote this summary:

- In Matthew, the women arrived toward dawn, there is a rock in front of it. There is a violent earthquake, and an angel descends and rolls back the stone. In Mark, the women arrive at the tomb at sunrise and the stone had been rolled back. In Luke, when the women arrive at early dawn, they find the stone already rolled back.
- In Matthew, an angel is sitting on the rock, and in Mark a youth is inside. In Luke, two men are inside.
- In Matthew, Mary Magdalene and the other Mary are there. In Mark, the two Marys and Salome. In Luke, Mary Magdalene, Mary the mother of James, Joanna, and "the other women" are present.

Do contradictory details tempt you to doubt the Bible?

Instead of giving up on it, how could you work through your doubts?

Martin's arguments sounded convincing. In light of all this, can we still consider the empty tomb story to be credible? Yes; and we'll see why.

Lord, when skeptics make credible arguments, give me the wisdom to see the truth clearly.

254

The Historical Core of the Tomb Story

"He is not here; he has risen!"

LUKE 24:6

We've heard a skeptic's argument about contradictions between the gospel accounts of Jesus's resurrection. With so many differences, can we still trust that Jesus rose?

"Look at the core of the story," says Bill Craig, resurrection scholar. "It's the same: Joseph of Arimathea takes the body of Jesus and puts it in a tomb, the tomb is visited by a small group of women followers of Jesus early on the Sunday morning following his crucifixion, and they find that the tomb is empty. Even if there are some differences concerning the names of the women, the exact time of the morning, the number of the angels, and so forth, those discrepancies wouldn't bother a historian."

Historians research to find the facts. The fact of there being differences between the empty tomb narratives suggest there were multiple, independent writers who each had their own perspective—which is exactly what the Bible claims.

Remember what we learned about different perspectives in eyewitness testimony? It would be more disturbing if the gospel authors had identical details, as though they had worked out what to say together instead of telling the truth as they remembered it.

Have you ever remembered an event different from someone else you know?

How would you describe the core of the resurrection story to someone else?

Lord, help me trust the truth of your resurrection.

The Contradiction of the Ladies' Names

On the first day of the week, very early in the morning, the women took the spices they had prepared and went to the tomb.

LUKE 24:1

Even if the core of the resurrection story is the same between all the gospel accounts, are the differences between them insurmountable? Let's take a closer look at the contradiction of the women who visited Jesus's tomb.

Dr. Michael says: "In Matthew, the women present at the tomb are Mary Magdalene and the other Mary. In Mark, the women present at the tomb are the two Marys and Salome. In Luke, Mary Magdalene, Mary the mother of James, Joanna, and the other women are present at the tomb."

How does expert Bill Craig reconcile these differences?

"None of the gospels pretend to give a complete list," says Bill. "They all include Mary Magdalene and other women, so there was probably a gaggle of these early disciples that included those who were named and probably a couple of others. I think it would be pedantic to say that's a contradiction."

Instead of pointlessly arguing over the exact list of names who visited the tomb, it would be better to look at what they found when they got there. Again, beyond the minor differences, they all found the tomb empty. Jesus had risen!

What did the women do in every version of the story?

Who can you tell about the risen Jesus?

Lord, like the women who visited your tomb, make me excited to tell others about you.

The Contradiction of Jesus's Jonah Prophecy

For as Jonah was three days and three nights in the belly of a huge fish, so the Son of Man will be three days and three nights in the heart of the earth.

MATTHEW 12:40

Jesus was crucified on Friday and rose again on Sunday morning. That's one full day, two full nights, and part of two days. But when the Pharisees pressed Jesus about his identity and asked him for a sign, Jesus specifically mentioned the sign of the prophet Jonah.

Matthew 12:39–40 says, "He answered, 'A wicked and adulterous generation asks for a sign! But none will be given it except the sign of the prophet Jonah. For as Jonah was three days and three nights in the belly of a huge fish, so the Son of Man will be three days and three nights in the heart of the earth.'"

Did Jesus get his own prophecy wrong?

"Some well-meaning Christians have used Matthew 12:40 to suggest Jesus was crucified on Wednesday rather than on Friday, in order to get the full time in there!" says Bill Craig. "But most scholars recognize that according to early Jewish time-reckoning, any part of a day counted as a full day."

This is another example of how discrepancies can be explained or minimized with some background knowledge or by just thinking them through with an open mind.

> Is your mind open to the world's arguments but closed to God's truth?
>
> How is Jonah's message to Nineveh like Jesus's message to the world?

Lord, give me an open mind when it comes to your word.

257

Can the Witnesses be Trusted?

So the women hurried away from the tomb, afraid yet filled with joy, and ran to tell his disciples.

MATTHEW 28:8

Let's go back to Sunday morning. The gospels agree on the empty tomb being discovered by women who were friends and followers of Jesus. Does their admiration of Jesus make their testimony untrustworthy?

"Actually," says Bill Craig, "this argument backfires on people who use it. Certainly these women were friends of Jesus. But when you understand the role of women in first-century Jewish society, what's really extraordinary is that this empty tomb story should feature women as the discoverers of the empty tomb in the first place."

In first-century Palestine, women were on a very low rung of the social ladder. Women's testimony was regarded as worthless. They usually weren't even allowed to serve as legal witnesses in a Jewish court of law!

"In light of this," says Bill, "it's absolutely remarkable that the chief witnesses to the empty tomb are these women who were friends of Jesus. Any later legendary account would have certainly portrayed male disciples as discovering the tomb—Peter or John, for example. The fact that women are the first witnesses to the empty tomb is most plausibly explained by the reality that—like it or not—they *were* the discoverers of the empty tomb! This shows that the gospel writers faithfully recorded what happened, even if it was embarrassing."

Did social status matter to Jesus when calling disciples or choosing friends?

Should social status matter to you?

Lord, you embraced all people regardless of social status. Help me do the same.

258

Why Didn't Christians Cite the Empty Tomb?

But God raised him from the dead, freeing him from the agony of death, because it was impossible for death to keep its hold on him.

ACTS 2:24

More than one skeptic has claimed that none of the apostles, including Peter, bothered to point to the empty tomb in their preaching.

Resurrection scholar Bill Craig strongly disagrees with this claim.

"The empty tomb *is* found in Peter's speech," he insists. "He proclaims in verse 24 that 'God raised him from the dead, freeing him from the agony of death.'

"Then he quotes from a psalm about how God would not allow his Holy One to undergo decay. This had been written by David, and Peter says, 'I can tell you confidently that the patriarch David died and was buried, and his tomb is here to this day.' But, he says, Christ 'was not abandoned to the realm of the dead, nor did his body see decay. God has raised this Jesus to life, and we are all witnesses of it.'"

It is unreasonable to criticize the early Christian speakers because they didn't use the words "empty tomb." They were more concerned with advising people how to live in the love which emptied the tomb in the first place.

How do you feel when someone tells you something you already know?

How can you show someone else Jesus's love?

Jesus, give me the chance to express your love this week.

Three More Arguments for the Empty Tomb

But Christ has indeed been raised from the dead,
the firstfruits of those who have fallen asleep.

1 CORINTHIANS 15:20

Peter's speech in Acts 2 isn't the only argument for the apostles' belief in Jesus's empty tomb. Bill Craig gives three additional reasons to believe:

"First," he says, "the empty tomb is definitely implicit in the early tradition that is passed along by Paul in 1 Corinthians 15, which is a very old and reliable source of historical information about Jesus.

"Second, the site of Jesus's tomb was known to Christians and Jews alike. So if it were not empty, it would be impossible for a movement founded on belief in the resurrection to have come into existence in the same city where this man had been publicly executed and buried.

"Third, Jewish writings after the death of Jesus don't deny the historicity of the empty tomb. In other words, there was nobody claiming that the tomb still contained Jesus's body. The question always was, 'What happened to the body?'

"Based on the evidence, it's the best explanation for what happened," Bill says. "God raising Jesus from the dead doesn't contradict science or any known facts of experience. As long as the existence of God is possible, and I think there are good independent reasons for believing that he does exist, it's possible that he acted in history by raising Jesus from the dead."

Would you be tempted to tell a lie if the answer could be easily checked?

What is your favorite reason for believing Jesus's tomb is empty?

Lord, help me defend your empty tomb to people who question it.

260

If God Exists . . .

All your words are true; all your
righteous laws are eternal.

PSALM 119:160

In his argument for the proof of the empty tomb, Bill Craig says as long as God is possible, the resurrection is possible. Before we move on to further evidence for the resurrection, let's pause and consider some of the arguments for God's existence.

It would be convenient to look at Psalm 119:160 and conclude the Bible to be a trustworthy source in itself for God's existence. If God's words are true and he wrote them in the Bible, we should be able to believe them. But this argument is easily dismissed on the basis of circular reasoning. Critics don't like the argument that God wrote the Bible and the Bible says God exists.

Are there other reasons Christians can point to as evidence for God's existence? After all, if God is a hoax, then making the case for Christ is pointless. All we'd be able to do is prove a man named Jesus existed, did some unexplainable things, and died on a cross. Without God's existence and Jesus's identity as God, our faith would be pointless.

Fortunately, we'll see—for a number of reasons—God really exists, Jesus is really his Son, and we can be filled with his Holy Spirit when we recognize the true nature of the universe in light of God's love.

> **What reasons do you already have to believe God exists?**
>
> **How would you answer someone who says God is a hoax?**

God, show me the truth, both in the Bible
and in the world that you exist.

261

Pascal's Wager

*I delight in your decrees; I will
not neglect your word.*

PSALM 119:16

Blaise Pascal was a brilliant inventor, mathematician, scientist, philosopher, and theologian who made important contributions in every area of his studies. In his teenage years, he invented a mechanical calculator able to do time-consuming calculations. He later conducted experiments with barrels of water to come up with a principle for fluid mechanics known as Pascal's Law.

On November 23, 1654, Pascal had a religious vision, revitalizing his previously dead faith in the Christian God. He began writing theological texts. He carried a card with Psalm 119:16 around with him and made his most famous contribution to theology: Pascal's Wager.

Pascal believed even if we didn't have any evidence for God's existence, it would still be better to live as though he did than to live as though he didn't. If God does not exist but we believe in him, we may miss out on a few worldly pleasures but our death will be final and we will cease to exist. If God exists but we don't believe in him, we'll spend eternity separated from him in Hell. If God exists and we believe in him, we'll have eternal rewards in heaven.

Pascal believed, based on logic alone, it would be better to believe in God.

How would you explain Pascal's Wager to someone?

Why do the benefits of belief in God outweigh the risks of disbelief?

*Lord, don't let me neglect your word.
Help me know you better.*

Thomas Aquinas' Unmoved Mover

"You are worthy, our Lord and God, to receive glory and honor and power, for you created all things, and by your will they were created and have their being."

REVELATION 4:11

In the 13th century, priest and philosopher Thomas Aquinas wrote *Summa Theologica* in which he gave five ways to understand the existence of God. Aquinas' ways are a great place to begin our search for God.

The first way Thomas Aquinas uses to understand God is the Unmoved Mover argument. It's based on the principle of motion. Let's imagine a rock. The rock doesn't move on its own. It takes something else to move the rock. If the rock moves because it was hit by a stick, then something must have moved the stick which moved the rock.

This principle fits with Isaac Newton's first law of motion, which states objects at rest stay at rest and objects in motion stay in motion unless acted upon by an unbalanced force.

When we look at the universe, we see things in motion everywhere. The world spins on its axis as it revolves around the sun, which is traveling through space as well. All this motion, Aquinas says, had to have its start somewhere

God set the universe into motion with a word at the very beginning. He is the force outside of our existence which caused everything to move.

> How would you explain Aquinas' Unmoved Mover argument to someone?
>
> How does Newton's first law of motion support Aquinas' argument?

Lord, you move the universe according to your pleasure, but nothing can move you where you don't want to go.

263

Thomas Aquinas' First Cause

I make known the end from the beginning, from ancient times, what is still to come. I say, 'My purpose will stand, and I will do all that I please.'

ISAIAH 46:10

Thomas Aquinas' second argument for God's existence is similar to the first. Just like all motion must have started with an initial push, every effect must be preceded by a cause.

The principle of cause and effect—also called *causality*—is taught in elementary school. Every effect has a cause. If we stub our toe on the coffee table, the effect is pain in our toe. The cause might be because someone moved the furniture around. For the coffee table to exist in the first place, someone must have built it. For someone to build a coffee table, someone must have cut down a tree and milled the wood. For the tree to be there, it must have been planted at some point. And so on.

The relationship of cause and effect goes back through time to the very beginning of everything, when something must have been the first cause which led to every following effect. Thomas Aquinas says the first cause is God.

Not only was God the original cause of everything, he is still the cause of everything. Nothing happens outside of his purposes. Isaiah 46:10 says, "I make known the end from the beginning, from ancient times, what is still to come. I say, 'My purpose will stand, and I will do all that I please.'"

What effects do you cause in the people around you?

How well do your purposes line up with God's?

Lord, nothing can stop your causes from coming to the affects you desire.

Thomas Aquinas' Necessary Being

Lord, you have been our dwelling place throughout all generations.

PSALM 90:1

The third of Thomas Aquinas' ways to understand God's existence is an argument of possibilities.

He says there are two types of beings in the universe: possible beings and necessary beings. If our parents had never met, we would never have been born, so it was possible for us not to exist. We then are possible beings.

The second kind of being, a necessary being, does not depend on something else for its existence. No parents necessary!

Aquinas says because the universe is full of possible beings, it is possible for nothing to exist. Since people do exist, there must be another kind of being who holds all the possible beings together. So just like every effect needs a cause, every possible being needs a necessary being to exist. The necessary being is God.

Psalm 90, attributed to Moses, says the same thing. God is above all living things, our life is only made possible by his immortality. He does not need us as we need him, but since we do exist, we know he loves us and wants a relationship with us.

How do you feel about being a possible being instead of a necessary being?

What is the proper response to God since we depend on him for our existence?

Lord, keep me and protect me so I can give you praise.

Thomas Aquinas' Degrees of Perfection

*For all have sinned and fall
short of the glory of God.*

ROMANS 3:23

When we were little and drew self-portraits, we probably had sticks for arms and our face might not have had a nose. If we attended art classes and practiced regularly, our self-portraits got better. People might recognize us from our painting. If we spent our whole life practicing, at some point we might be able to do a self-portrait approaching camera quality. What does this have to do with God?

In his fourth way to understand God's existence, Thomas Aquinas says goodness exists on a spectrum with perfection on the furthest end. As we got better at painting self-portraits, our work would more closely resemble ourselves, but it would never be a perfect likeness. How is it possible for us to understand what perfection is without actually being able to achieve it?

We were made in the image of a perfect creator, but we have fallen from perfection by choosing ourselves over him. Romans 3:23 says, "For all have sinned and fall short of the glory of God."

God's glory is perfection in every sense. He is perfectly good, perfectly just, perfectly loving, and he calls us to be like him. Matthew 5:48 says, "Be perfect, therefore, as your heavenly Father is perfect."

How? By leaning into Jesus and accepting his perfect covering for our sins.

How well can you draw a self-portrait?

Why should we strive toward perfection?

*God, you are perfect. Help me
lean on you when I am not.*

Thomas Aquinas' Final Cause

For in him all things were created: things in heaven and on earth, visible and invisible, whether thrones or powers or rulers or authorities; all things have been created through him and for him.

COLOSSIANS 1:16

The final way Aquinas understood God's existence is as the *final cause*—a term coined by ancient philosopher Aristotle which means a purpose or end goal.

When we look at nature, we see evidence of predictable design. If we plant an acorn, we get an oak tree, not a plush giraffe. Orange trees grow oranges, not orangutans. The final cause, or purpose, of an acorn is to become an oak tree. The final cause of an orange tree is to grow oranges.

Intelligent beings can determine their own purposes, but non-intelligent things which show purpose must have been designed by an intelligent being to act in a certain way. This being is God.

Colossians 1:16 says basically the same thing. But not only do the acorns have a final cause to become oak trees, they share a final cause with all of creation (including us!) to live for God's glory. According to Isaiah 55:12, "all the trees of the field will clap their hands." Why are they clapping? Because God exists and is worthy of applause.

What is your final cause?

How can you join in creation and praise the creator?

Lord, guide me to do your purposes more than my own.

The Unreasonable Effectiveness of Math

> *"Where were you when I laid the earth's foundation? Tell me, if you understand."*
>
> **JOB 38:4**

William Lane Craig, or Bill as we've been calling him, is a fan of using mathematical principles as evidence for God's existence.

Is there an equation to prove God? Not exactly. It'd be better to say God made the universe with mathematical principles baked in and equations can work only because God has ordered them to.

Believe it or not, math is pretty incredible. Using math, we're able to build better buildings, put people into space, and predict the existence of subatomic particles years before they can be proven with billions of dollars of research equipment.

Not only is math useful, some people consider it to be beautiful. Mathematician Bertrand Russell once said, "Mathematics, rightly viewed, possesses not only truth, but supreme beauty—a beauty cold and austere, like that of sculpture, without appeal to any part of our weaker nature, without the gorgeous trappings of painting or music, yet sublimely pure, and capable of a stern perfection such as only the greatest art can show."

Although Russell did not believe in God, he recognized in mathematics the qualities of God's perfection. God is the author of the universe, in both its beauty and its usefulness, and he gave us many ways to recognize him, even through math.

Have you ever considered math to be beautiful?

Why do you think God gave us math?

God, you are a God of order and beauty. Help me remember you when I'm doing math.

268

The Law of Human Nature

So I find this law at work: Although I want to do good, evil is right there with me.

ROMANS 7:21

If we don't love how God gave us math, maybe a basic understanding of right and wrong would be a more relatable proof of his existence. In his book *Mere Christianity*, C. S. Lewis calls our understanding of right and wrong the Law of Human Nature, or the Moral Law.

"Think of a country where people were admired for running away in battle, or where a man felt proud of double-crossing all the people who had been kindest to him. You might just as well try to imagine a country where two and two made five. Men have differed as regards what people you ought to be unselfish to—whether it was only your own family, or your fellow countrymen, or everyone. But they have always agreed that you ought not to put yourself first. Selfishness has never been admired."

This Law of Human Nature, Lewis says, is the only law which we intuitively understand, but continually break. We want things to be fair, but we are unfair to others. Still, we appeal to a common sense of fairness or rightness which must exist higher than our ability to meet it.

Paul says in Romans 7:21: "So I find this law at work: Although I want to do good, evil is right there with me." Fortunately, God—who is the ultimate in rightness and fairness—has made a way for us to be right with him through Jesus Christ.

How does the Moral Law point to God?

How can you overcome your tendencies to be selfish?

God, you are the only perfect one, and by your perfection, I know I'm not perfect and I need you.

The Existence of Love

*Whoever does not love does not know
God, because God is love.*

1 JOHN 4:8

If appealing to the mind through math or morality isn't enough to convince us of God's existence, let's look at something closer to the heart: Love.

Although some people attribute love to a series of chemical reactions in the brain, it is more complex than anything science could explain. The idea of putting someone else's interests above our own flies in the face of self-preservation, which is a cornerstone of human behavior. How then can we show love and feel love if it doesn't make good sense to do so?

We were made in the image of a loving God. First John 4:8 says, "Whoever does not love does not know God, because God is love."

Our ability to feel love is only possible because God exists. Our ability to show love is only possible because he loves us. First John 4:19 says, "We love because he first loved us."

In what way do you feel most loved?

How do you show love to others?

*God, thank you for loving me and making
it possible for me to love others.*

The Unmet Desire

> *"What no eye has seen, what no ear has heard, and what no human mind has conceived"—the things God has prepared for those who love him—these are the things God has revealed to us by his Spirit.*
>
> **1 CORINTHIANS 2:9–10**

We're familiar with sadness and joy, hunger and thirst, contentment and restlessness, but there's another feeling out there that's harder to pin down. In fact, we don't even have an English word for it. *Sehnsucht* (pronounced "Zane-zookt") is a German word to describe a longing for which there is no satisfaction to be found. It's like being homesick for a place we've never been.

But how can we know of a place like that? Because the Spirit has revealed it to us.

First Corinthians 2:9–10 says, "'What no eye has seen, what no ear has heard, and what no human mind has conceived'—the things God has prepared for those who love him—these are the things God has revealed to us by his Spirit. The Spirit searches all things, even the deep things of God."

Have you ever felt Sehnsucht?

What could you pray when you are feeling this way?

Lord, you made me to be with you in eternity. Help me long for you.

271

Evidence of Appearances

Then Jesus told him, "Because you have seen me, you have believed; blessed are those who have not seen and yet have believed."

JOHN 20:29

After looking at a number of proofs for God's reality, it's time to look at whether his son Jesus actually rose from the grave. We have seen compelling evidence the tomb was empty, but it is another thing to suggest Jesus Christ came back to life.

The first problem to overcome is the lack of any eyewitness accounts of Jesus's resurrection. "That's exactly right," agrees Dr. Gary Habermas, author of a number of books on Jesus's resurrection.

"When I was young," says Habermas, "I was reading a book by C. S. Lewis, who wrote that the New Testament says nothing about the resurrection. I wrote a real big 'No!' in the margin. Then I realized what he was saying: Nobody was sitting inside the tomb and saw the body start to vibrate, stand up, take the linen wrappings off, fold them, roll back the stone, wow the guards, and leave."

Doesn't this hurt the idea that Jesus rose again?

"No," says Habermas, "because science is all about causes and effects. We don't see dinosaurs; we study fossils. We may not know how a disease originates, but we study its symptoms. Maybe nobody witnesses a crime, but police piece together the evidence after the fact."

Why don't you need to see something happen to know it really did?

Before we study it, how convinced are you of Jesus's resurrection?

Lord, show me the truth of your resurrection.

DAY 262

Jesus's Other Tomb?

Early on the first day of the week, while it was still dark, Mary Magdalene went to the tomb and saw that the stone had been removed from the entrance.

JOHN 20:1

People who argue against Christianity are always trying to put Jesus back in the grave. That was the case in 2007 when newspapers and TV stations announced Jesus's bones had been found in an ancient tomb in Jerusalem. Academy Award-winning director James Cameron brought international fame to the tomb by producing a documentary called, *The Lost Tomb of Jesus* which aired on the Discovery Channel.

The film claimed the Talpiot Tomb was the final resting place of Jesus and his family. Yes, they alleged he was married and had a son. And if Jesus's bones were in this tomb, there's no way he rose from the dead and ascended into heaven as the Bible reports (see Acts 1:6–11).

The documentary's "proof" was that this tomb had several notable names inscribed on the ossuaries (containers which hold the bones of dead people). These names included Jesus, the son of Joseph, Mary, Matthew, Joseph, and Judas. In addition, a soil sample from the tomb dated back to the time Jesus lived.

All the hype quickly had people talking. But hype doesn't equal fact. Soon experts dug into the claims of the film and figured out the story didn't add up.

> **Why might a filmmaker claim to have made an important discovery about Jesus's tomb?**
>
> **Do you think the tomb in question was Jesus of Nazareth's tomb?**

Lord, help me dig deeper when claims against you are made.

273

No, Just the Other Jesus's Tomb

Now Jesus himself was about thirty years old when he began his ministry. He was the son, so it was thought, of Joseph.

LUKE 3:23

Amos Kloner helped lead the excavation of the Talpiot Tomb in 1980. When asked about the 2007 documentary, he said, "It makes a great story for a TV film, but it's completely impossible. It's nonsense."

One of the most outspoken critics was Bible scholar Ben Witherington III. Ben pointed out numerous problems, including:

- Jesus was never called "son of Joseph" by his followers.
- Joseph's adult home was Nazareth. There's no reason he would have been buried alone in Jerusalem with Jesus' "family" added to the grave later.
- There's no historical evidence Jesus was married or had a son.
- No DNA evidence.
- Mary, Joseph, and Jesus, were common names.

The experts quickly arrived at the same conclusion: The story of Jesus's bones being found was questionable. But the headlines and hype confused a large number of people.

Do you share a name with anyone you know?

How would you answer someone who claimed Jesus's bones had been found?

Jesus, give me the words to defend your truths.

274

Things Dead People Don't Do

> *When he had received the drink, Jesus said, "It is finished." With that, he bowed his head and gave up his spirit.*
>
> **JOHN 19:30**

It was well-documented that Jesus was a historical figure who died by crucifixion. There was no way he could have survived the cross. Jesus was dead.

Dead people don't do much. In fact, here are a few more things dead people don't do:

- Mow the lawn.
- Do the dishes.
- Compete in the Olympics.
- Build robots capable of doing homework so we don't have to.
- Tell jokes or laugh at jokes.

Dr. Gary Habermas looks at the case of Jesus's death and what happened later and adds one more item.

"Here's how I look at the evidence," says Dr. Habermas. "First, did Jesus die on the cross? And second, did he appear later to people? If you can establish those two things, you've made your case, because dead people don't normally do that."

But did people actually see Jesus after he died on the cross? Yes, a lot of people, in fact.

What are some more things dead people don't do?

What is something nice you can do for someone else (since you are not dead)?

Lord, be alive in me and help me live for you.

Resurrection Witnesses: Paul's Encounter

*And last of all he appeared to me
also, as to one abnormally born.*

1 CORINTHIANS 15:8

What evidence is there to say people actually saw Jesus after he died and was placed in a tomb?

"I'll start with evidence that virtually all critical scholars will admit," says Gary Habermas. "Nobody questions that Paul wrote 1 Corinthians. Two places in that letter, he affirms that he personally encountered the resurrected Christ. He says in 1 Corinthians 9:1, 'Am I not an apostle? Have I not seen Jesus our Lord?' And he says in 1 Corinthians 15:8, 'Last of all he appeared to me also.'"

Paul, formerly Saul, encountered Jesus on the road to Damascus. Before the encounter, he did everything he could to stamp out Christianity. He was present at the stoning of a Christian named Stephen (Acts 7:58), and he was "breathing out murderous threats against the Lord's disciples" (Acts 9:1). Then he met Jesus.

Acts 9:3–5 says, "As he neared Damascus on his journey, suddenly a light from heaven flashed around him. He fell to the ground and heard a voice say to him, 'Saul, Saul, why do you persecute me?'

"'Who are you, Lord?' Saul asked.

"'I am Jesus, whom you are persecuting,' he replied."

Why is Paul's testimony important to Jesus's resurrection?

How has encountering Jesus changed you?

Encountering the resurrected Jesus changed Paul. It can change us too.

Lord, change me and give me a purpose for you.

276

Resurrection Witnesses: Five Hundred People

After that, he appeared to more than five hundred of the brothers and sisters at the same time, most of whom are still living, though some have fallen asleep.

1 CORINTHIANS 15:6

Paul's experience with Jesus on the road to Damascus was life-changing, but one man's testimony isn't always compelling. That's why Paul mentioned in 1 Corinthians 15:6 how Jesus "appeared to more than five hundred of the brothers and sisters at the same time."

Jesus appearing to Paul is great. Showing himself to five hundred people is amazing. But the big number of witnesses isn't the most impressive part of Paul's claim. By mentioning "most of whom are still living," Paul was inviting doubters to test whether he was telling the truth.

Since 1 Corinthians was written within twenty years of Jesus's crucifixion, it would have been fairly easy to find one of these five hundred people who saw the risen Christ. It's not as if these witnesses would have easily forgotten it.

Today, there are millions of people who have encountered Jesus. If we've accepted him into our life as Lord and Savior, we are one of them. We may not have seen Jesus in person, but our experience is no less impressive. In fact, Jesus calls us blessed:

If five hundred people saw something, would you believe it happened?

Could you testify Jesus rose again even though you haven't seen him?

"Because you have seen me, you have believed; blessed are those who have not seen and yet have believed" (John 20:29).

Lord, help me tell others about my experiences with you.

279

Resurrection Witnesses: Mary Magdalene

Mary Magdalene went to the disciples with the news: "I have seen the Lord!" And she told them that he had said these things to her.

JOHN 20:18

John 20:11–18 tells about a special encounter between Jesus and Mary Magdalene at the tomb.

After discovering Jesus's missing body, Mary met two angels sitting inside the tomb who told her Jesus wasn't there. "At this, she turned around and saw Jesus standing there, but she did not realize that it was Jesus. He asked her, 'Woman, why are you crying? Who is it you are looking for?'

"Thinking he was the gardener, she said, 'Sir, if you have carried him away, tell me where you have put him, and I will get him.'

"Jesus said to her, 'Mary.'

"She turned toward him and cried out in Aramaic, 'Rabboni!' (which means 'Teacher')" (John 20:14–16).

The last time Mary saw him, he was beaten, bloody, and nailed to a cross. No wonder she didn't recognize Jesus immediately! But when he called her name, she knew it was Jesus.

Jesus is calling our name as well. He wants us to know him, not only for the sacrifice he made on the cross, but as our risen Lord. We can get to know him better by reading the Bible and trusting him with our prayers.

Are you as excited to recognize Jesus in your life as Mary Magdalene was?

How could you deepen your relationship with Jesus?

Lord, help me hear your call and recognize you.

Resurrection Witnesses: Other Women

*Suddenly Jesus met them. "Greetings,"
he said. They came to him, clasped
his feet and worshiped him.*

MATTHEW 28:9

In Matthew's Gospel, Jesus followed up his meeting with Mary Magdalene with an encouraging roadside encounter after their visit to the tomb.

Matthew 28:1–10 mentions Mary Magdalene and the other Mary, but suggests other women were present too. If Mary Magdalene still couldn't believe her eyes when Jesus appeared to her, he gave her another reason to believe by meeting the whole group of women as they left the tomb.

This wasn't just wishful thinking. The unnamed group of ladies "came to him, clasped his feet and worshiped him" (Matthew 28:9). If the risen Jesus didn't have an actual body, the women wouldn't have been able to clasp his feet.

There are times in our Christian walk where we have an amazing encounter with Jesus and immediately start doubting whether it happened. Those doubts can lead us on paths of our choosing. What we need in those times is another encounter with Jesus like Mary and the other women had. The best way to have an encounter is to open our Bible, clasp his words, and go where he tells us to go.

What do you do when Jesus doesn't feel real to you?

Where do you think he's telling you to go?

Lord, when I have doubts, make yourself known through your Word.

Resurrection Witnesses: Cleopas Plus One

One of them, named Cleopas, asked him,
"Are you the only one visiting Jerusalem
who does not know the things that have
happened there in these days?"

LUKE 24:18

Luke 24 tells the story of a couple of travelers on the road from Jerusalem to Emmaus who encountered a mysterious stranger. The travelers, one of whom is named Cleopas, were talking about Jesus when the stranger asked for more details.

Cleopas told him how the religious elites had killed a mighty prophet named Jesus. Now their hopes of Jesus being the Messiah were dead.

The stranger pointed to Old Testament prophecies concerning how the Messiah had to suffer before entering glory. Of course, the mysterious stranger was Jesus himself, but Cleopas and the other traveler didn't recognize him until dinner time.

Luke 24:30–32 says, "When he was at the table with them, he took bread, gave thanks, broke it and began to give it to them. Then their eyes were opened and they recognized him, and he disappeared from their sight. They asked each other, 'Were not our hearts burning within us while he talked with us on the road and opened the Scriptures to us?'"

Jesus can have this effect on our hearts when we engage the Scriptures with him too!

> **When was the last time your heart burned within you when reading the Bible?**
>
> **What is it about giving thanks which prepares us to see Jesus?**

Lord, thank you for revealing your love to me.

Resurrection Witnesses: The Eleven Plus Others

While they were still talking about this,
Jesus himself stood among them and
said to them, "Peace be with you."

LUKE 24:36

When Cleopas and his traveling companion realized the mysterious stranger who joined them was Jesus, they immediately headed back to Jerusalem to find his disciples. The eleven disciples—Judas was no longer in the picture—had a surprise visitor too: Jesus (Luke 24:36).

"Peace be with you," is a good greeting when popping into existence among people, because it must seem pretty scary. Sadly, the greeting didn't do much to help the disciples.

Luke 24:37 says, "They were startled and frightened, thinking they saw a ghost."

Jesus wasn't a ghost though. To put all fears to rest, he asked them for a bit of food and he ate it in front of them.

Jesus came back to remind them of the Old Testament prophecies, to tell them what he told Cleopas: The promised Messiah had to suffer and Jesus is the promised Messiah. Death had no power over him.

Death doesn't need to have power over us either. As Christians, we are confident death is only temporary. Jesus's peace is real in our lives when we put our trust in his sacrifice and his resurrection.

Does death worry you?

How can you live in peace when death is around you?

Lord, help me overcome fear like
you overcame death.

Resurrection Witnesses: Thomas

A week later his disciples were in the house again, and Thomas was with them. Though the doors were locked, Jesus came and stood among them and said, "Peace be with you!"

JOHN 20:26

The account of the resurrected Jesus's visit with his disciples is recorded in both Luke and John, but with minor differences. In John's gospel, Thomas wasn't present. So when the disciples told Thomas what happened, it seemed too good to be true.

Thomas' specific reply is found in John 20:25: "Unless I see the nail marks in his hands and put my finger where the nails were, and put my hand into his side, I will not believe."

Fast forward one week when Jesus popped by for another visit. Jesus called Thomas aside and said, "Put your finger here; see my hands. Reach out your hand and put it into my side. Stop doubting and believe" (John 20:27).

Jesus may not have been physically present when Thomas talked to the other disciples, but he is still omniscient and omnipresent. We don't need to stick our fingers where the nails were to trust in Jesus. He hears our prayers, our words, and our thoughts. And just like he did with Thomas, he's ready to prove himself to us too.

How has Jesus proven himself to you?

What is something you'd like him to overhear you saying?

Jesus, you are always with me. Guide my thoughts and words to be worthy of being overheard.

282

Resurrection Witnesses: Seven Apostles Fishing

> *Early in the morning, Jesus stood on the shore, but the disciples did not realize that it was Jesus. He called out to them, "Friends, haven't you any fish?" "No," they answered.*
>
> **JOHN 21:4–5**

When Jesus originally called Peter, James, and John to follow him, they were fishing on the Sea of Galilee. In the final chapter of John's gospel, Peter, James, and John are fishing again.

Only they weren't catching fish.

Then someone from shore shouted out a suggestion to fish on the other side of the boat. With nothing to lose, they took his suggestion and their nets filled with fish. Sound familiar? Jesus did the same miracle with them at the beginning of his ministry in Luke 5:1–11.

John immediately recognized what was happening. John 21:7 says, "Then the disciple whom Jesus loved said to Peter, 'It is the Lord!' As soon as Simon Peter heard him say, 'It is the Lord,' he wrapped his outer garment around him (for he had taken it off) and jumped into the water."

When we recognize Jesus's call to action in our life, we should be ready to jump ship like Peter did. Jesus still needs us to be fishers of men, and his presence in our life will be bait to draw others to him.

How did Peter's reaction differ from the miracle in Luke to the one in John?

Are you ready to jump ship and follow Jesus?

Lord, help me boldly follow you wherever you call me to go.

283

Resurrection Witnesses: The 11 Commissioned

Then Jesus said to them, "Do not be afraid. Go and tell my brothers to go to Galilee; there they will see me."

MATTHEW 28:10

Any doubts the disciples had about Jesus's resurrection must surely have been put to rest by the time he saw them in Galilee. Since death didn't seem to affect Jesus's ability to get around, maybe the disciples thought he would continue his earthly ministry.

When Jesus met with his disciples on the mountain in Galilee, he knew his earthly ministry would continue, but he wasn't going to keep up his appearances. It was time for the disciples to work!

Matthew 28:19–20 says, "Therefore go and make disciples of all nations, baptizing them in the name of the Father and of the Son and of the Holy Spirit, and teaching them to obey everything I have commanded you. And surely I am with you always, to the very end of the age."

As followers of Jesus, this Great Commission (as it is called) is for us too. Like the women at the tomb, our excitement at discovering Jesus should be clear to all. Like the travelers on the road, our conversations should involve what Jesus has done. Like the apostles, we are called to live boldly and testify to Jesus's power.

Who could you talk to about Jesus today?

What would you tell them?

Lord, may I make more disciples for you wherever I go.

Resurrection Witnesses: The Final Appearance

*While he was blessing them, he left them
and was taken up into heaven.*

LUKE 24:51

For forty days, Jesus's resurrection had been visible to individuals, large crowds, and doubting and faithful believers alike. Acts 1:3 says, "After his suffering, he presented himself to them and gave many convincing proofs that he was alive. He appeared to them over a period of forty days and spoke about the kingdom of God."

After giving his disciples their instructions to go out and spread the gospel, Jesus prepared himself for a grand exit from earth. But his disciples still had questions.

Acts 1:6–9 says, "Then they gathered around him and asked him, 'Lord, are you at this time going to restore the kingdom to Israel?'

"He said to them: 'It is not for you to know the times or dates the Father has set by his own authority. But you will receive power when the Holy Spirit comes on you; and you will be my witnesses in Jerusalem, and in all Judea and Samaria, and to the ends of the earth.'

"After he said this, he was taken up before their very eyes, and a cloud hid him from their sight."

Unlike his humble arrival in Bethlehem, Jesus left in a cloud of glory. We don't know when he'll be back, but we must be prepared when he comes.

> **How can you prepare for Jesus's return?**
>
> **How can the Holy Spirit help you spread the gospel?**

*Lord, may I be found spreading
your love when you return.*

Corroboration from Acts

You killed the author of life, but God raised him from the dead. We are witnesses of this.

ACTS 3:15

The gospels indeed contain a wealth of Jesus sightings. These weren't fleeting observations of a shadowy figure by one or two people. There were multiple appearances to numerous people, several of which were confirmed by more than one gospel or by the 1 Corinthians 15 creed.

"Just look at Acts," says scholar Gary Habermas, referring to the New Testament book recording the launch of the church. Not only are Jesus's appearances mentioned regularly, but details are provided and the theme of the disciples being witnesses are found in almost every context.

Indeed, Acts is littered with references to Jesus's appearances. The apostle Peter says in Acts 2:32, "God has raised this Jesus to life, and we are all witnesses of it." In Acts 3:15 he repeats, "You killed the author of life, but God raised him from the dead. We are witnesses of this." He confirms to Cornelius in Acts 10:41 that he and others "ate and drank with him after he rose from the dead."

The Bible clearly shows Jesus didn't stay buried. His resurrection wasn't just a rumor started by his disciples. Jesus was seen by many. We serve the risen Lord whose love overcame death to bring us life!

What does the amount of testimony evidence suggest about Jesus's resurrection?

What does new life in a risen Christ mean to you?

Lord, help my life be a witness to my friends that your resurrection is real.

Mark's Missing Conclusion

> *"But go, tell his disciples and Peter, 'He is going ahead of you into Galilee. There you will see him, just as he told you.'"*
>
> **MARK 16:7**

After looking at all the evidence for Jesus's resurrection in the gospels and elsewhere, it may be troubling to note how Mark's gospel is light on mentions of Jesus's post-resurrection appearances. In fact, the earliest manuscripts don't have Mark 16:9–20.

"I don't have a problem with that whatsoever," says Gary Habermas. "Sure, it would be nice if he had included a list of appearances, but here are some things for you to think about:

"Even if Mark does end [at Mark 16:8] which not everyone believes, you still have him reporting that the tomb is empty, and a young man proclaiming, 'He is risen!' and telling the women that there will be appearances.

"You can close your favorite novel and say, 'I can't believe the author's not telling me the next episode,' but you can't close the book and say, 'The writer doesn't believe in the next episode.' Mark definitely does. He obviously believed the resurrection had taken place. He ends with the women being told that Jesus will appear in Galilee, and then others later confirm that he did."

> Can you find a Bible passage to support the resurrected Jesus's meeting with his disciples in Galilee?
>
> How can you proclaim "He is risen" to someone you know?

> *Lord, make my next episode with you even better than the last.*

Hopeful Hallucinations?

God has raised this Jesus to life,
and we are all witnesses of it.

ACTS 2:32

Since people don't typically rise again after being dead for a few days, what if there was a logical solution for Jesus's post-resurrection appearances? Maybe the witnesses really believed they saw Jesus, but could they have been seeing a hallucination instead?

Dr. Gary Collins, the psychologist we met with to determine if Jesus was crazy, has this to say on the topic:

"Hallucinations are individual occurrences. By their very nature only one person can see a given hallucination at a time. They certainly aren't something which can be seen by a group of people. Neither is it possible that one person could somehow induce an hallucination in somebody else. Since hallucinations exist only in this subjective, personal sense, it is obvious that others cannot witness it."

Gary Habermas concurs. "There are several other arguments why hallucinations can't explain away his appearances," he says. "The disciples were fearful, doubtful, and in despair after the crucifixion, whereas people who hallucinate see what they expect to see."

Since Peter was hard-headed and James was a skeptic, they weren't ideal candidates for hallucinations. No, the people who testified they saw Jesus weren't dreaming it up. Jesus is better than we could dream up anyway!

> **Have you ever seen something which wasn't really there?**
>
> **How would you answer someone who said Jesus's resurrection appearances were hallucinations?**

Jesus, your love is no hallucination.

Jesus vs. Aliens and Bigfoot

They replied, "Believe in the Lord Jesus, and you will be saved—you and your household."

ACTS 16:31

In 2013, Public Policy Polling conducted a survey on the differences between Democratic, Republican, and Independent voters with regard to conspiracy theories. They asked questions about the moon landing, aliens, and Bigfoot, among other topics.

According to their research, only 7% of people believe the moon landing was faked (6% Democrat, 5% Republican, 17% Independent), 29% of people believe aliens exist (28% Democrat, 28% Republican, 41% Independent), and 14% of people believe in Bigfoot (12% Democrat, 15% Republican, 19% Independent). These numbers don't reflect the people who were unsure on these topics; only the people who confidently said they believed in them.

When it comes to Jesus, critics of Christianity try to put Jesus in the same category as aliens and Bigfoot. They say there's not enough evidence to support the belief that the Son of God died on a cross and rose again to be seen by hundreds of his followers. But Christians don't have to rely on shaky video footage to support their claims.

What evidence have you seen for the existence of aliens or Bigfoot?

Why do some people struggle to believe in Jesus when so much evidence exists?

We have history, archaeology, and documentary evidence on our side! If we are wrong about aliens or Bigfoot, our lives won't change much. If we are right about God's sacrifice and love, nothing will ever be the same!

Lord, may your existence be more real to me than conspiracy theories.

289

What Jesus's Resurrection Means

*Brothers and sisters, we do not want you
to be uninformed about those who sleep
in death, so that you do not grieve like the
rest of mankind, who have no hope.*

1 THESSALONIANS 4:13

When loved ones die, it is easy to be overwhelmed by sadness. And while it's true we won't see them on earth again, if they were fellow believers in Christ, we will see them again.

In 1 Thessalonians 4:13, Paul compares death to sleep because one day, we'll wake up in new bodies, free from sin and pain. This current life will seem like a dream to the reality which awaits. This belief in a better future after death gives us hope, unlike those who believe our existence ends in the grave.

It will always be sad when a loved one dies. Even Jesus cried when his friend Lazarus died (John 11:35), and Jesus knew he was about to bring Lazarus back to life! But our sadness is mingled with hope. Why?

First Thessalonians 4:14 says, "For we believe that Jesus died and rose again, and so we believe that God will bring with Jesus those who have fallen asleep in him."

We share in Jesus's resurrection! We will rise again too and live with God forever, perfectly restored to Him.

Why wouldn't non-Christians have hope?

Who is one person you'd like to make sure joins you in Jesus's resurrection?

Lord, give me hope in my sadness.

Sadducees: The Original Resurrection Deniers

That same day the Sadducees, who say there is no resurrection, came to him with a question.

MATTHEW 22:23

Denying the resurrection was one of the defining characteristics of the Sadducees. They dominated the Sanhedrin, the group who governed Jewish affairs.

They rejected the idea of fate, believing humans alone were responsible for the good or evil choices they made. They also believed the soul died with the body, so there was no afterlife.

Matthew 22 records a conversation between Jesus and some Sadducees who tried to make him look foolish. The Sadducees painted a scenario where the widow of an eldest brother married a younger brother who then died himself. The widow repeated the process until she had married each of the seven brothers in the family. Matthew 22:28 records their question: "Now then, at the resurrection, whose wife will she be of the seven, since all of them were married to her?"

Since the Sadducees didn't believe in resurrection in the first place, they didn't really expect an answer. Still, Jesus answered them wisely. He corrected their assumptions about resurrection as well as their view of God.

God is not distant or uncaring. He's alive and loves us now and forever. The resurrection of Jesus paved the way for our own resurrection with him.

How did Jesus answer the Sadducees in Matthew 22:29–33?

Have you ever asked a question to make someone else look foolish?

Lord, forgive me when I treat others poorly. Help me remember how I'm supposed to live for you.

Heaven vs. New Heaven & New Earth

> *But in keeping with his promise we are*
> *looking forward to a new heaven and a*
> *new earth, where righteousness dwells.*
>
> **2 PETER 3:13**

While the Sadducees did not believe in any kind of afterlife, Jesus taught differently. He referred to his father in heaven and said believers who endure persecution will be rewarded greatly there (see Matthew 5:12).

Heaven is the holy dwelling place of God and his angels (Matthew 18:10). Contrary to depictions from pop culture, heaven isn't made of clouds where people sit around with their new wings and play harps.

After receiving judgment at heaven's throne, we'll be taken to a new heaven and a new earth, where God will dwell with us for eternity, as he did with Adam and Eve before sin entered the picture.

And as Jesus was resurrected into a new body following his death, so will his followers get new bodies too. In 2 Corinthians 5:4, Paul refers to our bodies as tents for our souls: "For while we are in this tent, we groan and are burdened, because we do not wish to be unclothed but to be clothed instead with our heavenly dwelling, so that what is mortal may be swallowed up by life."

Revelation 21 has some descriptions of what our new home will look like, but no matter how it looks, we'll dwell there in holiness with God which is the best part by far.

What did you think about heaven before today?

Why is dwelling with God the best part of our eternal existence?

Lord, I can't wait to be with you face to face.

Jesus & Hell

Do not be afraid of those who kill the body but cannot kill the soul. Rather, be afraid of the One who can destroy both soul and body in hell.

MATTHEW 10:28

Most people think of Jesus's message in terms of his love. We should love our neighbors and our enemies. We should love God with all our heart. He showed us love by taking our punishment on the cross. So, it might surprise us how often Jesus talked about hell.

In Matthew 18:9, Jesus associated hell with fire. In Mark 9:48, he said it is a place where the worms who eat the dead do not die and the fire is never quenched. In Matthew 8:12, he describes it as a place of darkness, "where there will be weeping and gnashing of teeth." In fact, Jesus talked more about hell than he did about heaven.

Hell is obviously not a good place, but who is it for? Second Thessalonians 1:8-9 says, "He will punish those who do not know God and do not obey the gospel of our Lord Jesus. They will be punished with everlasting destruction and shut out from the presence of the Lord and from the glory of his might."

Why would Jesus, Lord of love, talk about hell so much? Simple. He didn't want anyone to go there. Especially not when the alternative is so much better. Jesus believed in hell. We should too. And we should make sure our loved ones know the way to avoid it.

Why do you think hell is hard to talk about?

Do you know where your soul is headed after death?

Lord, hell is real, but you made a way for me to get to heaven. Thank you.

293

DAY 283

How Not to Be Saved

*For, "Everyone who calls on the name
of the Lord will be saved."*

ROMANS 10:13

The Sadducees were wrong. The afterlife is real. There are only two ways to go: Eternal presence with God or eternally without him in hell. The choice is clear, but how do we get there?

Some people think of God as holding a balance in Heaven, weighing each deed on a scale between good and evil. If the good outweighs the evil, they think they'll be good enough to spend eternity with him.

Some think hell is a hoax and God will just let everyone into glory. Others think all religions lead to God.

While God is eternally fair, his scales will always find our good deeds lacking. Romans 3:10 says, "There is no one righteous, not even one."

Since Jesus spoke more about hell than he did heaven, we know hell isn't a hoax. And Jesus clearly said in John 14:6 no one comes to the Father except through him, so not every religion leads to the one true God.

If we aren't good enough to avoid a very real hell, how do we get to heaven? We believe in Jesus, accept his gift of salvation on our behalf, and ask him to be our Savior. Romans 10:13 says, "Everyone who calls on the name of the Lord will be saved."

Have you accepted Jesus as your Savior?

How can you tell others about Jesus so they can believe too?

Lord, give me the opportunity to speak to someone about you today.

294

Not a "Get Out of Hell" Pass

> *What good is it, my brothers and sisters,*
> *if someone claims to have faith but has*
> *no deeds? Can such faith save them?*
>
> **JAMES 2:14**

Romans 10:13 says salvation is available to anyone willing to call on Jesus's name. According to Ephesians 2:8-9, there's nothing we've done to earn salvation: "For it is by grace you have been saved, through faith—and this is not from yourselves, it is the gift of God—not by works, so that no one can boast."

So is that it? Once we accept Jesus's gift of salvation, can we do whatever we want and not worry about the eternal consequences?

While our salvation is secured by Jesus's sacrifice, our actions will show whether our faith in his sacrifice is genuine. James 2:14 says, "What good is it, my brothers and sisters, if someone claims to have faith but has no deeds? Can such faith save them?"

James isn't saying salvation can be earned. He's saying it should be shown through our actions. If we are saved, we'll want to live for Jesus's glory more than our own. We'll want to be kind, patient, and loving. If we say we're Christians but we don't show any resemblance to Christ, we should ask ourselves if our faith is genuine or if we are treating salvation like a "Get out of Hell" pass.

How does Matthew 25:31–46 illustrate this lesson?

How can your actions better show what you believe?

> *Lord, may my faith be alive and*
> *my salvation be obvious.*

How Sacrifice Leads to Resurrection

> *"For whoever wants to save their life will
> lose it, but whoever loses their life for
> me and for the gospel will save it."*
>
> **MARK 8:35**

Jesus's resurrection didn't happen until after his crucifixion. For new life to happen, death must come first. This principle isn't limited to literal resurrection. Jesus invites us to experience resurrection in every area of our lives. How?

Mark 8:34-35 says, "Then he called the crowd to him along with his disciples and said: 'Whoever wants to be my disciple must deny themselves and take up their cross and follow me. For whoever wants to save their life will lose it, but whoever loses their life for me and for the gospel will save it.'"

The cross was a shameful way for prisoners to die, but Jesus told his followers it was the key to new life. This wasn't just some shocking thing for Jesus to say; he would take up his own cross in time. To truly follow Jesus, we need to be willing to face shame, to deny our own wants, and to put the interests of others first.

Maybe this means doing housework for our parents with a good attitude (which we may not feel like doing). Maybe we should look for someone who needs a friend—Jesus was drawn to society's outcasts, after all. However it looks, allowing our wants to die will always lead to new life in the areas we need it most.

What is one thing you could sacrifice to have new life?

Who came to mind when you read about someone needing a friend?

> *Lord, help me be willing to put my wants to
> death so I can have resurrection in my life.*

Coming to the Father, Getting the Spirit

For there is one God and one mediator between God and mankind, the man Christ Jesus, who gave himself as a ransom for all people. This has now been witnessed to at the proper time.

1 TIMOTHY 2:5–6

During the last supper before he was crucified, Jesus told his disciples what would happen. He knew he would die on a cross. This is the background when he told his disciples in John 14:6, "I am the way and the truth and the life. No one comes to the Father except through me."

Jesus was comforting his disciples by showing them the necessity of his actions. Unless he went to the cross, there would be no way to the Father. Also, he wouldn't be able to send the Holy Spirit.

John 14:16–17 says, "And I will ask the Father, and he will give you another advocate to help you and be with you forever—the Spirit of truth. The world cannot accept him, because it neither sees him nor knows him. But you know him, for he lives with you and will be in you."

Since Jesus *did* go to the cross, there *is* a way to the Father, and we can pray to him through the Holy Spirit. With the Spirit inside us, we can pray confidently, believing God will answer our requests (see Mark 11:24). And when we don't know how to pray, the Spirit will pray on our behalf (see Romans 8:26).

Jesus's death and resurrection gave us access to the full power of the Trinity. Praise God!

Why can you have confidence when you pray?

What would you like to talk to God about in prayer today?

Jesus, thank you for being my way to the Father, and for sending the Spirit.

297

The Other Side of the Cloud

> *"In my vision at night I looked, and there before me was one like a son of man, coming with the clouds of heaven. He approached the Ancient of Days and was led into his presence."*
>
> **DANIEL 7:13**

After Jesus's resurrection, he appeared to a lot of people for forty days before ascending into heaven. Acts 1:9 says, "After he said this, he was taken up before their very eyes, and a cloud hid him from their sight."

What was happening on the other side of the cloud?

Daniel 7:13–14 says, "In my vision at night I looked, and there before me was one like a son of man, coming with the clouds of heaven. He approached the Ancient of Days and was led into his presence. He was given authority, glory and sovereign power; all nations and peoples of every language worshiped him. His dominion is an everlasting dominion that will not pass away, and his kingdom is one that will never be destroyed."

Jesus the Messiah was crowned King of Kings! People on earth wanted him to be king over Israel, but Jesus was waiting for a different coronation. When the soldiers crowned him with a crown of thorns at the cross, Jesus knew it was the path to his true crown in heaven. Today, he sits on the throne and waits for the right time to usher his people into the perfect kingdom to come.

Have you ever had to endure something bad to get something great afterward?

How does the hope of a great thing make the bad thing bearable?

Lord, be king of my life as you are in heaven.

Let the Dead Rest in Peace

For we know that our old self was crucified with him so that the body ruled by sin might be done away with, that we should no longer be slaves to sin—because anyone who has died has been set free from sin.

ROMANS 6:6–7

If our beloved pet hamster died, we might give it a little funeral and bury it somewhere in the yard. We wouldn't get the shovel out the next day, dig it up, and put it back in the hamster ball for old times' sake. That's just wrong.

When Jesus was crucified, our sins were crucified with him. Our old sins, our current sins, and our future sins have all been paid for by Christ's death. They were buried with him in the tomb. Then Jesus rose again, sin-free. Our sins stayed dead.

Why is sin so tempting when the reality of it is as gross as playing with a dead hamster? Because sin puts us in God's place and we like to feel important. It is in our old nature to live for ourselves first. Philippians 2:21 says, "For everyone looks out for their own interests, not those of Jesus Christ."

But we have been set free from sin. The tomb is wide open. It's time to let our sins rest in peace. Sure, we'll make mistakes, and there's always forgiveness available when we do, but we shouldn't camp out in the tomb.

We should do what Jesus did when he rose again: Spend time with the living and show God's power over death.

> Do you see sin as something gross or hard to talk or even think about?
>
> How can you look out for Jesus' interests more than your own?

Jesus, help me leave my dead sins alone.

Living in the Already, But Not Yet

> *But our citizenship is in heaven. And we eagerly await a Savior from there, the Lord Jesus Christ.*
>
> **PHILIPPIANS 3:20**

Our sins were paid for in full at the cross. At the tomb, Jesus proved he was God by rising from the dead. When we put our faith in his sacrifice and resurrection, we are welcomed into his family and our citizenship is changed from earth to heaven.

But...

We aren't in glory yet. Our sins have been forgiven, but we still have temptations to sin daily. We are children of God, but we sometimes rebel against our Heavenly Father. We live in the "already, but not yet" period of history between Jesus's resurrection and our own perfection.

Paul says in Philippians 3:20–21, "But our citizenship is in heaven. And we eagerly await a Savior from there, the Lord Jesus Christ, who, by the power that enables him to bring everything under his control, will transform our lowly bodies so that they will be like his glorious body."

Someday, Jesus will return to earth and we'll be transformed fully into his likeness, free from temptation and death. Today, we still deal with the fallen world, but we are not alone. We have the Holy Spirit inside us, connecting us to the Father through the Son.

When Jesus said, "It is finished," on the cross, he was right, but he's giving us time to tell the world about him.

> **Who can you tell about Jesus while you still have time?**
>
> **What exactly would you like to tell them about Jesus?**

> *Lord, give me the words to express your love to others so they can be citizens of heaven too.*

300

Circumstantial Evidence

I have come into the world as a light, so that no one who believes in me should stay in darkness.

JOHN 12:46

According to Dr. Alexander Metherell, there was no medical way Jesus lived beyond the cross. William Lane Craig argued Jesus's body was definitely placed into Joseph of Arimathea's tomb. Multiple witnesses saw Jesus outside the tomb after his death.

It would be easy to settle the case with what we've learned so far, but there's one more form of evidence available to bolster our case for Christ: circumstantial evidence. Also known as "indirect evidence," circumstantial evidence is made up of clues which point to a logical conclusion.

If a powdered donut went missing at breakfast time and no one saw the thief in action, we still might be able to find out who took it using circumstantial evidence. Does anyone have powdered sugar on their hands or clothes? Is someone not eating as much as they usually do? Did anyone have time they couldn't account for? If the clues all point to the same person, there's a good chance this person is guilty of taking the powdered donut.

How does this relate to Jesus? We're going to look at some circumstantial evidence to support the existence and actions of Jesus Christ. If an event as extraordinary as the resurrection of Jesus had really occurred, history would be packed with indirect evidence to back it up.

> **When is one time you used clues to come to a logical conclusion about something?**
>
> **What kind of circumstantial evidence do you think exists for Jesus?**

Lord, help me follow the clues to their logical conclusion.

Brick by Brick

I write these things to you who believe in the name of the Son of God so that you may know that you have eternal life.

1 JOHN 5:13

As in the case of the missing powdered donut, circumstantial evidence is plural rather than singular. One clue doesn't make a strong case on its own.

To make a case using indirect evidence, it must be built like a solid wall, brick by brick.

To make the case for Christ, we'll turn to J.P. Moreland, a professor at the Talbot School of Theology with a background in history, philosophy, and science. Can J.P. show us any convincing circumstantial evidence to show Jesus rose from the grave? Things that are not in dispute by anybody? Actually, yes. J.P. will show us:

- The disciples died for their beliefs.
- Skeptics were convinced and converted.
- Key social structures going back centuries changed almost overnight.
- Communion and baptism took prominence as religious practices.
- The church emerged on the scene.

Why isn't one piece of circumstantial evidence enough to make a case?

What do you think the bonus reason will be?

As we evaluate each item on the list, we'll build our case brick by brick. When the circumstantial evidence is added to the rest of the evidence we've seen, the case for Christ becomes indisputable.

Jesus, you leave an impression everywhere you go. May others see your impression in my life.

302

Exhibit 1: The Disciples Died for Their Beliefs

*However, if you suffer as a Christian,
do not be ashamed, but praise God
that you bear that name.*

1 PETER 4:16

When Jesus was crucified, his followers were discouraged. They no longer had confidence Jesus had been sent by God because they believed anyone crucified was cursed by God. So they dispersed.

After a short time, the disciples regathered and committed themselves to spreading a very specific message—Jesus Christ is the Messiah who died on the cross, returned to life, and appeared to them alive.

"Why did they do this?" asks J.P. Moreland. "Because they were convinced beyond a shadow of a doubt that they had seen Jesus Christ alive from the dead. They spent the rest of their lives proclaiming this, without any payoff from a human point of view. They faced a life of hardship. They often went without food, slept exposed to the elements, were ridiculed, beaten, and imprisoned. And finally, most of them were executed in torturous ways.

"The apostles were willing to die for something they had seen with their own eyes and touched with their own hands," says J.P. "When you have eleven credible people with no ulterior motives, with nothing to gain and a lot to lose, who all agree they observed something with their own eyes—that's something extremely difficult to explain away.."

> **Would you risk being killed for something you didn't believe to be true?**
>
> **What is something you would be willing to die for?**

*Lord, the disciples believed in your resurrection.
Help me believe just as strongly.*

303

Exhibit 2A: The Conversion of James, Jesus's Brother

For even his own brothers did not believe in him.

JOHN 7:5

What is it about brothers in the Bible? In the Old Testament, Joseph told his older brothers about dreams in which they all worshiped him. (Not exactly a great way to make friends.) His brothers reacted by tossing Joseph in a pit, selling him into slavery, and telling their father that a wild animal killed Joseph.

Things aren't much better in the New Testament. Jesus's half-brothers James, Joses (more commonly Joseph), Simon, and Judas are mentioned in the Bible. But according to John 7:5, "Even his own brothers did not believe in him." How could this be? By growing up with Jesus, they would've seen he was different. But maybe it was too much for them to believe their brother was God's Son.

Wait! Didn't Jesus's brother James write a book in the Bible? Yes, he did. But he didn't believe Jesus's claims until after Jesus died. Once Jesus rose from the dead, he appeared before James to tell his brother the good news (1 Corinthians 15:7).

After seeing his older brother face-to-face, James became one of Jesus's most committed followers. He was a leader in the church at Jerusalem. Some experts say James' change of heart is one of the strongest arguments for the resurrection of Jesus Christ.

How would it feel to be one of Jesus's half-siblings?

What are some ways your relationships with siblings or friends could be better than Joseph's?

Lord, as I draw closer to you, help my relationships with others to be better.

Exhibit 2B: The Conversion of Saul to Paul

They only heard the report: "The man who formerly persecuted us is now preaching the faith he once tried to destroy."

GALATIANS 1:23

We've heard about Paul's conversion on the road to Damascus (Day 265), but just how significant was his decision to follow Christ?

"As a Pharisee," says Professor J.P. Moreland, "he hated anything that disrupted the traditions of the Jewish people. To him, this new counter-movement called Christianity would have been the height of disloyalty. In fact, he worked out his frustration by executing Christians when he had a chance." Remember the stoning of Stephen (Acts 7:58)?

"Suddenly," continues J.P., "he doesn't just ease off Christians but joins their movement! How did this happen? Well, everyone agrees Paul wrote Galatians, and he tells us himself in that letter what caused him to take a 180-degree turn and become the chief proponent of the Christian faith. By his own pen he says he saw the risen Christ and heard Christ appoint him to be one of his followers."

Galatians 1:11–12 says, "I want you to know, brothers and sisters, that the gospel I preached is not of human origin. I did not receive it from any man, nor was I taught it; rather, I received it by revelation from Jesus Christ."

Whether Jesus appeared to us in a vision or we heard about him in church, he is still calling people to himself.

What is your conversion story?

What is Jesus calling you to do for him?

Lord, give me the strength and wisdom to follow you like Paul did.

305

Exhibit 3: Drastic Changes to Judaism

> *But now, by dying to what once bound us,*
> *we have been released from the law so that*
> *we serve in the new way of the Spirit.*
>
> **ROMANS 7:6**

At the time of Jesus, the Jews had been persecuted for seven hundred years by the Babylonians, Assyrians, Persians, and now by the Greeks and the Romans. But we still see Jews today, while all those other empires are gone. Why?

Professor J.P. Moreland answers, "Because the things that made the Jews Jews—the social structures that gave them their national identity—were unbelievably important to them. They believed these institutions were entrusted to them by God."

Then Rabbi Jesus showed up, taught lower-middle class people for a few years, got in trouble with the authorities, and got crucified.

"But five weeks after he's crucified," says J.P., "over ten thousand Jews are following him and claiming that he is the initiator of a new religion. And get this: They're willing to give up or alter all five of the social institutions that have been taught since childhood have such importance both sociologically and theologically."

"Something *very* big was going on!" exclaims Moreland.

Indeed, when Jesus rose again, everything changed.

> Why would these Jews throw out hundreds of years' worth of religious instruction?
>
> How has serving Jesus changed your own practices?

> *Lord, change my actions and practices*
> *to reflect your priorities.*

Exhibit 4A: Communion

While every religion has certain rituals and practices, Christianity's sacraments—or outward signs of an inward faith—are different from the rest. Communion and baptism specifically celebrate the death and resurrection of Jesus Christ.

"Consider Communion for a moment," says Professor J.P. Moreland. "What's odd is that early followers of Jesus didn't get together to celebrate his teachings or his miracles. They came together regularly to have a celebration meal for one reason: to remember that Jesus had been publicly slaughtered in a grotesque and humiliating way."

It does seem a bit strange to celebrate the death of someone you love instead of focusing on the awesome things they did while alive.

"Here's why," answers J.P. "They realized that Jesus's death was a necessary step to a much greater victory. His murder wasn't the last word—the last word was that he had conquered death for all of us by rising from the dead. They celebrated his execution because they were convinced that they had seen him alive after being laid in the tomb."

If Jesus had remained in the tomb, his death would have been something to mourn. Because he rose again, it became something to be celebrated.

> **How would you explain Communion to someone who had never seen it before?**
>
> **How does the knowledge of Jesus's sacrifice inspire you to live better?**

Lord, help me sin less because I'm already counted as sinless in God's sight.

307

Exhibit 4B: Baptism

> *Or don't you know that all of us who*
> *were baptized into Christ Jesus*
> *were baptized into his death?*
>
> **ROMANS 6:3**

The practice of baptism wasn't new in Jesus's day. John was baptizing people before Jesus came along, after all. But Christianity gave it new meaning.

"The early church adopted a form of baptism from their Jewish upbringing, called proselyte baptism," says J.P. Moreland, "When Gentiles wanted to take upon themselves the laws of Moses, the Jews would baptize those Gentiles in the authority of the God of Israel. But in the New Testament, people were baptized in the name of God the Father, God the Son, and God the Holy Spirit—which meant they had elevated Jesus to the full status of God."

If communion focuses primarily on Jesus's sacrifice for our sins, baptism paints a fuller portrait of his death, burial, and resurrection.

"By going under the water," says J.P., "you're celebrating his death, and by being brought out of the water, you're celebrating the fact that Jesus was raised to newness of life."

Different churches handle baptism differently, but the focus of every baptism is on identifying with Jesus's death and resurrection. It is a way of showing other people our new life in Christ.

> **How does your church do baptism?**
>
> **Why is it important for other people to see outward signs of your faith?**

> *Lord, I am yours through and through. Help*
> *me live in the newness of life you give.*

308

Exhibit 5: The Emergence of the Church

> *Keep watch over yourselves and all the*
> *flock of which the Holy Spirit has made you*
> *overseers. Be shepherds of the church of*
> *God, which he bought with his own blood.*
>
> **ACTS 20:28**

When culture shifts in a certain direction, historians look for events to explain it.

"OK," says J.P. Moreland, "then let's think about the start of the Christian church. There's no question it began shortly after the death of Jesus and spread so rapidly that within a period of maybe twenty years it had even reached Caesar's palace in Rome. Not only that but this movement triumphed over a number of competing ideologies and eventually overwhelmed the entire Roman empire."

Today, two thousand years later, we're still gathering to celebrate the life, death, and resurrection of Jesus Christ. We're still applying what he taught and singing praises to him in churches around the world every week.

"Look," says J.P., "if someone wants to consider this circumstantial evidence and reach the verdict that Jesus did not rise from the dead—fair enough. But they've got to offer an alternative explanation that is plausible for all five of these facts.

"Remember, there's no doubt these facts are true; what's in question is how to explain them. And I've never seen a better explanation than the resurrection."

> **How would you account for the rise of the church if Jesus didn't rise from the grave?**
>
> **What is your favorite part about church today?**

Lord, I believe in the church and I believe in you!

Bonus Exhibit: How Jesus is Still Changing People

See, I am doing a new thing! Now it springs up;
do you not perceive it? I am making a way in
the wilderness and streams in the wasteland.

ISAIAH 43:19

With all the circumstantial evidence pointing toward the resurrection, the case for Christ seems conclusive. We would be in good company for believing the Bible's account of Jesus's life, death, and resurrection really happened.

Sir Lionel Luckhoo—the brilliant attorney whose 245 consecutive murder acquittals earned him a place in *The Guinness Book of World Records* as the world's most successful lawyer—once said, "I say unequivocally that the evidence for the resurrection of Jesus Christ is so overwhelming that it compels acceptance by proof which leaves absolutely no room for doubt."

But J.P. Moreland says there's another reason to believe.

"It's the ongoing encounter with the resurrected Christ that happens all over the world, in every culture, to people from all kinds of backgrounds and personalities—well educated and not, rich and poor, thinkers and feelers, men and women," he said. "They all will testify that more than any single thing in their lives, Jesus Christ has changed them."

Around the world, Jesus is still doing miracles and changing people—which is definitely not something a dead man can do.

How has Jesus changed your life?

Which example of circumstantial evidence do you find most compelling?

Jesus, you still change hearts and lives.
Change mine to be more like yours today.

Answered Prayers

And my God will meet all your needs according to the riches of his glory in Christ Jesus.

PHILIPPIANS 4:19

One of the ways we know God is still working and changing lives is when he answers the specific prayers of his children.

Ten-year-old Jocelyn just returned to Chile with her mother and sister. Her dad and older brothers were still in the United States. Jocelyn awoke to the sound of crashing and breaking, wondering why her sister was being so loud so early in the morning. In reality, the noise was from an earthquake.

Jocelyn's mom burst into her room, saying, "Come stand in the doorway with me." Her mom said Jesus would take care of them. Once the earth stopped moving, they weren't hurt, but the electricity and phones didn't work. When Jocelyn wrote to Focus on the Family's *Clubhouse* magazine about the 2010 event, she said her mom was worried because she wanted everybody to know they were safe.

They prayed God would make a way for them to communicate with their loved ones. Just then a man from their church knocked on the door. He let Jocelyn's mom go to his house to call her dad, brothers, grandma, and aunts. Right after she hung up, the electricity went off in his house.

God is active all over the world. He hears our prayers and gives us what we need. He knows the thing we need most is his love, but he delights in giving us what we ask for too!

> **How has God answered your specific prayers?**
>
> **What is something you'd like to pray specifically for right now?**

Lord, help me trust you to answer my prayers in the best way.

311

Not a Drive-Thru Restaurant

Do not be anxious about anything, but in every situation, by prayer and petition, with thanksgiving, present your requests to God.

PHILIPPIANS 4:6

Some Christians treat God like a drive-thru. We bow our heads in prayer and give our order. Then we expect God to answer as soon as we "pull forward." And if God doesn't do what we ask, we get angry or think he doesn't hear us.

God always hears our prayers, and he wants us to pray about everything. Philippians 4:6 says, "Do not be anxious about anything, but in every situation, by prayer and petition, with thanksgiving, present your requests to God."

But prayer is much more than asking for something. This acrostic might be helpful:

P = Praise. Acknowledge his amazing power. Praise him for being active and alive in our life.

R = Repent. Admit our failures. Ask for forgiveness.

A = Ask. Tell God our desires. Ask for his help.

Y = Yield. Let God know that we want to serve him. Tell him we want to follow his will for our life.

> **Are your prayers mostly requests?**
>
> **What will you praise God for today?**

Prayer isn't putting in an order. It's connecting with God, which is much more satisfying.

Lord, forgive me when I treat you like a drive-thru.

312

Heart, Soul, and Mind

Jesus replied: "'Love the Lord your God with all your heart and with all your soul and with all your mind.'"

MATTHEW 22:37

When Jesus was being quizzed by the religious professionals of his day, one of them asked him which commandment was the greatest. Matthew 22:37–40 captures his response:

"Jesus replied: "'Love the Lord your God with all your heart and with all your soul and with all your mind." This is the first and greatest commandment. And the second is like it: "Love your neighbor as yourself." All the Law and the Prophets hang on these two commandments.'"

To answer the experts in Jewish law, Jesus quoted from Deuteronomy 6:5, a passage faithful Jews would repeat twice daily. To love God with heart, soul, and mind was to love him with every aspect of their being.

If God has our heart, we won't try to love other things more than we love him. If God has our soul, we are securely held through life and death. If God has our mind, we will think about his truths and strive to see the world as he does.

When we love God with everything we are, we'll naturally love the things he does. We'll show his love to all the people around us. Our neighbors aren't just the people whose house is next to ours. Our neighbors include everyone, even the people who look and act nothing like us.

Do you love God with your heart, soul, and mind?

How can you show some love to your neighbor today?

Lord, help me love you most then show me how to love like you do.

313

Hair-Raising Reality

> *Are not five sparrows sold for two pennies? Yet not one of them is forgotten by God. Indeed, the very hairs of your head are all numbered. Don't be afraid, you are worth more than many sparrows.*
>
> **LUKE 12:6–7**

Our hair is pretty strong. Scientists say if we weaved all the hair on our head into a rope, it'd be strong enough to lift a giraffe! Blondes have the most hair, averaging 150,000 hairs per head. Redheads tend to have the least with 90,000. (However, blondes have the thinnest hair, so it's good they have more of it.)

A human hair grows about one centimeter per month. Nine out of ten hairs on our head are growing right now. The other hair is resting and will eventually fall out.

Those are some hair-raising facts. Here's something even more amazing: God knows the number of hairs on our heads. In Luke 12, Jesus explains to a crowd of thousands how God is actively involved in their lives. Jesus uses a sparrow, a very common bird, as an example to show the people how much God cares about his creation. If not one sparrow is forgotten, think about how much more concern God has for our lives (Luke 12:6–7).

God loves us wholeheartedly, right down to the last hair on our heads. He knows our needs, our wants, our dreams, and the things about ourselves we don't tell anyone else. And he *still* loves us!

How have you seen God actively working in your life recently?

How can you trust God with the things in your life which make you want to pull your hair out?

> *Lord, help me know you as intimately as you know me.*

314

What Our Mouths Say

Do not let any unwholesome talk come out of your mouths, but only what is helpful for building others up according to their needs, that it may benefit those who listen.

EPHESIANS 4:29

When the Holy Spirit lives inside us, our lives change. One of the ways this change becomes obvious is by the words we speak.

Luke 6:45 says, "A good man brings good things out of the good stored up in his heart, and an evil man brings evil things out of the evil stored up in his heart. For the mouth speaks what the heart is full of."

When our hearts are full of love for God, our mouths will be ready to share the gospel and build people up. When our hearts are full of selfishness, our words will come out twisted and mean.

James 3:9–10 says, "With the tongue we praise our Lord and Father, and with it we curse human beings, who have been made in God's likeness. Out of the same mouth come praise and cursing. My brothers and sisters, this should not be."

Ephesians 4:29 backs up the message: "Do not let any unwholesome talk come out of your mouths, but only what is helpful for building others up according to their needs, that it may benefit those who listen."

When we believe in Jesus's resurrection, we need to invite his new life into every area of our own, including the words we use.

Do you hear the Holy Spirit living in you when you speak?

How can you build someone else up today?

Lord, fill my heart with love so it comes out in my words.

315

The B-I-B-L-E

Heaven and earth will pass away, but my words will never pass away.

MARK 13:31

Here are some interesting facts about the Bible's history:

- The books of the Bible weren't divided into chapters until about 800 years ago.
- The chapters were divided into verses in 1551.
- Before 1440, only churches could afford a Bible.
- Most Bibles were written in Latin.
- John Wycliffe translated the Bible into English in 1382.

Today, nine out of ten families in the United States own a Bible, but how many "stand alone" on its power to help us live well? Second Timothy 3:16–17 says, "All Scripture is God-breathed and is useful for teaching, rebuking, correcting and training in righteousness, so that the servant of God may be thoroughly equipped for every good work."

Since we have a book containing God's inspired words for teaching, training, and equipping for good works, it's something that deserves our time. It really is the book for us.

How often do you read the Bible for yourself?

What is your favorite verse in the Bible?

God, may I love your word and stand alone on its power.

Dirty Cups

> *"Woe to you, teachers of the law and Pharisees, you hypocrites! You clean the outside of the cup and dish, but inside they are full of greed and self-indulgence."*
>
> **MATTHEW 23:25**

While Jesus spoke with kindness to nearly everybody he met, there was one group of people he spoke harshly to—the religious leaders.

In Matthew 23:25, Jesus said, "Woe to you, teachers of the law and Pharisees, you hypocrites! You clean the outside of the cup and dish, but inside they are full of greed and self-indulgence." Jesus went on to say it's imperative to clean the inside of the cup first, then the outside will be clean.

Jesus wasn't talking about "cups." He was talking about our hearts. Many of the religious leaders in Jesus's day were stuck being, well . . . religious. They did all the "right" things by praying in public, giving money to God's work, and memorizing the Scriptures. Many Pharisees took pride in following God's laws. But being a Christian isn't about following a list of dos and don'ts. It is about having a relationship with Jesus Christ.

Instead of outward actions, Jesus is more concerned about our inward beliefs and purity. Our actions should come from a sincere heart that wants to follow God—not from the desire of having other people look at us and say, "What a good person."

Are you motivated to do good so people see it or because you want to please God?

Is your cup ready to drink from or does it need a good washing?

> *Jesus, keep me from hypocrisy. May I be motivated by pleasing you alone.*

317

Delfin's Story: Part 1

Have mercy on me, LORD, for I am faint; heal
me, LORD, for my bones are in agony.

PSALM 6:2

There will be times in life when it feels like God is against us. That's how ten-year-old Delfin Cruz felt when a traumatic brain injury landed his up-and-coming hockey career in the penalty box. He prayed for months for God to heal him without improving.

Delfin thought, *How can there be a God if he can't make me better?*

After another disappointing doctor's visit, he told his mom, "I don't want to be on God's team anymore."

"If you are not on God's team," she said, "there is only one other team you can be on."

She explained how Satan can attack, bringing discouragement and causing people to turn away from God. She even got a little mad, telling Delfin how God might be using this struggle for a bigger purpose.

Delfin was at the end of his rope when something changed in his heart. It was as if Delfin saw Jesus clearly for the first time. God loved him. Jesus had everything under control. Delfin understood he could be mad at his circumstances, but he couldn't be mad at God and blame him for what happened. God had allowed the concussion for a reason, even if Delfin didn't understand it.

> **When have you felt like God wasn't listening?**
>
> **Why does it make sense to be on God's team, even when it feels like you are losing?**

Lord, may I stay committed when it feels
like things aren't going my way.

318

Delfin's Story: Part 2

*The LORD has heard my cry for mercy;
the LORD accepts my prayer.*

PSALM 6:9

In spite of the brain injury preventing him from doing the sport he loved, Delfin Cruz decided to stay on God's team. After making the decision, Delfin's struggles didn't immediately disappear. His ten-year-old brain was fighting to get better. And he was fighting to stick close to God.

Six months passed without any real improvement. Delfin started the new school year at a new school—a Christian school. Now every subject he studied was geared toward God. Delfin dove deep into theology and gained a better knowledge of God.

A year later, he still couldn't play hockey until a neurologist cleared him to compete in contact sports. The night before his appointment, he prayed, "God, if you don't want me to play sports again, then I won't. I will follow you."

The next day the doctor performed some balance and memory tests on Delfin. Then she shook his hand and said, "Go be a kid. Go play sports. Have fun."

Delfin jumped for joy. God had given him back the sport he loved. Delfin promised to stay humble and grateful. Instead of playing sports for personal glory, he'd play for God's glory.

How did God reward Delfin for his willingness to follow when he didn't know if he would be healed?

If God hadn't healed Delfin, should it have made a difference in Delfin's decision?

*Lord, help me follow you,
especially when it's hard.*

Whose Team Are We On?

*If anyone acknowledges that Jesus is the Son
of God, God lives in them and they in God.*

1 JOHN 4:15

Together, we have studied history, sifted archaeology, asked questions, and analyzed answers with open minds. The evidence we've found has built an airtight case.

Jesus fulfilled the Old Testament prophecies of a coming Savior. The Gospel writers had carefully recorded Jesus's life story. His teachings and actions were accurately copied and passed down through the centuries. Historians recognized the impact Jesus had on the world. Science showed how the people and places he touched were real.

Then there was Jesus himself. Not only did he claim to be God, but he proved it through his miracles, the love he showed by willingly dying on the cross, and the power he displayed by rising from the dead and appearing to hundreds of his followers.

How could we say there is no God and deny the truth about Jesus in the face of this overwhelming avalanche of facts?

Like Delfin Cruz, it is time for us to make a decision. Whose team are we on?

First John 4:15 says, "If anyone acknowledges that Jesus is the Son of God, God lives in them and they in God."

Will we acknowledge Jesus? Is God alive in us? And if so, what does that mean?

**How sure are you
Jesus really lived, died,
and rose again for you?**

**What questions do you still
have about Jesus?**

*Lord, help me remember everything I've
learned about you in my studies.*

Jesus of Many Names

That at the name of Jesus every knee should bow, in heaven and on earth and under the earth.

PHILIPPIANS 2:10

Most people have three names—a first, middle, and last. For many years, the title of longest personal name belonged to Adolph Blaine Charles David Earl Frederick Gerald Hubert Irvin John Kenneth Lloyd Martin Nero Oliver Paul Quincy Randolph Sherman Thomas Uncas Victor William Xerxes Yancy Zeus Wolfeschlegel-steinhausen-bergerdorff, Sr.; and that's with the shortened version of his last name!

Jesus was known by even more. He was called the Son of God, Holy One, King, Emmanuel, Prince of Peace, Messiah, Master, Lamb of God, Bread of Life, Rock, Deliverer. All of Jesus's names have special meanings and allow us to know more about his character.

We can even call Jesus our "friend." (see John 15:15)

But he's much more than that. Bible scholar Daniel B. Wallace warns, "We need to quit turning Jesus into our buddy. He's the sovereign Lord of the universe, and we need to understand that and respond accordingly."

Jesus is the most powerful name in the history of the world. Just the mention of his name causes people to bow in reverence (Philippians 2:10). We should show similar reverence as we serve Christ. He is, after all, the King of Kings.

Which of Jesus's names is your favorite?

How much power does Jesus's name have in your life?

Lord, you deserve respect. Thank you for counting me as your friend.

Implication #1: Divine Insights

"Why do you call me, 'Lord, Lord,' and do not do what I say?"

LUKE 6:46

After looking at the evidence, we can see historically, logically, and truthfully how Jesus is the Son of God, but what does this mean for us personally?

We'll look at eight implications—meaningful relationships logically connected by a set of facts—which should change our thinking and behavior in light of Jesus's reality.

Implication #1: If Jesus is the Son of God, his teachings are more than just good ideas from a wise teacher. They are divine insights on which we can confidently build our lives.

In Luke 6:46-49, Jesus says, "Why do you call me, 'Lord, Lord,' and do not do what I say? As for everyone who comes to me and hears my words and puts them into practice, I will show you what they are like. They are like a man building a house, who dug down deep and laid the foundation on rock. When a flood came, the torrent struck that house but could not shake it, because it was well built. But the one who hears my words and does not put them into practice is like a man who built a house on the ground without a foundation. The moment the torrent struck that house, it collapsed and its destruction was complete."

Why isn't listening to Jesus good enough?

How can you put his teaching into practice today?

Jesus, help me build on the foundation you lay.

322

Implication #2: Making Decisions

But love your enemies, do good to them, and lend to them without expecting to get anything back. Then your reward will be great, and you will be children of the Most High, because he is kind to the ungrateful and wicked.

LUKE 6:35

Implication #2: If Jesus sets the standard for right and wrong, we can now have a firm foundation for how we make choices and decisions rather than basing what we do on what feels good or fulfills our selfish desires.

Ethics, or the study of right and wrong, can be based on many different things. One popular belief says what is right for one person may be wrong for another, so we really can't judge people based on what they say or how they act. While we recognize God as the only one qualified to judge a person's motivations, Jesus has given us clear instructions on how to know if we ourselves are living ethically.

Jesus invited us to follow his example of self-sacrifice, of loving our enemies and our neighbors with both words and deeds.

Luke 6:35 says, "But love your enemies, do good to them, and lend to them without expecting to get anything back. Then your reward will be great, and you will be children of the Most High, because he is kind to the ungrateful and wicked."

What do you base right and wrong on?

How was Jesus the ultimate example of self-sacrifice?

We are most like Jesus when our decisions reflect his priorities. That doesn't leave room for selfishness or hate—only love.

Lord, make my motivations right. Help me honor you with my decisions.

323

Implication #3: Jesus is Alive & Available

Peace I leave with you; my peace I give you. I do not give to you as the world gives. Do not let your hearts be troubled and do not be afraid.

JOHN 14:27

Implication #3: If Jesus did rise from the dead, he's still alive today and available for us to encounter on a personal basis.

Jesus really died, but he didn't stay dead. He rose again, ate with his disciples, was seen by a lot of people, and ascended to heaven to be crowned King of Kings. Since he isn't still in the grave, he's available to interact with whenever we need him. We can talk to him through prayer and hear from him by reading the Bible.

Jesus said in Matthew 28:20, "And surely I am with you always, to the very end of the age."

Since he is with us right now, we can have his peace in our lives (John 14:27). He presents our prayers to his Father on our behalf (Romans 8:34). He invites us to be one filled with the fullness of God (Ephesians 3:17–19). His grace is sufficient for us, and when we are weak, he is strong (2 Corinthians 12:9).

Jesus isn't some impersonal god who we say a prayer to and leave at the altar. He goes with us and before us. He cares about what we care about. He fights on our behalf. He loves us unconditionally and wants us to love him in return, not in some distant future, but right now.

How should Jesus's presence change your behavior?

What do you hear Jesus telling you today?

Lord, you are always there for me.

324

Dig Deeper—The Location of Emmaus

According to Luke 24, Jesus appeared post-resurrection on the road to Emmaus and walked with two disciples, chatting about the recent events in Jerusalem. It wasn't until they sat down to eat in Emmaus when Jesus revealed his identity before disappearing.

Like Jesus at the end of the story, the city of Emmaus disappeared from the world map a long time ago. According to Luke 24:13, the distance from Jerusalem to Emmaus was about seven miles. For many years, people thought Emmaus was another name for Nicopolis, about forty miles too far.

But in 2019, archaeologists may have solved the riddle of Emmaus' location while researching another biblical site. Professor Israel Finkelstein, an archaeologist based at Tel Aviv University and Thomas Römer, a professor of biblical studies at the College de France, have discovered compelling evidence linking the New Testament town of Emmaus with the Old Testament town of Kiriath-Jearim.

Kiriath-Jearim is located on a hill west of Jerusalem around the right distance described for Emmaus. In the Old Testament, it temporarily hosted the Ark of the Covenant after it was recovered from the Philistine army (see 1 Samuel 7:1–2). Between the Old and New Testaments, the site was an important military outpost during the Maccabean revolt. Around 66 AD, the site was refortified by the Romans and hosted the 10th Roman Legion.

Both the book of Maccabees and the historian Josephus provided lists of the towns around Jerusalem which were fortified during the Maccabean revolt. Most of those cities have been identified, but neither list referred to Kiriath-Jearim, even though archaeology has proven it was one of the fortified sites. Instead, both mention another name: Emmaus.

As archaeologists look for additional proof of Emmaus' location, we can take comfort in knowing that to date, no archaeological discoveries have proven the Bible's historical record to be false.

Implication #4: Jesus Gives Eternal Life

"I am the Living One; I was dead, and now look, I am alive for ever and ever! And I hold the keys of death and Hades."

REVELATION 1:18

Implication #4: If Jesus conquered death, he can open the door of eternal life for us too.

In John 10:14–18, Jesus says, "I am the good shepherd; I know my sheep and my sheep know me—just as the Father knows me and I know the Father—and I lay down my life for the sheep. I have other sheep that are not of this sheep pen. I must bring them also. They too will listen to my voice, and there shall be one flock and one shepherd. The reason my Father loves me is that I lay down my life—only to take it up again. No one takes it from me, but I lay it down of my own accord. I have authority to lay it down and authority to take it up again. This command I received from my Father."

Jesus told the Pharisees he wasn't just willing to die for his followers, he *would* die, but he would come back to life and continue being the good shepherd. Not only that, but he would bring his sheep with him to eternal life.

Jesus isn't just the shepherd, he's the gate through which the sheep pass to get to eternal life. John 10:9 says, "I am the gate; whoever enters through me will be saved. They will come in and go out, and find pasture."

How can you recognize Jesus's voice better?

In what ways is Jesus the good shepherd?

Lord, thank you for leading me to eternal life.

Implication #5: Jesus Can Help Me

And God is able to bless you abundantly, so that in all things at all times, having all that you need, you will abound in every good work.

2 CORINTHIANS 9:8

Implication #5: If Jesus has divine power, he has the supernatural ability to guide me, help me, and transform me as I follow him.

If we decided to go on a road trip to somewhere new, there's a few things we'd want to have in the car: snacks (because all road trips require snacks, right?), a map or a GPS device, and fuel.

The Christian life is like a road trip toward Jesus. He gives us the food we need to keep up our strength. In John 6:51, Jesus says, "I am the living bread that came down from heaven. Whoever eats this bread will live forever. This bread is my flesh, which I will give for the life of the world."

He gave us the Bible as a map and the Holy Spirit to be our GPS. Jesus is the way (John 14:6), the Bible lights our path (Psalm 119:105), and when we get lost we can ask for the wisdom we need to get back on track (James 1:5).

Jesus provides the fuel we need to do God's will here on earth (2 Corinthians 9:8).

The difference between a road trip and the Christian life is that cars break down, while Christ transforms us into better followers over time. We are new creations becoming more like our Creator every day (Colossians 3:10).

How are you being transformed into the image of God?

What good works will you abound in today?

Jesus, give me direction and transform me as I go.

327

Implication #6: Jesus Understands & Comforts

> *Therefore, since Christ suffered in his body, arm yourselves also with the same attitude, because whoever suffers in the body is done with sin.*
>
> **1 PETER 4:1**

Implication #6: If Jesus personally knows the pain of loss and suffering, he can comfort and encourage me in the midst of the struggles and setbacks that I face.

Jesus was the prophesied Son of Man from the Old Testament who came to earth so his throne could be established, not just over Israel, but over the whole world. But he was also the prophesied man of suffering.

Isaiah 53:3–5 says, "He was despised and rejected by mankind, a man of suffering, and familiar with pain. Like one from whom people hide their faces he was despised, and we held him in low esteem. Surely he took up our pain and bore our suffering, yet we considered him punished by God, stricken by him, and afflicted. But he was pierced for our transgressions, he was crushed for our iniquities; the punishment that brought us peace was on him, and by his wounds we are healed."

Jesus understands our suffering perfectly, so he is able to comfort us perfectly. Through Jesus, we can see our suffering as a chance to become more like Christ.

Jesus has been where we are and he'll walk with us where we need to go.

How can suffering be a good thing?

How could you encourage someone else who is suffering?

Lord, you understand my sufferings. May my suffering make me more like you.

328

Implication #7: Jesus Loves Me & I Can Trust Him

> *And we know that in all things God works for the good of those who love him, who have been called according to his purpose.*
>
> **ROMANS 8:28**

Implication #7: If Jesus loves me as he says, he has my best interests at heart. That means I have nothing to lose and everything to gain by committing myself to him and his plans.

When we love someone, we want what's best for them. This doesn't always mean giving them what they want; it means giving them what they need. Jesus loves us.

Romans 5:8 says, "But God demonstrates his own love for us in this: While we were still sinners, Christ died for us." There's no way God wanted to put his Son through a torturous death, but he allowed it because he loves us. Jesus was willing to take our punishment for the same reason.

In fact, it isn't just that God loves us. The Bible says he *is* love. First John 4:16 says, "And so we know and rely on the love God has for us. God is love. Whoever lives in love lives in God, and God in them."

We trust the people who love us. Since God loves us completely, we can trust him completely. Romans 8:28 says, "And we know that in all things God works for the good of those who love him, who have been called according to his purpose."

In what area is God asking you to trust him?

Who are some other people you love and trust completely?

> *Lord, you know what is best for me. Help me trust your plans more than my own.*

Implication #8: Jesus Is Worthy of Worship

The Son is the radiance of God's glory and the exact representation of his being, sustaining all things by his powerful word. After he had provided purification for sins, he sat down at the right hand of the Majesty in heaven.

HEBREWS 1:3

Implication 8: If Jesus is God, then as my Creator he rightfully deserves my allegiance, obedience, and worship.

Jesus was more than a good teacher and healer. He was God in the flesh. Hebrews 1:3 says, "The Son is the radiance of God's glory and the exact representation of his being, sustaining all things by his powerful word. After he had provided purification for sins, he sat down at the right hand of the Majesty in heaven."

As God, Jesus deserves our worship, love, and obedience.

We can sing to him. Ephesians 5:19–20 says, "speaking to one another with psalms, hymns, and songs from the Spirit. Sing and make music from your heart to the Lord, always giving thanks to God the Father for everything, in the name of our Lord Jesus Christ."

We can dedicate our work to him. Colossians 3:17 says, "And whatever you do, whether in word or deed, do it all in the name of the Lord Jesus."

We can serve others. First Peter 4:11 says, "If anyone serves, they should do so with the strength God provides."

> **How will you praise Jesus today?**
>
> **What is one way you could serve someone in God's strength?**

Jesus, you are beyond praiseworthy!

330

The Leap of Faith

Now faith is confidence in what we hope for and assurance about what we do not see.

HEBREWS 11:1

Knowledge of who Jesus is and what he's done won't be enough. We need faith. Matthew 14:25–29 tells us this story about Peter:

"Shortly before dawn Jesus went out to them, walking on the lake. When the disciples saw him walking on the lake, they were terrified. 'It's a ghost,' they said, and cried out in fear.

"But Jesus immediately said to them: 'Take courage! It is I. Don't be afraid.'

"'Lord, if it's you,' Peter replied, 'tell me to come to you on the water.'

"'Come,' he said.

"Then Peter got down out of the boat, walked on the water and came toward Jesus."

If we really have faith in Jesus, we'll follow Peter's example and swing our legs out over the edge of the boat and step down onto the water.

Faith isn't wishful thinking; it is confidence in the person of Jesus Christ. Hebrews 11:1 says, "Now faith is confidence in what we hope for and assurance about what we do not see."

We don't need to know all the answers to trust in the one who does.

Are you ready to put your faith in Jesus?

What is a practical way you can step out on faith like Peter did?

Lord, take my hand and lead me out onto the water. I want to be with you.

331

Believe

For Christ also suffered once for sins, the righteous for the unrighteous, to bring you to God. He was put to death in the body but made alive in the Spirit.

1 PETER 3:18

Doubts may cause us to stumble, but with all the evidence for Jesus, it would take more faith to be an atheist—someone who doesn't believe in God—than to be a Christian. We know faith is involved, but how do we actually become a Christian?

As usual, the Bible is our guide! John 1:12 says, "Yet to all who received him, to those who believed in his name, he gave the right to become children of God." With mathematical precision, this verse spells out what it takes to enter into an ongoing relationship with God and be adopted into his family: believe + receive = become.

What do we believe? Jesus is the Son of God who died to rescue us and pay the penalty for every wrong we have committed.

Our sins separate us from God, who is holy and morally pure. We can't save ourselves with any amount of good deeds. We need the cross of Jesus to bridge the gulf between us and God.

Believing in Jesus's sacrifice and resurrection to save us from our sins is the first step toward becoming a Christian.

Do you believe Jesus died for your sins because he loves you?

How would you explain this step of Christian belief to a non-Christian?

Jesus, I believe you died for my sins to bring me to God.

332

Receive

> *For the wages of sin is death, but the gift of*
> *God is eternal life in Christ Jesus our Lord.*
> **ROMANS 6:23**

Christianity is unique. Non-Christian religions are based on a "do" plan. Their followers have to *do* something to earn their way into someone's favor. *Christianity* is based on the "done" plan. Jesus has *done* on the cross what we cannot do for ourselves: He has paid the death penalty we deserve for our wrongdoings so we can become children of God.

The Bible says Jesus offers forgiveness and eternal life as a free gift:

- "For the wages of sin is death, but the gift of God is eternal life in Christ Jesus our Lord" (Romans 6:23).
- "For it is by grace you have been saved, through faith—and this is not from yourselves, it is the gift of God—not by works, so that no one can boast" (Ephesians 2:8–9).
- "He saved us, not because of righteous things we had done, but because of his mercy" (Titus 3:5).

> **If you prayed this prayer, who can you tell about it?**
>
> **How can you show others you are a member of God's family?**

Dear Jesus, I know I've made lots of mistakes. I'm sorry for the selfish and bad things I've done. I believe you took the punishment for my wrongdoings so I could be forgiven. I know you died for me and rose from the dead. I receive your gift of forgiveness and eternal life. I trust you as Lord. Please help me to follow you from this day forward. Amen.

333

Become

> *Therefore, if anyone is in Christ, the new creation*
> *has come: The old has gone, the new is here!*
>
> **2 CORINTHIANS 5:17**

After taking the step of faith and giving our life to Jesus, according to John 1:12 we have become children of God. We have been adopted forever into his family through the historical, risen Jesus. The apostle Paul said, "Therefore, if anyone is in Christ, the new creation has come: The old has gone, the new is here!" (2 Corinthians 5:17).

Over time, as we follow Jesus's teachings, we will see him transform our priorities, our values, and our character.

Philippians 2:12–13 says, "Therefore, my dear friends, as you have always obeyed—not only in my presence, but now much more in my absence—continue to work out your salvation with fear and trembling, for it is God who works in you to will and to act in order to fulfill his good purpose."

We work out our salvation in the same way athletes work out to become better at their sport. It takes practice to give up what we want so Jesus can have his way with our lives. Over time, our spiritual muscles will grow.

It won't be comfortable because muscles grow by constant tearing and healing. The tearing happens when we submit to God; the healing happens when he works in us. As our muscles grow, we'll be able to do more for his glory, which we'll be rewarded for in heaven!

How can you strengthen your spiritual muscles today?

What does Matthew 16:27 say about heavenly rewards?

> *Lord, help me work out my salvation*
> *and grow my spiritual muscles.*

334

Faith Like a Child

> *And he said: "Truly I tell you, unless you change and become like little children, you will never enter the kingdom of heaven."*
>
> **MATTHEW 18:3**

Kids have it rough. Adults can do what they want (within reason), say what they want (usually), and go where they want (most of the time). Kids don't have those freedoms. They have to do what adults say, be respectful whether they feel like it or not, and go where the adults tell them to go.

It may not feel fair, but parents set up boundaries and guidelines for kids to keep us safe. Good parents are trustworthy. When they restrict our freedoms, we know it is for a good reason. And being a kid isn't all bad because we don't have to worry about grown-up stuff.

According to Jesus, being a kid is pretty awesome. In fact, before someone can come to faith in him, they have to become like a child.

Matthew 18:3–4 says, "And he said: 'Truly I tell you, unless you change and become like little children, you will never enter the kingdom of heaven. Therefore, whoever takes the lowly position of this child is the greatest in the kingdom of heaven.'"

To put our faith in Christ, we need to trust him like we would trust our parents. We have to know beyond doubt he has our best interest in mind, even when it doesn't feel like it. When we give Jesus our wholehearted faith, he says we are the greatest in God's kingdom.

How well do you trust Jesus?

How has he proven himself trustworthy to you in the past?

Lord, help me trust you more every day.

335

Decision Time

"I told you that you would die in your sins; if you do not believe that I am he, you will indeed die in your sins."

JOHN 8:24

At the beginning of this devotional, we looked at why some people have doubts about Jesus. Throughout the year, we've looked at evidence like a detective or journalist would, drawing our conclusions based on the weight of the facts. In the end the decision is ours and ours alone. Nobody else can choose what team we're on. It's up to us.

Perhaps after reading testimony from expert after expert, listening to argument after argument, seeing the answers to question after question, we've found the case for Christ to be conclusive. If so, let's follow the equation of faith—believe + receive = become—with enthusiasm!

On the other hand, maybe questions still linger. Fair enough. We should talk about our doubts with a parent, pastor, or family member who follows Jesus.

We should never approach our decision about Christ casually. There's a lot riding on our conclusion. As Jesus declared, "If you do not believe that I am he, you will indeed die in your sins" (John 8:24).

Those are tough words. But they're offered out of authentic love and concern. No decision we make in life is as important as what we decide about the case for Christ.

Why shouldn't you put off making a decision until later?

How important do you feel like this decision is to you?

Lord, don't let me put off my decision. Help me trust I'm making the right one.

Completely Clean

As far as the east is from the west, so far has
he removed our transgressions from us.

PSALM 103:12

We probably don't love to wash the dishes. But dishwashing soap can be fun. Here's an experiment:

Gather a shallow plate or bowl, a little bit of water, some black pepper, and a drop of dishwashing soap. Start by pouring some water into the bowl. Sprinkle pepper all over the surface of the water. Dip your finger into the water. What happens? Not much, right? Now dab some dishwashing liquid onto your finger. Put that finger into the bowl and voilà! The pepper rushes to the edge of the dish. Amazing, huh? While this fun experiment can teach something about the scientific principle of surface tension, it's also what Christ does to sin in our life.

Before we ask Jesus to be our Savior, our lives are peppered with sin. We can attempt to clean ourselves up by dipping our finger into acting nicer or speaking more kindly, but nothing truly works. Only Christ can clean up our lives.

Just like when soap hits the water, when Jesus enters our lives our sins are instantly pushed away. Psalm 103:12 says, "As far as the east is from the west, so far has he removed our transgressions from us." God doesn't just remove our sins to the edge of the dish. They're totally forgiven. Because of Jesus, we can stand before God as redeemed and holy.

If you are a believer, how does it feel to be completely clean?

Who is one person you could show this experiment to?

Lord, thank you for washing my
sins and making me clean.

337

Be Sharp

*As iron sharpens iron, so one
person sharpens another.*

PROVERBS 27:17

Let's imagine a race. Two people are given dull axes and told to chop down Christmas trees. One immediately starts chopping wildly. The other takes out a whetstone and sharpens the axe blade before taking a swing. Who would win?

It might be surprising, but a sharp axe beats brute strength every time. Similarly, exerting a lot of effort doesn't always lead to an effective life for Christ. Ecclesiastes 10:10 says, "If the axe is dull and its edge unsharpened, more strength is needed, but skill will bring success." So how can we sharpen our skills when it comes to living for Jesus?

One of the best ways is to find a friend who shares our beliefs and ask to be accountability partners. We could meet regularly to find out what God is teaching us, pray for each other, and talk about problems and successes. If we can't think of a good accountability partner, we could ask our mom, dad, or youth pastor. Proverbs 27:17 tells us it's important to have somebody in our lives to make us sharper.

Our own individual efforts can only get us so far. Instead of working harder, we need to work smarter and find a friend who can help us grow closer to Christ.

Who do you know who loves God and wants to grow in their relationship with Jesus?

How could you challenge each other to be closer to God?

*Lord, help me find someone in my life
who can keep me close to you.*

The Battle Doesn't Stop

*"Do not suppose that I have come to
bring peace to the earth. I did not come
to bring peace, but a sword."*

MATTHEW 10:34

It would be comforting to think salvation came with the promise of an easy life, but it didn't. Far from it. Jesus himself recognized the effect he had on the world in Matthew 10:34.

Once we've made clear whose side we're on in the spiritual battle, we should expect attacks. First Peter 5:8 warns, "Be alert and of sober mind. Your enemy the devil prowls around like a roaring lion looking for someone to devour."

Fortunately, we aren't defenseless. Second Corinthians 10:3–4 says, "For though we live in the world, we do not wage war as the world does. The weapons we fight with are not the weapons of the world. On the contrary, they have divine power to demolish strongholds."

What are our weapons? According to Hebrews 4:12, we are armed with the Bible, our two-edged sword. One edge cuts toward the enemy, revealing lies intended to harm us. The other edge cuts toward us, revealing the areas of our lives which need God's attention.

How can God's armor help you in the spiritual battle? (Check Day 76 for a reminder.)

What areas of your life can the Bible help you cut out?

The battle doesn't stop when we become Christians, but the victory is assured. "But thanks be to God! He gives us the victory through our Lord Jesus Christ" (1 Corinthians 15:57).

*Lord, give me strength in the
battle against the enemy.*

Mustard Seed Faith

> *He replied, "Because you have so little faith. Truly I tell you, if you have faith as small as a mustard seed, you can say to this mountain, 'Move from here to there,' and it will move. Nothing will be impossible for you."*
>
> **MATTHEW 17:20**

The Bible tells the story of a father who desperately wanted his son to be healed. Jesus's disciples tried and failed. When the Lord heard this, he asked for the boy to be brought to him. The father came to Jesus and pleaded, "If you can do anything, take pity on us and help us."

"If you can?" Jesus replied. "Everything is possible for one who believes."

The boy's father exclaimed, "I do believe; help me overcome my unbelief!"

Immediately, Jesus healed the boy.

Now, was the boy healed because of the strength of the father's faith? No. The father had little faith. He wanted to believe, but he had been disappointed so many times he had difficulty believing. The father simply had faith in the right person— Jesus. The ultimate truth is this: faith is only as good as the one in whom it's invested.

Jesus said, "If you have faith as small as a mustard seed, you can say to this mountain, 'Move from here to there,' and it will move. Nothing will be impossible for you" (Matthew 17:20). Through God's power, our little faith can accomplish big things.

Do you have the faith to move mountains?

If God doesn't do what you want, why can you still have faith in him?

> *Lord, my faith may not be big, but you are. Help me believe. Take away my unbelief.*

Christian Morality

And God is faithful; he will not let you be tempted beyond what you can bear. But when you are tempted, he will also provide a way out so that you can endure it.

1 CORINTHIANS 10:13

Morality is the ability to tell right from wrong. Because of sin, people have a tendency toward immorality.

King David recognized it in Psalm 51:5: "Surely I was sinful at birth, sinful from the time my mother conceived me."

Paul said it about everyone in Romans 3:23: "For all have sinned and fall short of the glory of God." And specifically about himself in Romans 7:19: "For I do not do the good I want to do, but the evil I do not want to do—this I keep on doing."

So how do we choose to do what is right? Does the Bible say people can't be moral at all?

People *can* choose to be good and do good apart from God's help, but no one besides Jesus has ever chosen good every time. Fortunately, God provides help.

First Corinthians 10:13 says, "... And God is faithful; he will not let you be tempted beyond what you can bear. But when you are tempted, he will also provide a way out so that you can endure it."

> **Would you consider yourself moral or immoral?**
>
> **Why should we want to be moral people?**

We'll still mess up, but that's why God gives forgiveness when we need it.

Lord, help me reflect your love and goodness to the world around me.

341

Giving Generously

You will be enriched in every way so that you can be generous on every occasion, and through us your generosity will result in thanksgiving to God.

2 CORINTHIANS 9:11

Generosity is one identifying mark of a moral person. Its opposite—selfishness—is so common it is often excused, or is even praised as wisdom by people who want to justify their own selfish behavior.

God has given different people different gifts. For example, some people have a lot of money and others do not. Why the difference?

Second Corinthians 9:11 says, "You will be enriched in every way so that you can be generous on every occasion, and through us your generosity will result in thanksgiving to God." When we are generous with the gifts and abilities God has given us, others will recognize the love of God through us.

First John 3:17 shows the flip side: "If anyone has material possessions and sees a brother or sister in need but has no pity on them, how can the love of God be in that person?"

If we want other people to experience God's love, we can use the gifts God has given to bless others. In fact, if we don't, we're sinning and showing a lack of God's love. We may not always be able to give money, but we can always give our time and attention to someone else.

What gifts has God given you which you might be able to give someone else?

How will you show God's love to someone today?

Lord, keep me from being selfish with the blessings you meant for me to give freely to others.

God-Vision Goggles

What we have received is not the spirit of the world, but the Spirit who is from God, so that we may understand what God has freely given us.

1 CORINTHIANS 2:12

With their big eyes and huge pupils, owls have amazing night vision. If we wanted to see as well as an owl in the dark, we'd need night-vision goggles. The technology has changed over the years, but basically the goggles gather and amplify any available light.

Everybody wears goggles. They might not be night-vision goggles, but we all see the world through a particular "lens." When we asked Christ into our life, we became a new creation (2 Corinthians 5:17). At that moment, it's like we put on "God-vision goggles." Instead of looking at purple mountains' majesty, we now see God's majesty in magnificent mountains.

As a Christian, we naturally view life through a Christian worldview. Scientists and scholars who don't believe in God see things differently. When people choose to assume there is no God, they miss seeing God's handiwork in the world around them.

When we read articles and books written by various experts, we should question the kind of goggles these writers wear. As we read and learn more about the Bible, we can test and approve what is right or wrong according to God's Word.

How can you make sure your goggles are seeing the light in the darkness?

How would difficult times look using God-vision goggles?

Jesus, help me see things the way they really are by understanding them with the Holy Spirit's help.

343

Honor Your Parents

> *"Honor your father and your mother,*
> *so that you may live long in the land*
> *the LORD your God is giving you."*
>
> **EXODUS 20:12**

Included in the Ten Commandments given to Moses by God on Mount Sinai, sandwiched between keeping the Sabbath holy and not murdering people is the following commandment: "Honor your father and your mother, so that you may live long in the land the LORD your God is giving you" (Exodus 20:12).

Is honoring your parents really as serious as not murdering people?

How we treat our earthly parents (and authority figures in general) is a reflection on how we feel about God's authority. Plus, the call for us to honor our parents comes with a promise. If the nation of Israel followed this commandment, they would live long in the promised land.

Children who honor their parents are naturally part of successful families, and they grow up to be people who honor God. Also, if children didn't honor their parents, the chances of them reaching adulthood at all went down significantly. (Check out Exodus 21:17.)

The other detail of this commandment is it applies to everyone, not just kids. Grown-ups must also honor their parents and authority figures, because everyone made in the image of God is worthy of our respect (and that's *everyone*).

What does Proverbs 30:17 say about rolling your eyes at your parents?

How could you honor your parents today?

> *Lord, help me give respect to my parents,*
> *even when I don't feel like it.*

344

Spending Time with Other Christians

And let us consider how we may spur one another on toward love and good deeds, not giving up meeting together, as some are in the habit of doing . . .

HEBREWS 10:24–25

Four out of five American adults call themselves Christians, but only about one out of five attends church on Sundays.

Growing as a Christian means acting more like Jesus, which takes time, understanding, and encouragement, which are some of the purposes of a church. Our journey to become more like Jesus goes better when we learn from a godly pastor and build relationships with other Christians.

Numerous times in God's Word we're instructed to gather with other believers. If we need another reason to attend church, we should remember how Jesus went to worship services. Luke 4:16 tells us, "[Jesus] went to Nazareth, where he had been brought up, and on the Sabbath day he went into the synagogue, as was his custom."

Notice the words "as was his custom." It wasn't like he had to go. Jesus understood everything about God and his Word. Still, he made a point to go to church. We shouldn't simply do it out of obedience. We ought to attend church with anticipation, expecting it to change us to be more like Jesus.

How can you prepare your heart to get the most out of church?

Why are relationships with other Christians valuable?

Lord, may I love spending time in your church with other people who love you.

What Are We Training For?

For physical training is of some value, but godliness has value for all things, holding promise for both the present life and the life to come.

1 TIMOTHY 4:8

When the Covid-19 pandemic went global in 2020, most of the world's sporting events were cancelled or postponed. Almost overnight, the athletes who spent their lives training for these specific events had nothing to do.

This isn't to say sports aren't important. God wants us to take care of our bodies and sports can be a great way to do it. First Corinthians 6:19–20 says, "Do you not know that your bodies are temples of the Holy Spirit, who is in you, whom you have received from God? You are not your own; you were bought at a price. Therefore honor God with your bodies."

But the Bible also makes clear that while sports can be part of a healthy lifestyle, they are no replacement for exercising our spiritual muscles through prayer, reading God's Word, living out his love for others, and spreading the gospel.

First Timothy 4:8 says, "For physical training is of some value, but godliness has value for all things, holding promise for both the present life and the life to come."

If we have strong bodies and win games while on earth, our achievements are temporary. If we train our spiritual lives for godliness, we'll be winning others to Christ while on earth and gaining rewards in heaven!

What does your spiritual workout routine look like?

How could you combine physical and spiritual exercises?

Lord, make my body strong, but make my faith stronger.

346

See a Need, Fill a Need

"The King will reply, 'Truly I tell you, whatever you did for one of the least of these brothers and sisters of mine, you did for me.'"

MATTHEW 25:40

Piper Hayward didn't go to Africa thinking about clean drinking water. She was going to help orphans. She even brought a trunk full of school supplies. But once Piper got to the Maasai village, she was surprised to find girls about her age who were responsible for providing water. They had no time for school, because water was scarce and took a long time to carry.

Piper enjoyed helping the orphans, but when she returned home, she couldn't get the "water girls" out of her mind. She set up a coin drive in her school. Soon Piper's friends and family members began collecting coins in Illinois, Texas, and other states. In less than a year, enough money had been raised to drill a 600-foot well and install a pump and generator. Now the village would enjoy clean water and everybody could have a chance to go to school.

When Piper saw a need, she worked to fix it. Anytime we help someone in need, we honor God and further his kingdom. In Matthew 25, Jesus tells a parable in which the king commends his true followers for helping the hungry, sick, and imprisoned, saying, "Whatever you did for one of the least of these brothers and sisters of mine, you did for me."

What needs do you see around you?

How could you fill them? (Don't just think about this. Get out there and do it!)

Lord, help me see the needs around me and work hard to fill them.

On Being Young

Don't let anyone look down on you because you are young, but set an example for the believers in speech, in conduct, in love, in faith and in purity.

1 TIMOTHY 4:12

It's easy to be overlooked when we're young. Adults have their own problems to deal with and not all of them are good at seeing our problems as worth their time. Jesus was an adult who understood the importance of children. In Matthew 18:10, he told his disciples, "See that you do not despise one of these little ones. For I tell you that their angels in heaven always see the face of my Father in heaven."

Kids are important. We have the same value before God as everyone else. When dealing with an infinite God, the difference between elderly people and kids is infinitesimally small. He cares more about how we reflect his attributes than how many years we've been around.

The apostle Paul agreed in his letter to a young pastor named Timothy. While people sometimes treat others differently based on their age, Paul told Timothy not to worry about his youth. First Timothy 4:12 says, "Don't let anyone look down on you because you are young, but set an example for the believers in speech, in conduct, in love, in faith and in purity."

Godliness doesn't have an age requirement. We can be an example of God's love no matter how old we are.

What aspect of God's holiness will you focus on today?

How could the words you use show others you are a Christian?

Lord, help me be bold in my love for you, no matter what others think.

The Secret to Giving

Each of you should give what you have decided in your heart to give, not reluctantly or under compulsion, for God loves a cheerful giver.

2 CORINTHIANS 9:7

Larry Stewart—Kansas City's Secret Santa—knew how to give. But for twenty-five years, nobody knew his name.

Over the course of his life, Stewart gave away over $1 million. He'd go to a thrift store, the bus station, a laundromat, or a fast-food restaurant and look for somebody in need. Then he'd go over, give some money (sometimes $1,000 at a time), and say, "God bless you."

During a 2006 interview with *USA Today*, Stewart said before he began giving away his millions, "Part of my daily prayer was, 'Lord, lift me up and let me be a better witness to you and for you and somehow reach more people.' I had no idea this is what he had in mind."

Part of being a follower of Jesus is giving. God has given us so much. We reflect God's giving nature when we give to others. Plus, when we freely give, it shows we recognize God as Lord over everything we have.

We don't have to give away millions like Larry Stewart to please God. The amount isn't as important as how we give our gift. Second Corinthians 9:7 says, "Each of you should give what you have decided in your heart to give, not reluctantly or under compulsion, for God loves a cheerful giver."

What things could you give to bless someone else?

How could you prepare yourself to give cheerfully?

God, give me a generous heart that cheerfully gives.

Simply Trustworthy

*All you need to say is simply 'Yes' or 'No';
anything beyond this comes from the evil one.*

MATTHEW 5:37

The phrases, "I'm telling the truth," and, "No, really, I swear," are kind of funny. When we hear them, we should be able to trust the person talking, but these phrases usually have the opposite effect. Often, the people most likely to swear they are trustworthy are the people who have a history of lying.

Being trustworthy is beyond important. It should be one of the identifying characteristics for all Christians. Since the message of Jesus's love is already pretty unbelievable, he knew his followers would have to be known as trustworthy people so the incredible things they say would be believed.

Matthew 5:37 says, "All you need to say is simply 'Yes' or 'No'; anything beyond this comes from the evil one."

Maybe lying has been a problem for us though. If we're new to this whole Christianity thing, that's okay. Habits don't always change overnight, but we *are* new creations thanks to Jesus. Colossians 3:9–10 says, "Do not lie to each other, since you have taken off your old self with its practices and have put on the new self, which is being renewed in knowledge in the image of its Creator."

Trustworthiness starts with us trusting in Jesus's power to heal our sins, then letting them go.

How trustworthy are you?

What are some of the benefits of being trustworthy?

*Lord, help me be honest so others will
believe me when I talk about you.*

Keep Going and Going and Going

*Rejoice always, pray continually, give
thanks in all circumstances; for this is
God's will for you in Christ Jesus.*

1 THESSALONIANS 5:16–18

The ocean continually moves. What other things keep going and going and going?

- The sun always shines.
- The earth continually rotates and revolves.
- Time constantly moves forward.

God created many things to function constantly. In 1 Thessalonians 5:16–18, the apostle Paul tells us three things we should always be doing: rejoicing, praying, and giving thanks.

Living out this command may seem pretty impractical. But as followers of Jesus, we should look at these things like breathing.

Praying continually means holding an open conversation with God throughout the day. Rejoicing always recognizes how our current situation (no matter how rough it feels right now) is temporary, and our future with God will be joyful forever. No matter what's going on in life, we can trust that God's love for us will keep going, and going, and going.

What are some things you can pray about today?

What are some things you can praise God for today?

*Lord, may I pray, praise, and
rejoice without stopping.*

351

Shine

In the same way, let your light shine before others, that they may see your good deeds and glorify your Father in heaven.

MATTHEW 5:16

Our eyes are amazing. They work like little cameras in our heads. As light enters the lens, tiny muscles in the iris decide how much or how little to let in. The light passes through a protective sheet called the cornea, then it's focused to point on the retina at the back of the eye where little receptors called rods and cones send electrical signals to the brain through the optic nerve. Our brain then interprets the signals into an image we can understand.

Our ability to see depends on light. And our ability to see God depends on his light. First John 1:5 says, "This is the message we have heard from him and declare to you: God is light; in him there is no darkness at all."

In situations of pitch darkness, our eyes don't know what to do and will often send false messages to our brain. We end up seeing what we think we should see.

This world is a dark place, and people need God's light in order to see what's really here. That's where we come in. Jesus said in Matthew 5:16 it is our job to let God's light shine before others. How? Through the way we live, the things we do, and the power of his love working through us!

> **How can you shine today?**
>
> **How can you make sure the light others see is from God and not from you?**

Jesus, help me do good deeds, but help others see you because of them.

352

More Than Meets the Eye

Do not conform to the pattern of this world, but be transformed by the renewing of your mind. Then you will be able to test and approve what God's will is—his good, pleasing and perfect will.

ROMANS 12:2

In 1984, America was introduced to *The Transformers*, an animated television series based on a line of toys imported from Japan.

Ironically, each *Transformers* toy was made by being cast from plastic mold. Liquid plastic is poured into a specially designed container which cools and conforms to the desired shape. These parts are then assembled into the toy, which can transform from one object into another.

The Bible warns Christians against conforming. The world wants people to fit into the mold of sin and selfishness, but God wants us to be transformed into people who live for him.

Romans 12:2 says, "Do not conform to the pattern of this world, but be transformed by the renewing of your mind. Then you will be able to test and approve what God's will is—his good, pleasing and perfect will."

Our transformation happens when we give our mind to God, thinking about good things (see Philippians 4:8) and memorizing scripture. Like *The Transformers*, there's "more than meets the eye" to Christians, and only when our minds are transformed by God will we be battle-ready against the spiritual forces of this world.

> **If you could transform into an object, what would it be?**
>
> **What things will you think about to renew your mind?**

Lord, transform me into your likeness so I'm ready to do your will.

353

Conflict Resolution

"But if they will not listen, take one or two others along, so that 'every matter may be established by the testimony of two or three witnesses.'"

MATTHEW 18:16

Sin happens. It shouldn't, but because we live in a fallen world it does. Conflicts happen because of sin.

When we have disagreements or conflicts with our friends or family, it can mess up our relationship with God. Jesus doesn't want anything to come between us and God, which is why he said in Matthew 5:23–24, "Therefore, if you are offering your gift at the altar and there remember that your brother or sister has something against you, leave your gift there in front of the altar. First go and be reconciled to them; then come and offer your gift."

Matthew 18:15–16 says to address people one-on-one before bringing others into the conflict. The fewer people who get involved, the quicker resolution can happen.

By going directly to the person we're struggling with, we show them respect, which can help in healing hurts. It also gives them a chance to tell us their side of the conflict. By listening and showing respect, our human relationships can heal so our heavenly relationship can thrive.

How would you feel if someone talked about you instead of to you?

How does listening and respect lead to forgiveness?

Lord, heal my human relationships so I'm not distracted from our relationship.

Of Mistakes and Dog Vomit

As a dog returns to its vomit, so
fools repeat their folly.

PROVERBS 26:11

Books and dogs are both great. It's hard to feel lonely when curled up with either one. But while books won't greet us at the door wagging their tails, they'll also never throw up something they ate only to eat it again. Let's face it, sometimes dogs are gross.

Unfortunately, we aren't much better than dogs.

Proverbs 26:11 says, "As a dog returns to its vomit, so fools repeat their folly."

Mistakes are only accidental the first time. Each mistake we make comes with an opportunity to learn from it. For this reason, when we repeat a mistake, we are actually making a worse mistake than the original one.

The best way to avoid repeating mistakes is repentance. Repentance isn't just feeling bad for the mistakes we make. It is actively changing our behavior in order to go somewhere new.

Second Corinthians 7:10 says, "Godly sorrow brings repentance that leads to salvation and leaves no regret, but worldly sorrow brings death."

And when we repent and learn from our mistakes, there will be rejoicing in heaven. It's all there in God's book, which really is man's best friend.

> **What are some mistakes you find yourself repeating?**
>
> **How can you change your behaviors to get different results?**

Lord, keep me from making the
same mistake twice.

Arguing Online (or Anywhere Else)

*Don't have anything to do with foolish
and stupid arguments, because you
know they produce quarrels.*

2 TIMOTHY 2:23

The creators of social media sites like Facebook and Twitter didn't create foolish arguments, but they did make them easier to have. From our comfortable position behind the screen, we can say just about anything to just about anyone. It may feel like we're exercising our free speech when we blast our opinions onto the internet or enter into arguments just for the fun of it, but the Bible tells us there's a better way.

Second Timothy 2:23–26 says, "Don't have anything to do with foolish and stupid arguments, because you know they produce quarrels. And the Lord's servant must not be quarrelsome but must be kind to everyone, able to teach, not resentful. Opponents must be gently instructed, in the hope that God will grant them repentance leading them to a knowledge of the truth, and that they will come to their senses and escape from the trap of the devil, who has taken them captive to do his will."

What does it mean to gently instruct others? It means approaching people who hold different opinions with kindness not judgment, with knowledge not ignorance, and with humility not pride. Lastly, it means trusting God with the outcome instead of insisting on someone adopting our way of thinking.

Do you get into arguments which have nothing to do with you?

How can you increase your kindness, knowledge, and humility?

Lord, help me avoid foolish arguments.

356

Defending the Oppressed

Learn to do right; seek justice. Defend the oppressed. Take up the cause of the fatherless; plead the case of the widow.

ISAIAH 1:17

In Isaiah 1:17, we get to see the things God thinks are important: "Learn to do right; seek justice. Defend the oppressed. Take up the cause of the fatherless; plead the case of the widow."

When Jesus walked the earth, his ministry echoed these priorities. He healed the sick, helped widows, and encouraged his followers to care for the people in society no one seemed to care about. Then, he died so everyone could be made right with God.

The Bible is very clear when it comes to showing favoritism—or unfairly treating one person or group better than others. The Bible doesn't tell us to treat all people equally. It tells us to give special attention to those in society who have been cast aside by the wealthy and powerful.

Modern examples of doing right and seeking justice could include issues of racial privilege or rich vs. poor people. Before we say we're too young to do something about these things, we should realize God is the one in control of all things and we're never too young to pray. Then, we can look for opportunities to give our voice to those around us who can't speak for themselves.

Who do you feel God calling you to stand up for?

How could you pray for that person or group?

Lord, give me a heart for justice and help me show others the mercy you've shown me.

357

Be Still

*"The LORD will fight for you; you
need only to be still."*

EXODUS 14:14

The Israelites knew God was real when they followed Moses out of Egypt. Ten plagues had confirmed his power. The pillars of cloud and fire which led them by day and by night confirmed his presence. But as the Israelites came up to the Red Sea with the Pharaoh's chariots racing behind them, they wondered if God was good.

There will be times in our lives when we know God is real and that he's with us, but we may question his wisdom in allowing bad things to happen. Our fears can bring out the worst in us and cause us to doubt things which should never be doubted.

As Moses stood with the Red Sea in front of him, Pharaoh's chariots behind, and the people of Israel freaking out all around him, God told him, "I will fight for you. You need only to be still" (Exodus 14:14). And God came through. The Red Sea parted. Pharaoh's army was washed away. The Israelites were saved.

God won't always part the waters when we think he should, but he asks us to trust him anyway. God's goodness doesn't depend on our circumstances. He is good because he is God and we can be still because he loves us and always knows what is best.

**Have you ever
questioned God's
goodness?**

**How can you be still
when life gets crazy?**

*Lord, may I be still when I feel like freaking
out because I know you love me.*

358

Fast Track to Prayer

So we fasted and petitioned our God about this, and he answered our prayer.

EZRA 8:23

The word "breakfast" is a compound word made up of "break" and "fast." The "fast" which we break when we eat in the morning has nothing to do with the speed at which we eat, but the fact we're eating at all.

Fasting is when we stop doing something in order to focus our attention on something else. Usually, fasting is associated with food. So, when someone fasts, they stop eating and use the time they would have spent eating or preparing food to pray. And every time their stomach growl, it is a reminder to pray.

While fasting can be a good way to get our minds focused on prayer, it isn't a magic formula to make God answer our prayers in the way we want. God will do what God will do. He loves when we take prayer seriously, but we can't make him do something he doesn't want to do.

If there's something serious going on in our lives though, fasting can be a great way to make God's involvement a priority. We don't have to give up meals though. We can take a break from screen time, a favorite hobby, or maybe just dessert (we shouldn't refuse to eat our veggies and call it fasting, though).

God will always hear our prayers, and fasting is the fast-track to remembering to pray.

What is something you could give up to help you remember to pray?

How would fasting help you focus your attention?

Lord, make my prayer life more important to me than food.

The Grasp Reflex

> *I know what it is to be in need, and I know what it is to have plenty. I have learned the secret of being content in any and every situation, whether well fed or hungry, whether living in plenty or in want.*

PHILIPPIANS 4:12

When it comes to making wish lists for Christmases or birthdays, most of us have no problem filling up a page with stuff we want. Wanting more is something we're born with.

Babies have something called a "grasp reflex." When a baby's palm is lightly touched, the baby grabs hard onto whatever is in their hand. This reaction helps doctors see that the baby's nervous system is functioning normally.

Unfortunately, as some people grow, so do their grasp reflexes. The problem is this: when our hands are full of the world's stuff, we can't accept what God wants to give us.

The apostle Paul knew how to live with open hands. In Philippians 4:12, he says, "I know what it is to be in need, and I know what it is to have plenty. I have learned the secret of being content in any and every situation, whether well fed or hungry, whether living in plenty or in want."

How can you open your hands to what God has for you?

What are some things you might want to stop grasping?

What is the secret? Paul says in Philippians 4:13, "I can do all this through him who gives me strength." God will supply our needs and give us strength when we keep our hands open to him and free of the world's stuff.

> *Lord, open my hands and heart to you.*

Respecting Elders, Respecting God

Stand up in the presence of the aged,
show respect for the elderly and
revere your God. I am the LORD.

LEVITICUS 19:32

Elderly people are awesome: Grandparents who bake warm cookies on cold days. Older people from church who always have a kind word or a funny joke. The elderly neighbor who waves as we walk by their house.

With other older people though, it can be difficult to see their awesomeness. Some senior citizens smell funny or can't remember our names. Others insist on giving us food we can't imagine *anyone* enjoying. But these things don't make anyone any less awesome in God's eyes.

Leviticus 19:32 says, "Stand up in the presence of the aged, show respect for the elderly and revere your God. I am the LORD."

Showing respect isn't something we reserve just for the elderly folks. We are supposed to show respect to everyone. Why? Because when we give respect, we are showing respect to God too.

Not only is our respect for the elderly good for them, it is good for us too. When we respectfully listen to what older generations have to say, we can learn a lot! Job 12:12 says, "Is not wisdom found among the aged? Does not long life bring understanding?"

How can you show respect to an elderly person you know?

What is one question you think they could answer for you?

Next time we're tempted to brush someone off because they are elderly, we need to remember these verses and show respect.

God, help me show respect to the elderly.

361

The Riddle of Time

*Teach us to number our days, that
we may gain a heart of wisdom.*

PSALM 90:12

What comes once in a minute, twice in a moment, but never in a thousand years? The letter M. For many people, time management can be a riddle too. Since time is always passing, it may feel like an unlimited resource, but the Bible tells us there is wisdom in learning how to number our days (Psalm 90:12).

Salvation means we'll have an eternity to spend with God, but we won't live on earth forever. Our time here is limited. Every limited resource has a value. Wisdom is knowing the value of every minute of our day. That's why it is possible to waste time, because we're never going to get a minute back if we've spent it unwisely.

Ephesians 5:15-17 says, "Be very careful, then, how you live—not as unwise but as wise, making the most of every opportunity, because the days are evil. Therefore do not be foolish, but understand what the Lord's will is."

God's will for his children is to spread the gospel, to love others without expectations, and do the good works he's prepared for us in advance (Ephesians 2:10). And since we only have a little while to do them before we run out of time, it's important to get started right away!

How could you track the time you use throughout the day?

Would you say you use your time on things that matter?

*Jesus, help me value my time on earth by
spending it on things that will last.*

362

Ears vs. Mouths

My dear brothers and sisters, take note of this: Everyone should be quick to listen, slow to speak and slow to become angry, because human anger does not produce the righteousness that God desires.

JAMES 1:19–20

It's hard to listen to someone when we are yelling at them. We might be able to see their mouths moving, but actually hearing what they have to say is difficult. Maybe that's why James 1:19–20 says, "Everyone should be quick to listen, slow to speak and slow to become angry, because human anger does not produce the righteousness that God desires."

God made humans according to an incredible design. In fact, we were made in the image of God himself! When God made us, he gave us twice as many ears as mouths. We know God is a great listener because he listens to our every prayer. He even hears the prayers of our hearts which are never uttered aloud.

As Christians, we can listen to others like God listens to us. Sometimes, we'll hear things which will make us angry, but James says our anger doesn't help others see God's righteousness in us.

How can you listen better when someone is speaking to you?

Why is it important not to get angry before hearing someone's full story?

When non-Christians can only hear Christians yelling without listening, it is no wonder they can't believe in a God of love. We should be known for listening, then responding in love. That way, God's righteousness can be heard when we do speak to the world.

Lord, help me use my ears more than my mouth.

Hard Work is a Good Thing

> *People who refuse to work want things and get nothing. But the desires of people who work hard are completely satisfied.*
>
> **PROVERBS 13:4 (NIRV)**

While contentment should be the goal for our own wants, there are times when we need things for others. In Matthew 25:31–46, Jesus gave some examples of how Christians took care of the people around them. If we are going to feed the hungry and clothe people in need, we need food and clothes to give. We can trust God to provide for us, and one way he provides is by allowing us to work.

Work is a gift. In fact, since God gave Adam a job before sin entered the world (check out Genesis 2:15), we know it is a good thing.

The opposite of hard work is laziness. Proverbs says:

- "People who refuse to work want things and get nothing. But the desires of people who work hard are completely satisfied" (Proverbs 13:4 NIrV).
- "One who is slack in his work is brother to one who destroys" (Proverbs 18:9).
- "The craving of a sluggard will be the death of him, because his hands refuse to work" (Proverbs 21:25).

> **Do you complain when you need to do a job?**
>
> **What verse could you repeat to yourself when you are feeling lazy?**

There's actually a lot more in there. It's obvious hard work is valuable. Laziness may be easier, but hard work is what Christians should be known for.

Lord, help me work hard when I'd rather not.

The Things That Matter

Let us therefore make every effort to do what leads to peace and to mutual edification.

ROMANS 14:19

In spite of the different ways we look and act, all Christians have a few things in common. We are all sinners saved by grace. We all serve and worship Jesus. None of us deserve the love we've been given. We are all called to love God and to love our neighbors as ourselves.

Since these are the most important things we *could* have in common, we shouldn't have much to argue about, right?

In his letter to the Romans, the apostle Paul addressed one of the common arguments in the church at the time. Since many believers came out of Judaism, they were used to some foods being ritually unclean. Gentiles who became Christians didn't worry about what food they ate. Paul knew the argument wasn't helpful. And though he knew it was impossible for food to make someone ritually unclean (Jesus said so in Matthew 15), Paul suggested the Gentile Christians not eat the foods in question since it would have caused tension with their Jewish Christian friends.

Very few things in this world are worth arguing about. Romans 14:19 says, "Let us therefore make every effort to do what leads to peace and to mutual edification."

Instead of arguing over things which don't matter, let's strive for peace by focusing on the things that do!

> **What was the last argument you had with someone?**
>
> **What are the things that matter in Christianity?**

Lord, help me live at peace with my fellow Christians.

Being Jealous of Non-Christians

Do not let your heart envy sinners, but always be zealous for the fear of the LORD. There is surely a future hope for you, and your hope will not be cut off.

PROVERBS 23:17–18

It's tempting to look at non-Christians and feel like they're having all the fun. What rules do they have to follow, after all? But if Christianity is about following rules, we're doing it wrong. Christianity is first and foremost about having a relationship with God.

If the things in the world look tempting, it's because the devil is good at his job. Non-Christians may seem like they're having fun, but they're missing out on true joy. The best thing the world can offer is distraction, while God offers hope.

Proverbs 23:17–18 says, "Do not let your heart envy sinners, but always be zealous for the fear of the LORD. There is surely a future hope for you, and your hope will not be cut off."

Our future is bright because of our relationship with Christ. We have someone who loves us and will never leave us. When everything is said and done, we'll spend eternity with God, beyond the reach of pain or sin.

Non-Christians can't say the same thing. They may be able to distract themselves from the poor choices they make while on earth, but their eternity will look very different from ours. We won't have anything to be jealous of then. And really, we don't right now either.

Are you ever jealous because it looks like non-Christians are having more fun than you?

How could you have more joy in your relationship with God?

God, give me the right perspective so I'm not jealous of sinners.

Remember to Forgive

*Be kind and compassionate to one
another, forgiving each other, just
as in Christ God forgave you.*

EPHESIANS 4:32

As of 2017, Pastor Andy Davis has memorized forty-three books of the Bible. And with the help of his book, *An Approach to Extended Memorization of Scripture*, anyone can do the same.

Memorizing scripture is important, but it isn't the hardest thing a Christian can do. For some people, forgiveness is a lot harder. One verse we can memorize to help us is Ephesians 4:32: "Be kind and compassionate to one another, forgiving each other, just as in Christ God forgave you."

Forgiveness isn't pretending we haven't been hurt. Just like a physical wound, if we cover it up without cleaning it out, it will likely get infected. True forgiveness starts with Jesus's help. We let go of our right to feel hurt and we give it to God. Why should we give it to God instead of getting even or holding a grudge? Because God forgave us.

Matthew 6:15 says, "But if you do not forgive others their sins, your Father will not forgive your sins."

When we focus on the forgiveness we've been given, it makes it easier to forgive others. As Christians, we need to make sure our hearts are full of God's love, our minds are full of God's Word, and our relationships with others are full of forgiveness.

**Which do
you find harder:
scripture memorization
or forgiveness?**

**Why don't grudges
make sense?**

*Lord, help me forgive others when
I feel like getting even.*

Real Heroes

Those who walk righteously and speak what is right, who reject gain from extortion and keep their hands from accepting bribes, who stop their ears against plots of murder and shut their eyes against contemplating evil.

ISAIAH 33:15

Heroes come in all shapes and sizes. Some people look up to pop icons for their talents, but many pop stars lead broken lives and have risky habits. Some look up to political leaders for their ideals, but many leaders fail when tempted by the opportunity to benefit themselves over their country.

So how do we know who to look up to?

According to Isaiah 33:15, we should look up to people committed to justice who are free from corruption and committed to doing good. Almost like a superhero, right?

In comic books, heroes often overcome a rough beginning—orphaned and raised by the family butler, or their home planet exploded, or a beloved uncle was killed in a mugging—by allowing the injustice they experienced to inspire them toward giving justice to others. Fortunately, we don't need superpowers to be super people.

Real people are capable of loving justice, understanding mercy, and living with honor too. They can be found in churches and in our family. It's important to find role models who can help us live for what is right, instead of what is popular.

Who is someone you look up to?

How could you be a hero to someone else?

Lord, help me love justice and look up to the right people.

True Strength

*Be strong and take heart, all you
who hope in the Lord.*

PSALM 31:24

When we picture someone strong, we probably think of someone big with rippling muscles doing what needs to be done. That's certainly the image of strength coming through in movies and TV. Strength is the ability to do something big on your own, right? Wrong!

True strength has nothing to do with physical appearances or a lack of emotions. The popular image of strength is a lot closer to the definition of pride. The Bible's version of strength knows going solo is a bad idea. Biblical strength is knowing our hope—trust or confidence, not wishful thinking—is placed in God's love and ability to do good in every situation.

When our hope is in the Lord, we are confident everything will go according to his plan. Even when things aren't going well for us, God will work things out on our behalf.

Romans 8:28 says, "And we know that in all things God works for the good of those who love him, who have been called according to his purpose."

Our strength cannot be found in our-selves, no matter what our muscles look like. The strength of our hope is less important than the strength of the one we put our hope in, and God is plenty strong enough for our needs.

How strong is your hope?

Why can you trust God to work things out in the end?

Lord, don't let me try to be strong without you.

369

Endurance and Faith

We are hard pressed on every side, but not crushed; perplexed, but not in despair; persecuted, but not abandoned; struck down, but not destroyed.

2 CORINTHIANS 4:8–9

Paul endured a lot of hardship in his missionary journeys. He was rejected, shipwrecked, beaten, and left for dead (2 Corinthians 11:23–30 describes Paul's hardships in depth).

Philippians 1:21–24 says, "For to me, to live is Christ and to die is gain. If I am to go on living in the body, this will mean fruitful labor for me. Yet what shall I choose? I do not know! I am torn between the two: I desire to depart and be with Christ, which is better by far; but it is more necessary for you that I remain in the body."

When Paul wrote 2 Corinthians 4:8–9, he wasn't writing an inspirational speech. He had been hard-pressed, perplexed, persecuted, and struck down. Paul's bad experiences might have made him question God's goodness. Instead, Paul trusted God. He did not despair because he knew he hadn't been abandoned. This world can destroy many things, but it doesn't have the power to destroy our faith.

When we have a bad day (hopefully never as bad as Paul experienced), we have a choice to make: Will we have hope and place our faith in God or will we despair and abandon our faith? Paul made the right choice over and over again. So can we.

> **How can bad experiences help you see God's goodness?**
>
> **How does hope make a difference in your life?**

Lord, when I am persecuted, I know you won't abandon me. Help me look for your glory in every situation.

No Age Restrictions

Josiah was eight years old when he became king, and he reigned in Jerusalem thirty-one years. He did what was right in the eyes of the LORD and followed the ways of his father David, not turning aside to the right or to the left.

2 CHRONICLES 34:1–2

Amon was king over Judah in the Old Testament. He was 22 when he took the crown from his father Manassah. Amon's reign was short and evil. He ended up getting killed by his servants.

Amon's son Josiah wore the crown after him. Josiah was eight years old when he became king. Josiah couldn't have had a rougher start to his kingship, but he was one of the best Biblical kings since David.

Time after time, Josiah discovered new ways to serve God in the position of king. When he restored the temple to worship God, he discovered the Book of the Law, which gave him insight into how to worship better. He reinstated the Passover celebration as soon as he came of age, and according to 2 Chronicles 35:18, "none of the kings of Israel had ever celebrated such a Passover as did Josiah, with the priests, the Levites and all Judah and Israel who were there with the people of Jerusalem."

Josiah's youth didn't stop him from doing what God wanted.

There are no age restrictions on serving God. We may not be kings like Josiah, but God has given us a position to reach people for him. When we look for new ways to serve God, he'll help us too.

> **How could you learn to worship God better?**
>
> **Who is one person you could reach for God?**

Lord, make me like Josiah and help me serve you well.

371

Too Much Is Too Much

*If you find honey, eat just enough—
too much of it, and you will vomit.*

PROVERBS 25:16

Ancient Israelites didn't have candy like we do today. They did have honey though. And just like our parents warn us not to eat too much candy or it'll make us sick, Proverbs 25:16 says, "If you find honey, eat just enough—too much of it, and you will vomit."

Self-control, or self-discipline, is the ability to stop enjoying something before it becomes unenjoyable. God wants us to have good things. That's why he made bees who make honey. But he knows if we can't control ourselves, we'll turn something good into something bad.

Some people struggle with self-control because they think more of something will make them happy. In fact, they might be afraid to stop indulging in something because they've become accustomed to having too much. But 2 Timothy 1:7 says, "For the Spirit God gave us does not make us timid, but gives us power, love and self-discipline."

And Galatians 5:22–23 says, "But the fruit of the Spirit is love, joy, peace, forbearance, kindness, goodness, faithfulness, gentleness and self-control. Against such things there is no law."

If we have God living inside us, we have everything we need to exercise self-control. It's true for honey, candy, and every other good thing which comes from God!

What is something you struggle with self-control over?

How could the Holy Spirit help you in your struggle?

Lord, help me keep good things good by having self-control.

372

Choosing the Right Friends

Do not be misled: "Bad company corrupts good character."

1 CORINTHIANS 15:33

Friends are awesome. They make us laugh. We love spending time with them. We can help each other through tough times. God wants us to choose our friends carefully.

First Corinthians 15:33 says, "Do not be misled: 'Bad company corrupts good character.'"

Over time, friends grow to resemble each other. We use the same words, listen to the same music, watch the same movies, and treat other people the same way. When our friends are fellow believers, this can be a great thing!

But when our friends are not encouraging us to be like God, it can be a terrible thing. The book of Psalms opens this way: "Blessed is the one who does not walk in step with the wicked or stand in the way that sinners take or sit in the company of mockers, but whose delight is in the law of the LORD, and who meditates on his law day and night. For the LORD watches over the way of the righteous, but the way of the wicked leads to destruction" (Psalm 1:1–2, 6).

Not only should we pick our friends carefully, we should be good friends to the ones we have. That way, we won't be the ones dragging our friends toward destruction.

> **Do your friends encourage you toward godliness or away from it?**
>
> **How could you befriend people who will encourage you?**

Lord, help me choose my friends wisely and be a good influence on the friends I have.

373

Running the Marathon

They will soar on wings like eagles;
they will run and not grow weary,
they will walk and not be faint.

ISAIAH 40:31

Marathon runners train for months to be able to run 26.2 miles in a single session. Without proper training, marathon runners could seriously injure themselves. In fact, the race itself is a memorial to a runner named Pheidippides who ran the distance from Marathon to Athens (26.2 miles) before he fell down and died.

Running a sprint—a quarter mile or less—isn't very dangerous. The fastest athletes still train for months, but anyone in just about any shape can handle a sprint without injury.

The saying, "life is a marathon, not a sprint," may be overused, but it's true, especially when it comes to the Christian life. The apostle Paul used running metaphors often in his letters (see 1 Corinthians 9:24–27, Philippians 3:12–14, Galatians 5:7 for a few).

In the Old Testament, Isaiah recognized the difficulty of long-distance running, and added encouragement.

The Christian life isn't easy. Doubts may cause us to stumble, but when we place our trust in God, we'll run without getting weary. Let's run well and win the prize we've been promised!

How far can you run without getting tired?

In a race or in your faith, what should you do when you fall down?

Jesus, help me run well for the whole distance.

Reading, Preaching, Teaching

Until I come, devote yourself to the public reading of Scripture, to preaching and to teaching.

1 TIMOTHY 4:13

In his letter to Timothy, the apostle Paul gave the following advice: "Until I come, devote yourself to the public reading of Scripture, to preaching and to teaching" (1 Timothy 4:13).

When we read the Bible, we're reading the very Word of God. If the God who made the universe, who controls time and space and is able to answer prayers according to his will, took the time to write us instructions on how best to live, it makes sense to spend a few minutes each day reading it. Even better, we can share what we're learning with others.

Preaching and teaching God's Word to others helps us all live better together. If we are encouraged by a specific verse, we should share it. If we find a passage challenging, we should ask others for help understanding it. Christianity is designed to be both a personal *and* a community thing.

But we shouldn't just read the Bible and talk about it. We need to live it out. "Be diligent in these matters; give yourself wholly to them, so that everyone may see your progress. Watch your life and doctrine closely. Persevere in them, because if you do, you will save both yourself and your hearers" (1 Timothy 4:15–16).

> **What is something you've learned from the Bible worth sharing with others?**
>
> **What is something you've read in the Bible you have questions about?**

Living out what we learn helps others and ourselves and will keep us from stumbling back into doubt.

Lord, help me read, preach, and teach for my own sake and for others.

Talking with Non-Christians

> *Be wise in the way you act toward outsiders;*
> *make the most of every opportunity. Let your*
> *conversation be always full of grace, seasoned with*
> *salt, so that you may know how to answer everyone.*
>
> **COLOSSIANS 4:5-6**

Some Christians see Christianity as an excuse to avoid the rest of the world. They quote verses like James 4:4—"Therefore, anyone who chooses to be a friend of the world becomes an enemy of God."—but they use them out of context. Being a friend of the world is living to look just like non-Christians. It has nothing to do with avoiding non-Christians altogether.

God has given us a mission to spread the gospel. If we look for excuses not to talk to non-Christians, the devil will be happy to help us find them. We do need to be wise with how we talk to the world, but we shouldn't avoid it.

Colossians 4:5-6 says, "Be wise in the way you act toward outsiders; make the most of every opportunity. Let your conversation be always full of grace, seasoned with salt, so that you may know how to answer everyone."

If we love the gospels, we'll be able to talk about it patiently and in a way that makes it appealing to the world. It means we'll be able to back up what we say with knowledge of the Bible and our lives will show our words to be true.

How can you season your conversations with salt?

Do you ever shy away from talking to non-Christians?

If our faith leads us to hide, it may not be true faith. True faith spreads the gospel whenever it can.

Lord, give me confidence so I can share my faith.

Don't Stop Here

> *For this very reason, make every effort to*
> *add to your faith goodness; and to goodness,*
> *knowledge; and to knowledge, self-control...*
>
> **2 PETER 1:5–7**

When our journey began, we started with skepticism. Can the gospels be trusted? Did Jesus really exist? Did he actually die? Did he rise again? How can we know for sure?

Our search led us to examine piece after piece of evidence until we built a rock-solid case for Christ. If we believe Jesus came, died, and rose again to set us free from sin, we are now counted as God's children. We have gone on a journey and ended up at faith in Christ.

We did what we set out to do. Now we're good forever, right?

In a letter to the whole church for all time, the apostle Peter encourages us not to stop at simple faith. In becoming Christians, we aren't just safe from punishment after death. We've been invited to live with divine power right now. Faith is just our starting point.

We'll never be able to add to our salvation—because it is a gift from God—but we can add strength to our faith, allowing us to love like God himself. Our love will help others come to know God. We can *be* the case for Christ to a doubting world.

How can you keep going in your faith?

How could your love make a case for Christ to someone else?

> *God, help my faith grow into love*
> *which brings others to faith.*

MEET LEE STROBEL

Lee Strobel is the bestselling author of more than twenty books. Lee's journey from atheism to faith in Christ has been documented in *The Case for Christ*, *The Case for Faith*, *The Case for a Creator*, *The Case for the Real Jesus*, and *The Case for Grace*. He currently serves as director of the Lee Strobel Center at Colorado Christian University.

Lee holds a Master of Studies in Law degree from Yale Law School and a journalism degree from the University of Missouri. He is the former legal editor of the *Chicago Tribune*, receiving Illinois' highest honors for both investigative reporting and public service journalism from United Press International.

Lee also wrote *The Case for Hope*, *The Case for Christianity Answer Book*, *God's Outrageous Claims*, *Reckless Homicide*, *The Unexpected Adventure* (with Mark Mittelberg), *Inside the Mind of Unchurched Harry and Mary*, *What Jesus Would Say*, and his first novel, *The Ambition*. He has been interviewed on such TV networks such as ABC, Fox, Discovery, PBS, and CNN, and his articles have appeared in a variety of periodicals, including the online editions of the *Wall Street Journal* and *Newsweek*.

Lee and Leslie, who have been married for forty-three years, coauthored *Surviving a Spiritual Mismatch in Marriage*. Their daughter Alison is a novelist and coauthor (with her husband Daniel) of two books for children. And their son Kyle is a professor of spiritual theology at the Talbot School of Theology at Biola University.

Lee's website is www.LeeStrobel.com. His Twitter account is @LeeStrobel.

MEET JOSH MOSEY

Josh Mosey is a writer, conference speaker, and marketing professional with fifteen years of experience in retail book selling. He would like to help good authors succeed, himself among them. Josh is a PAL Member of the SCBWI and the author of *3-Minute Prayers for Boys* among other titles. Follow him online at joshmosey.wordpress.com

Check Out This Title by Lee Strobel

The Case for Heaven Young Reader's Edition

Investigating What Happens After Our Life on Earth

Lee Strobel

Is heaven real? What is it really like? Award-winning author Lee Strobel tracked down the evidence and provides answers to the questions children 8–12 ask about both heaven and hell in this young reader's edition of *The Case for Heaven* that is perfect for teaching your child about the biblical evidence for eternal life.

Every child wonders at some point what happens after we die—especially after the loss of a pet, a grandparent, or another loved one. Lee Strobel (*The Case for Christ*) understands your child's questions, and presents a kid-friendly examination of the evidence for heaven, packed full of research.

By the end of this book, your child will have a clearer understanding of the afterlife, as well as peace knowing that the Christian view of heaven is sound.

Available in stores and online!

Check Out This Title by Lee Strobel

The Case for Christ
Young Reader's Edition

Investigating the Toughest
Questions about Jesus

Lee Strobel

Is Jesus real? Was he actually born in a stable? Did he really come back from the dead? Aren't all the stories in the Bible about Jesus just that ... stories? Kids ages 8–12 can join in this incredible search for the truth about Jesus, including the answers that changed the life of investigative reporter and international bestselling author Lee Strobel.

Here's a book that finally answers the most important questions about the existence, life, death, and resurrection of Jesus. *The Case for Christ Young Reader's Edition*, based on the adult edition that has sold over 5 million copies, is packed full of well-researched, reliable, and eye-opening investigations. In these pages, Lee Strobel—an award-winning legal journalist—tackles the toughest questions head-on. He investigates the historical reliability, eyewitness testimonies, and scientific evidence of Jesus's birth, miracles, ministry, and resurrection.

Available in stores and online!